Praise for *The New Pilgrims*

"Tapping into the very latest 'turn' in ecclesi...... thinking, namely (im)migration, this book is a .... concerned about the future of the Church in America. Gleaning from history and social studies, surveys and statistics, interviews and personal experiences, as well as biblical and pastoral wisdom, Dr. Castleberry provides an inspiring and inviting account of the impact of immigration to Christian faith and community. Truly, *The New Pilgrims* shows us clearly *How Immigrants Are Renewing America's Faith and Values.* A must-read for all pastors, missionaries, and Christian leaders."

Veli-Matti Kärkkäinen

Professor of Systematic Theology, Fuller Theological Seminary
and Docent of Ecumenics, Faculty of Theology, University of Helsinki

"Without any exaggeration, *The New Pilgrims* is the best book I have read contextualizing the immigrant experience within the framework of God's agenda. Brilliant indeed. My prayer is that this book will fall into the hands of every pastor, educator, and leader in our nation and eventually around the world. This book, if read by our Christian political leaders, can change the game."

Samuel Rodríguez

President, National Hispanic Christian Leadership Council and ConEl

"No matter what position readers hold on the issue of immigration, Dr. Castleberry's book deserves a careful reading. His biblical theology of migration and thorough description of how immigrants are contributing to the renewal of American faith, positively impacting churches, families, schools, politics, and the economy, demands that readers ask the inevitable question: Is God sending immigrants to America in answer to our prayers for revival?"

George O. Wood

General Superintendent of the Assemblies of God (USA)

"As many American Christians fret over reports of the declining influence of the Christian faith in the United States, Joseph Castleberry points to signs of a hopeful future—for both the Church and the nation—fueled by the faith, ingenuity, and courage of new immigrants. In *The New Pilgrims*, Castleberry artfully weaves together personal stories with the insights of history, missiology, sociology, and economics, making a compelling case that the Church should embrace, rather than fear, the arrivals of immigrants."

Matthew Soerens

Field Director, Evangelical Immigration Table
and Coauthor of *Welcoming the Stranger*

"Joseph Castleberry has not only provided us with a book about a timely topic. His discussion has profound spiritual significance. Too often we believers talk in the abstract about 'immigration.' Castleberry offers a convincing—and biblically grounded—case here for the fact that we have special obligations toward those immigrants who are our sisters and brothers in Christ. We need them for the important gifts they bring as present-day 'pilgrims,' to enrich the life of the body of Christ in North America."

Richard Mouw

President Emeritus, Fuller Theological Seminary

"*The New Pilgrims* provides a brilliant analysis of the religious and spiritual impact of immigrants on society in the United States. I believe this book will expand our understanding of the true meaning of Christianity, strengthen our faith in God, and respect the religious diversity reinforced by immigrants. I congratulate Joe Castleberry for this wonderful piece of literature."

Andrew Young

Civil Rights Leader, Former U.S. Ambassador to the United Nations,
and Mayor of Atlanta

"*The New Pilgrims* is a well-documented, analytical, and visionary work that shakes the conscience of people of faith—as well as those who do not follow a religious path—on the need for a change of mindset toward the immigration phenomenon, thereby inviting the reader to revisit the values and principles that gave rise to and have shaped the path of the United States."

Jorge Madrazo
Former Attorney General, Republic of Mexico

"What is needed now more than ever in this difficult conversation about race and immigration is context—and *The New Pilgrims* certainly delivers on context. Dr. Joseph Castleberry tackles this urgent issue very effectively with historical and sociological insight and gives us a gospel-oriented vision of our country. As a Filipino and first-generation American myself, I hope to be one of the many who proudly take up the mantle of *The New Pilgrims*. This book is a must-read for all who want a fully informed view on the place of immigrants in our new society."

The Venerable Canon Dr. Jon I. Lumanog
Archbishop's Canon and Chief Operating Officer,
Anglican Church in North America

"If you've already decided how you stand on immigration, prepare to be pushed and prodded to see it differently. Dr. Castleberry has written a hopeful book that could change the dialogue. Weaving history, theology, and personal experience, he makes a compelling argument for a new way, or rather a very old way: The Lamb's Way."

Hattie Kauffman
Journalist, Author of *Falling into Place: A Memoir of Overcoming*
and Nez Perce Nation Member

"Put down all those books and articles bemoaning the spiritual decline of America and pick up *The New Pilgrims* and learn what God is doing through immigrants committed to Christ and to the church. Some will read Joseph Castleberry's book as patriots and welcome the promise of a better future for America. As Christians, we read it as believers who rejoice over the spiritual awakening that has already begun."

Leith Anderson

President, National Association of Evangelicals

"Dr. Joseph Castleberry will get you thinking. *The New Pilgrims* is a great read if you want clarity among so much confusion on the issue of immigration in America. Be prepared to be formed and informed. Be prepared to be challenged. Be prepared to see immigration from a whole different perspective—a spiritual one. I have seen many books on cross-cultural issues and immigration, and from my personal, pastoral perspective, this one is definitely the very best!"

Dr. Andrés G. Panasiuk

Founder, The Institute for Financial Culture & CompassLatino

"Castleberry breathes hope into America's dark times, masterfully building upon the foundation of his life experience and scholarship by using the power of testimony. The remarkable stories of immigrants who have not only brought the American church back from the brink but who continue to awaken it to a renewed future serve as powerful motivation for native-born American believers to return to biblical principles of kindness, hospitality, justice, and mercy toward the 'New Pilgrims.' This book is not mere happy talk to prop up a sagging church but rather a call to thoughtfully discern the transformative move of the Spirit for our day."

Lois E. Olena

Associate Professor of Jewish Studies and Practical Theology at Assemblies of God Theological Seminary, and Executive Director of Society for Pentecostal Studies

"*The New Pilgrims* is a hope-filled dose of well-researched reality for those in the church who see the end of America's faith as a foregone conclusion. Castleberry compellingly tells the story of how God is using today's 'exiles and strangers' to rebuild his church and to engage, encourage, and equip new generations of believers."

Harold B. Smith

President and CEO, *Christianity Today*

"Only a very courageous president of a university situated within the mainstream of the Pentecostal-Evangelical tradition would be willing to speak out on immigration at this contested time in U.S. history. Yet *The New Pilgrims* is not only bold but also proclaims truth to power, beyond red and blue, precisely because it is biblically rooted, ecclesially situated, missionally impassioned, historically informed, sociologically alert, and theologically guided. May it signal new possibilities for the American dream even as it calls the North American church, even the church catholic, to live into the ministry of grace, reconciliation, and shalom that anticipates the coming reign of God."

Amos Yong

Professor of Theology & Mission at Fuller Theological Seminary, and Author of *The Future of Evangelical Theology: Soundings from the Asian American Diaspora*

"No person of faith should vote in another election or otherwise engage the issue of immigration before reading Dr. Castleberry's eye-opening book. It demonstrates that a system of justice is cherished by American and immigrant alike, but that current law does not reflect the realities causing the immigration crisis and is not working. The health of our churches and our communities is dependent upon both reforming the law and receiving the immigrant."

Jim Rice

Justice, Montana Supreme Court

Other Books by Joseph Castleberry

Your Deepest Dream: Discovering God's True Vision for Your Life

The Kingdom Net: Learning to Network Like Jesus

THE NEW PILGRIMS

How Immigrants Are Renewing
America's Faith and Values

Joseph Castleberry, Ed.D.

WORTHY®
PUBLISHING

The New Pilgrims *is dedicated to all of my friends and followers on social media.*

Follow me on Facebook at
www.facebook.com/joseph.castleberry
and on Twitter
@DrCastleberry

CONTENTS

ACKNOWLEDGMENTS

As the Roman historian Tacitus wrote in AD 98, "*Prospera omnes sibi vindicant, adversa uni imputantur.*" Translated it means, "Everyone claims credit for a success; a failure is blamed on one alone." Along those lines, Michael Clifford deserves a huge word of thanks for originally challenging me to write this book and for serving as its first reader. Ted Squires read the manuscript and recommended it to Byron Williamson at Worthy Publishing, who believed in it and brought it to print. Thanks to them, as well as to Sam Rodriguez at Worthy Latino.

Samuel Rodríguez of the National Hispanic Christian Leadership Conference (NHCLC) did much to inspire the book, including early feedback on the original draft. As always, Ted Terry gave me valuable advice at crucial points along the rocky road to publication. My wife, Kathleen Castleberry, a tough writing critic, made many solid suggestions for improvement. Dr. Joshua Ziefle, my American church history reader, corrected some of my misconceptions about the history of the Great Awakenings and other points of fact. Larry Barnett, a talented social and demographic researcher, read an early draft and made a major impact on the book to much benefit. Chuck Munson provided a very helpful reading as well, as did Gabriel Salguero. Dr. Wave Nunnally gave valuable advice on biblical Hebrew.

Larry Garza, Edgardo Montano, Fred Choy, Dr. Varun Laohaprasit, Dr. Isaac Canales, Andre and France Dutra, Saturnino González, Jessica Domínguez, Andrés Panasiuk, and Jesús de Paz gave me important emic accounts of the experience of *The New Pilgrims*. They have all contributed greatly to the book. I'm grateful also to my professors at Columbia University's Teachers College, who taught me the tools of social research that undergird the whole project. Jim Edwards taught me to write and Eliezer Oyola gave me my first formal lessons in Spanish, skills that contributed enormously to this project. The memory of Steve Halliday's coaching voice resounded in my head the whole time as I wrote. The members of Bethel Spanish Church in Othello, Washington, and Centro de Vida in Tacoma also inspired much of my understanding of the immigrant experience.

If you, the reader, decide that the book has succeeded, these people deserve big shares of the credit. If you deem it a failure, I alone should bear the blame.

INTRODUCTION

America—as G. K. Chesterton famously quipped—is "a nation with the soul of a church."[1] In making such a claim, Chesterton did not mean to say that America took a religious approach to religion. Rather, he meant that America took a religious approach to democracy and justice. "America," he wrote, "is the only nation in the world that is founded on a creed."[2] That creed did not come from an established church, a council of bishops, or even directly from any particular holy scripture but rather from the Declaration of Independence—"the only piece of practical politics that is also theoretical politics and also great literature. It enunciates that all . . . are equal in their claim to justice, that governments exist to give them that justice, and that their authority is for that reason just," naming "the Creator as the ultimate authority from whom these rights are derived."[3] America's creed, Chesterton said, did not so much treat divine things but rather human things.

Chesterton went on to extol America's creed in terms of its "vision of molding many peoples into the visible image of the citizen," and in so doing, "making a home out of vagabonds and a nation out of exiles."[4] Such a national quest, he reckoned, amounted to an admirable "spiritual adventure."[5] If America had the soul of a church, the creed of that church declared all people equal, and even more than equal. Everyone was welcome.

1

While the American creed does not rest exclusively on the particular claims of any one religion, it nevertheless assumes a belief in God rooted in the teachings of particular religions. From the beginning of the nation, Christianity has played the dominant role in American religion, but other religions have always found a home here and a role in supporting America's creed. Nevertheless, the feeling in the air today suggests that *faith in America*—in both senses of the phrase—has declined.

On one hand, many have lost faith in America in recent years and strongly question the traditional sense of America's mission to be a guiding light for democracy, freedom, and human equality in the world. We have paid a high cost in lives and treasure in our recent Middle Eastern wars. Unfortunately, we have suffered painful reversals of our gains in rebuilding Iraq and Afghanistan as united, free nations. This lack of return for sacrifice has provoked many Americans to wonder whether we should stay home and let the world take care of itself.

> From the beginning of the nation, Christianity has played the dominant role in American religion.

On the other hand, the weakened status of organized religion in America causes many to believe that faith itself has declined. Considerable evidence has mounted over the last fifty years that faith has indeed declined in America. Conservative Christians lament the moral decay that has resulted from the Sexual Revolution of the 1960s and '70s. They fear persecution as they lose one religious freedom case after another in federal and state courts. They sting at the rise of a new, militant atheism that has arisen to mock the Bible. They recoil from the constant ridicule of popular media and liberal elites in the arts, politics, education, and other sectors. They mourn the decline and collapse of America's historic Protestant churches—whether Episcopal, Methodist, Congregationalist, Presbyterian, Lutheran, or Baptist. They grieve as they observe the closing of ornately decorated, historic church buildings and their members move out to upstart churches in plain metal buildings or storefronts. They read reports that 70 percent of Christian youth abandon Christian faith during their late teens or twenties.[6]

Underneath these perceptions, the undeniable fact stands: the percentage of Christians in America shrank by 8 percent between 2007 and 2014, even as the percentage of nonreligious Americans has increased by 6 percent.[7] A palpable sense of decline hangs over many sectors of American Christianity like winter clouds, devoid of lightning and thunder and promising only cold water to put out whatever fire remains in the churches.

The news seems bad, but such evidence does not represent all of the facts. In the midst of decline, immigrants have been flooding into America, bringing with them powerful testimonies of faith. The chapters ahead will show how today's immigrants to America champion the values of the Pilgrims who landed at Plymouth Rock in 1620. They have a vision for personal opportunity and spiritual exceptionalism that come together in greatness for the noble nation they have come to help build. As they settle into their new lives, raise their children, and join our nation, they renew and restore America's faith, just as they have been doing since the Pilgrims landed in 1620.

Some will immediately argue that America does not have a faith but rather many faiths. Some will read this singular reference to faith as a claim that America has one legitimate faith—namely, Christianity. Others would argue that Christianity itself does not constitute a single faith. Catholicism, Eastern Orthodoxy, Ecumenical Mainline or Liberal Protestantism, and Evangelicalism, among others, sometimes offer very different visions of God and human behavior. Whatever the truth about the unity of Christianity as a religion, America does not have a single religion, offering a congenial home to Judaism, Buddhism, Hinduism, Islam, and other religions. At the same time, American history and culture undeniably owe a profound and eternal debt to Christianity, a fact we should remember as religious liberties come under increasing attack from secularist Progressives.

Since the beginning of American history, Christians have shared the North American continent with multiple faiths, in an exceptional way previously unknown to other nations of the world. Christians, for sure, have dominated American demography and culture, but never exclusively. Jews, a few Muslims, atheists, freethinkers, freemasons, and others have lived and prospered in America since the earliest days of European colonization. Underneath such diversity, Americans have traditionally regarded religious freedom as the queen of all freedoms, and freedom inherently implies the presence, protection, and proliferation of an almost limitless variety of faiths in America.

While recognizing the plural nature of religious faith in America, this book will focus on the faith of the overwhelming majority of today's immigrants, namely, Christianity. In 2012, 61 percent of legal immigrants identified themselves as Christians, compared to 83 percent of unauthorized immigrants and 75 percent of new permanent residents.[8] While 70 percent of Americans currently profess Christianity, roughly 75 percent of immigrants currently do so.[9] Immigrants confess Christianity in only slightly higher numbers than native-born Americans, but a close look at the faith of immigrants today reveals an amazing intensity and sincerity that will compound their effect on America's faith.

The conversion of immigrants to Christian faith (always a historic feature of American religion) and the high birthrates of both Christians and immigrants will maintain a stable, overwhelmingly Christian majority in the future. This fact does not apply to Europe or Canada, where the majority of immigrants do not profess Christian faith. Christian immigrants offer a great advantage to America that other nations do not enjoy, and even if the percentage of Christians in America does not increase in the future, the content of American faith will definitely show the influence of these new "high-octane" American believers.

While this book will make occasional reference to Jews, Muslims, Hindus, and Buddhists, readers should not look here for a detailed analysis of non-Christian fortunes in America.[10] Among non-Christian immigrants, the religiously unaffiliated make up the largest group at 23 percent, followed by Jews (1.9 percent), Muslims (0.9 percent), and Hindus and Buddhist (0.7 percent each). Their story deserves attention, and several authors have focused on them. Their story deserves attention, and several authors have focused on them.[11] They will undoubtedly make an important contribution to faith in America as the future unfolds. But this book focuses on the main event—Christian immigrants.

Despite the fact the majority of Americans have long identified with Christianity in one way or another, Christianity *per se* has not stood at center stage in America's public life over the last two centuries. In its place has stood "American Civil Religion," the faith illustrated in (and perhaps even created by) the public speaking of Washington, Jefferson, Lincoln, and many other public leaders who never publicly named Jesus Christ as their personal God and Savior.[12] Existing alongside but not independently of Christianity, Judaism, and other religions, American Civil Religion believes in a benevolent Creator God who intervenes in the affairs of humanity in favor of those who do good rather than evil. (The song "God Bless America" and other patriotic hymns testify to this latter point.) It generally offers salvation (and even Heaven) to those who do good and warns of punishment to those who do evil. It holds out

> Our founders recognized that the new American nation did not base its citizenship on ethnicity but rather on the acceptance of our creed.

the fundamental principles of American governmental culture—especially freedom—as being divinely inspired. It usually asserts the divine destiny of America to stand as a beacon of freedom, democracy, and commerce for all the world. As Chesterton noted, its scripture is the Declaration of Independence, which never mentions the name of Jesus Christ but does trust in "nature's God," who has given humanity "certain inalienable rights, among these life, liberty, and the pursuit of happiness."

Chesterton also recognized the role of immigrants in America's Civil Religion. In the Latin motto *e pluribus unum*, one out of many, our founders recognized that the new American nation did not base its citizenship on ethnicity but rather on the acceptance of our creed. Central to that creed was the concept of America as the natural home of all freedom seekers. The great poet Emma Lazarus penned a sonnet, "The New Colossus," that would adorn the base of the Statue of Liberty, the greatest symbol of America's civil religion:

> Not like the brazen giant of Greek fame,
> With conquering limbs astride from land to land;
> Here at our sea-washed, sunset gates shall stand
> A mighty woman with a torch, whose flame
> Is the imprisoned lightning, and her name
> Mother of Exiles. From her beacon-hand
> Glows world-wide welcome; her mild eyes command
> The air-bridged harbor that twin cities frame.
>
> "Keep ancient lands, your storied pomp!" cries she
> With silent lips. "Give me your tired, your poor,
> Your huddled masses yearning to breathe free,
> The wretched refuse of your teeming shore.
> Send these, the homeless, tempest-tost to me,
> I lift my lamp beside the golden door!"[13]

Such words remain so dear to the American soul that every patriot heart still beats to their cadence.

WATERED-DOWN CHRISTIANITY?

Some might consider American Civil Religion a watered-down form of Christianity, but in truth, it lacks the specificity to qualify as any form of Christianity. Throughout American history, politicians and other civic leaders have appealed to God in a generic way, but seldom to Jesus Christ. They have often quoted the Bible to support their arguments, though usually paying scant attention to its contextual meaning. The Ten Commandments stand as symbols of religiously sanctioned government, however shorn of their religious particularism and divested of any legal authority. Of the Ten Commandments, only three—killing, stealing, and giving false testimony in court—remain in force through our actual codes of law.

American Civil Religion's essential core brings elements of Judaism and Christianity (and values shared by other religions) into a generalized national faith that until recently has allowed national leaders to recognize God publicly without offending the followers of any particular religion. Yet despite the independent nature of civil religion, it depends on *specific* religious faiths to give it durable credibility with the population. Due to the recent rise of so-called atheist churches and the long history of Unitarianism notwithstanding, virtually no one attends church, temple, or mosque on a weekly basis to celebrate civil religion.[14] Faith requires religious specificity or particularism in order to thrive.

In speaking of immigrants renewing America's faith, I recognize that (1) immigrants have already replenished the demographic base of Christianity in America; (2) other religions have grown in America because of immigration, sometimes converting Americans to their faith even as some of their members convert to Christianity; (3) immigrants enhance the popular viability of American Civil Religion; and (4) immigrants offer promise for religious revival in American society as a whole—especially in terms of Christianity.

Let no one assume I have taken a dispassionate or even neutral position. My identity as a Christian minister and evangelist undoubtedly colors my view of the facts presented here. My enthusiasm for the renewal of Christianity promised by today's immigrants pervades this work. While the arguments offered here make heavy use of historical and sociological analysis, I do not offer this book as a work of social science but a mix of journalism, social sciences, history, biblical interpretation, futurism, ethics, political science, and, of course, theological perspective. The book offers an unflaggingly pro-American and pro-religious vision of a demonstrable, immigrant-led renewal of American religion, especially Christianity. It will describe how immigrants are transforming American faith in the present and how they may gain even greater influence in the near future. *For any religious American, the future appears brighter than we have imagined.*

1

THE NEW PILGRIMS

Finding an ancestor among the Pilgrims who landed on Plymouth Rock in 1620 stands as the Holy Grail for Americans who research their family tree. But many other iconic episodes have occurred in American history, such as

- the signing of the Declaration of Independence,
- Washington's crossing of the Delaware,
- the tragic defense of the Alamo,
- Lincoln's Emancipation Proclamation,
- the entry of immigrants through Ellis Island,
- the planting of the flag at Iwo Jima in World War II,
- the March on Washington and Martin Luther King's "I have a Dream" speech,
- the Woodstock Festival, and
- the rescue of victims of the 9/11 terrorist attacks.

People who took part in or had association with those events, as well as others, told (or still tell) about it for the rest of their lives.

But perhaps none of those events has the same enduring, iconic power as the landing at Plymouth Rock.

What special character did the Pilgrims have that made them such a source of pride for their descendants four hundred years later? They did not arrive as the first permanent British settlers in the Americas. That honor goes to the founders of Jamestown in Virginia. While the descendants of the *Mayflower* Pilgrims would have an important role in the American Revolution and the shaping of American democracy and the United States government, the role of Virginians like Washington, Jefferson, and Madison towers above them in the public's memory. Nevertheless, the Pilgrims of Plymouth hold a special place in the American heart.

> The Pilgrims stand apart from other settlers in early America precisely because they set the tone for what would become a nation founded on biblical values.

While I personally count in my family tree Jamestown founders from 1608 and ancient planters of Virginia as well as many other early American families, I confess I have never found a Pilgrim ancestor. Just recently, my friend Mitch Soule forced me to fold in the game of genealogy poker by trumping my Edward Gurganus of Jamestown with his George Soule, a signer of the Mayflower Compact.[1] The *Mayflower* Pilgrims stand supreme as the most coveted American ancestors.

The Pilgrims stand apart from other settlers in early America precisely because they set the tone for what would become a nation founded on biblical values. Their rigorous Reformed version of Christian doctrine did not last very long in colonial Massachusetts and probably never commanded the loyalty of more than about 20 percent of its citizens.[2] But it set a paradigm of rigorous commitment to a Christian faith that undergirds all aspects of life—personal standards, motivations, and ambitions; the family; community life; government; art and architecture; and other spheres of activity and being. The Pilgrims had come to America first and foremost in search of religious freedom. Their commitment to a totally integrated life of faith set the ideal standard for the religious life of the emerging nation, which in time would provide sanctuary—in both senses of the word—for many faiths to thrive, not only in worship but also in full-throated witness.

Not all citizens—usually not even a majority of them—would practice religion as vigorously as others, but devout religious practice would generally enjoy public approval, or at least tolerance, in America. Many other religious immigrants would follow the Pilgrims to Colonial America in large numbers—including French, Irish, and dissenting English Catholics, German Mennonites, English Baptists and Quakers, Scottish Presbyterians, British Methodists, Dutch Reformed, and others, including Jews and Muslims—all adopting a pilgrim status similar to that of the *Mayflower* immigrants. Their presence in America included commitment to a deeply held personal faith that informed their lives thoroughly. As a result, a new kind of religious nation gradually emerged, which the world had never seen before—a diverse, pluralistic nation where everyone's particular faith would come together to support a national faith-based mission.

Throughout most of the history of *Christendom*—defined as the community of nations that held Christianity as the religion established legally by the state—only one religion enjoyed sponsorship and tolerance in the nations of Western Europe. Starting with the Emperor Constantine's declaration of Christianity as the state religion of Rome and continuing through Charlemagne's Holy Roman Empire and other states, Christianity in the West meant "Roman Catholicism." When the Reformation took place in the sixteenth century, diverse forms of Protestantism arose and became the state religions of a handful of continental principalities and England. Religious wars arose and conflict boiled and simmered for over a hundred years. Many immigrants to the Americas in the seventeenth century—both Protestant and Catholic—faced persecution in their homelands for their dissenting approaches to faith. The Pilgrims of Massachusetts became, for America, a powerful, compelling symbol of all those immigrants who have ever left their homelands to pursue freedom of worship in America—not only Christian immigrants but also Jews, Muslims, and followers of other religions, old and new.

As America put together an unprecedented collection of diverse expressions of Christianity, it experimented with new ways of living out a national religious identity. At first, some individual colonies had different established churches—Congregationalism in Massachusetts, Anglicanism in Virginia—while others adopted relatively full religious freedom from the start—such as Pennsylvania and Rhode Island. As the new nation adopted the Constitution of the United States in 1789, its first amendment ensured the prohibition of an established national religion as well as protection for the free exercise of religion. It took a few decades for state establishment of particular churches to end, but once the First Amendment took hold, it inexorably led to the end of established churches in America.

Thus emerged a marvelous new phenomenon in statecraft—the first majority-Christian nation without an established church. The new nation had a decidedly *Judeo*-Christian character, and even the freethinking agnostics and atheists, who enjoyed tolerance and constitutionally protected freedom to not practice religion, recognized the biblical basis of the nation's culture. The prohibition of established religion meant that no particular church could have a monopoly on America's soul, and it also meant that Judaism, Islam, Hinduism, Buddhism, Native American religion, atheism, and any other religion would have a free religious market in which to declare its faith and seek or receive new adherents. Indeed, most Americans came to see such freedom as the most authentically Christian way to govern a nation. Freedom not to profess Christian faith enjoyed (imperfect) toleration, as did historic Christianity, new ways of expressing Christian faith, and other religions.[3]

Consequently, America has always allowed prayers at the beginning of public meetings. Our courts carry out business under the invocation of God's blessing. Our money declares "IN GOD WE TRUST." Ever since the days of George Washington at Valley Forge, our military has provided funding for chaplains from across the religious landscape, notably including Muslim chaplains who have recently ministered to American Muslim servicemen and women in the post-9/11 wars in the Middle East. Religious ministers of all faiths have long enjoyed a federal tax subsidy for their housing allowances. Until the Supreme Court ruling in *Engel v. Vitale* in 1962, prayer and Bible reading began the day at most public schools in America. All of these state-sponsored encouragements of religion contributed to the credibility of our national faith in a Creator God who endowed us with equal rights and dignity.

THE DECLINE OF FAITH IN AMERICA

Despite the robust commitment to religious freedom that has historically resulted in vibrant personal religion, the nation's embrace of Judeo-Christian principles seems to have seriously eroded in the past fifty years. Perhaps one of the only things the most convinced atheists share with the most conservative Christians is the denial of America's status as a Christian nation—the former because they never believed in such an identity and the latter because they believe we have completely forfeited it. No observer could possibly argue that the America's cultural elites and the communications media they control—the press, television, cinema—promote the cause of religion in America, and the fastest-growing religious affiliation in America today is those declaring "None." As the Pew Research Center reports, "One-fifth of the U.S. public—and a third of adults under 30—are religiously unaffiliated today."[4]

> The nation's embrace of Judeo-Christian principles seems to have seriously eroded in the past fifty years.

The increase in nonreligious people in America may reflect the mere fact that people feel more freedom to declare their atheism or agnosticism honestly and forthrightly. Devout Christians often consider that "lukewarm" or nominal Christians enjoy little real spiritual advantage over atheists. Most American Christians do not resent another person's rejection of faith, as little as the atheist's belief in a universe without a Creator may resonate with convinced believers. Christians have long understood the plain fact that most Americans do not attend church regularly and that many do not attend at all. But the widespread rejection of traditional moral values in American society contributes very powerfully to the sense that faith has suffered significant decline.

One reported trend causes the greatest distress to America's committed Christians and the greatest threat of faith's future decline in America: a number of studies suggest that 70 percent of young Protestants abandon church in their twenties.[5] Whether those reports adequately describe all segments of the diverse Christian community or not, they have received widespread reporting and contribute powerfully to a sense of decline. According to Robert Wuthnow, a prominent Evangelical sociologist who teaches at Princeton University, "Unless religious leaders take younger adults more seriously, the future of American religion is in doubt."[6]

CHRISTIAN RESPONSE

Those who value America's history as a majority-Christian nation naturally desire that it experience a new revival in the churches and an awakening to God among those Americans who do not profess or practice Christian faith. Christians who believe in the teaching authority of the Bible see God as "not willing that any should perish, but that all should come to repentance."[7] As a Christian minister for over thirty years, I have visited at least five hundred different Evangelical churches over my career. In all of them, people cry out in prayer for the salvation of America. Over the past fifty years, much evidence has accrued among our traditional population to suggest that our prayers may not have completely succeeded. It would appear that native-born American Christians have abandoned the faith in significant numbers, as the Christian population in America has declined by 5 percent over the past five years.[8]

ENTER THE NEW PILGRIMS

This tale of recent woes would almost certainly have spelled a more drastic decline in American Christianity had it not been for the massive entry of Christian immigrants into our national population over the past half century. As things stand now, immigrants and their children have kept Christian affiliation at a high level. But as the future unfolds, their effect on America's Christian population will become even more dramatic.

In order for a population to replace itself and maintain its numbers at a constant level, it has to reproduce. Because of infant mortality and other factors, the total fertility rate—that is, the average number of babies born for every two persons over the course of their lifetimes—must be at least 2.1 in developed countries like the United States.[9] At present, the only demographic groups in America that have a birthrate above the replacement level of 2.1 are immigrants and other social conservatives—immigrants at 2.9, white Evangelicals at 3.0, Mormons at about 3.0, Old Order Amish at about 7.0, and various Orthodox Jewish groups from 3.3 to 7.9.[10] In contrast, the low fertility rate of liberals threatens to decrease their numbers substantially in the next generation.[11] Together, the high entry and birthrates of immigrants offer hope for an actual rise in the

> As things stand now, immigrants and their children have kept Christian affiliation at a high level.

Christian population of America as well as a rise in population for many other faiths, such as Buddhism, Hinduism, and Islam. A secularist future for America seems less and less likely, even as a more religiously pluralistic future appears certain.

IMMIGRATION AND EVANGELICALISM

The role of immigrants in shoring up American Evangelicalism shines in the story of the Assemblies of God (AG), a leading Evangelical Protestant denomination. The AG, which completed one hundred years of existence in 2014, has a remarkable record of annual growth over the entire period of its work, showing positive growth every year since 1978 except for tiny declines in 1988 and 1989—years marked by the scandals involving AG televangelists Jim Bakker and Jimmy Swaggart.[12] From 2001 to the present, the entire net growth recorded by the denomination has come from ethnic minorities through immigration, a trend that probably began in about 1989.

Before 2001, the AG—like almost all other denominations—did not track the ethnic identity of its members, but the number of members from ethnic minority groups clearly began growing in the 1980s. By 2001, whites made up 70.6 percent of the denomination.[13] According to the 2000 census, whites made up 75.1 percent of the American population at that time.[14] By 2012, the number of white members in the AG had declined by about 20,000, and the percentage of whites had fallen to 59.2 percent. Hispanics, led by immigrants, grew from 16.3 percent to 21.7 percent.[15] The total minority population—overwhelmingly fed by immigration—had grown to almost 41 percent of the total membership.

According to Scott Temple, director of ethnic relations for

the General Council of the Assemblies of God (USA), if current growth patterns continue, the AG will become a *minority-majority* denomination by 2020, meaning that no ethnic or racial group will constitute a majority of the population.[16] This phenomenon puts the AG ahead of the national trend, as the Census Bureau expects the nation as a whole to reach minority-majority status in 2043.[17] By far, the lion's share of this growth among ethnic minorities has come from immigrants. Although virtually all Evangelical and Mainline churches have added immigrants to their rolls, the Assemblies of God has seen truly remarkable growth from immigration and the conversion of immigrants. How did the AG achieve so much success in attracting immigrants?

One of the key factors in the AG's growth has been its strong emphasis and success in foreign missions. While the American AG currently includes over 3.1 million adherents, its total worldwide constituency stood at over 67.5 million in 2013,[18] of which some 30 million live in Latin America, a major source of immigration to the United States.[19] The AG also has huge constituencies in South Korea, the Philippines, Nigeria, and other major source countries for immigrants to America.

A second key factor in AG success has been its strong emphasis on missionary work inside the United States. From its earliest days, the AG has understood the importance of allowing language groups to form their own ecclesial identities. After the founding of the denomination in 1914, Henry C. Ball founded a convention for Spanish-speaking pastors in 1918, followed by the founding of a German branch by European immigrants in 1922.[20] As new immigrant groups arose, "language fellowships" emerged for Filipinos (1943), Ukrainians (1943), Hungarians (1944), Polish

(1944), and Yugoslavians (1945). In 1973, the Assemblies established the most successful of these groups as self-governing districts with representation on the national governing council, the General Presbytery.[21] Recognizing in 1983 that immigration had been on the increase since its low point in 1970, the AG launched a new initiative, "Mission America," to reach the newcomers.

"How should Christians respond to the overwhelming tide of immigration—the influx of foreign, anti-Christian cultures and religions?" asked James Kessler rhetorically in the *Pentecostal Evangel,* the weekly magazine of the AG. "It is imperative that we take a new, long look at Christ's command and develop a responsible attitude toward Home Missions. America has become a mission field in the truest sense."[22] Ministry to new immigrants increased, and even as older groups assimilated into English-speaking churches and some of the early fellowships and districts dissolved, new immigrant groups raised the total number of language fellowships to twenty by 2014.[23]

From the beginning, early AG missionaries adopted the famous "Three-Self" principles of self-propagation, self-financing, and self-governance that Anglican missionary Roland Allen had articulated early in the twentieth century in the context of missions to China.[24] American church leaders applied the same principles of autonomy to diverse ethnic groups inside the United States. Rather than originating in cultural prejudice, such ethnically organized, ecclesial jurisdictions flowed out of an understanding that language differences create barriers that deter ministry to immigrants.[25] The motivation for separation of foreign language groups into their own districts always flowed from the initiative of those groups rather than from racial or ethnic prejudice on the part of the denomination. The missionary strategy arose out of a genuine concern in the denomination to reach those who have not heard the gospel.

Language districts allowed brand-new immigrants the opportunity not only to plant churches but also to supervise and govern them by themselves. This feature allowed for the development of ethnic leadership at the highest levels without competition or interference from native-born Americans. As a result of an enlightened polity and a focus on effective evangelistic strategy, AG immigrants have planted churches in their language or cultural groups and swelled the denomination's numbers. As their children have intermarried into the native-born population and adopted English as their first language, they have historically tended to filter into the mainstream of AG churches.

A NEW GENERATION OF
IMMIGRANT CHURCH LEADERS

Historically, many second-generation members of Spanish-speaking churches in the American AG assimilated into the English-speaking churches, but in recent years, an exceptional practice has become more common. More Latino members have remained in the Spanish-language districts despite a preference for English as their first language—or at least their strongest language. As the Hispanic districts have proliferated, a steady stream of new immigrants from Latin America has kept the use of Spanish strong. But many young ministers who grew up in the Hispanic districts operate primarily in English. Increasingly, the Spanish churches are becoming bilingual or even English-only churches.

The Florida Multicultural District offers an interesting example. Dr. Saturnino González, who serves as superintendent of the district and pastor of the five-thousand-member Iglesia El Calvario in Orlando, tells the story of how his district got a new name. The district, previously named the Spanish Southeastern District, decided to change its name when its churches from Georgia, South Carolina, and Alabama got numerous enough to start a new district, which became the Southern Latin District. González recalled when they formally set the other churches free to start a new district:

> The new district was birthed, and in that same meeting, a resolution came to the floor to change our name. We thought of several new names. But then, a new breed of ministers took the floor . . . a new generation of ministers took us by surprise. They went to the microphone when we were discussing the new name and they said, "Pastors, we're no longer Southeastern, but we want to consider the fact that we are no longer Spanish also." And then the discussion was, "If we say we're Spanish, does that mean that if I don't speak Spanish, I can't be part of the district?" To which we said, "No, you could be a part of us." Those were Hispanic ministers, young guys, who were credentialed with us but didn't speak Spanish.[26]

González recognized that something historic had begun to emerge in the meeting—a generational shift that would effect a profound change on the future.

In essence they were suggesting, "If we're going to look for a name, can we look for a name that does not say 'Spanish'?" It was a generational call that we weren't even thinking about. We were looking for a Florida Latin something or Florida Spanish. Those names came to the floor, but they were debated. You could sense that, while we were discussing the name, there was something spiritual in that floor, when we started saying, "Okay, it's Florida," but we now have a generation saying, "Please, let's look for a name that could be broader, that could reflect the mission of the church itself."[27]

As the meeting continued, creativity led to debate, which led to disagreement, which led to frustration. For more than an hour, the council deliberated and could not come up with a name that seemed suitable to everyone. Finally, after all the proposals for a new name had been rejected, Mabel Rojas, the wife of one of the pastors, stood up and said, "What about this? Florida Multicultural District of the Assemblies of God." As González recalled, "You could sense, everybody went, 'What?' You know, like, 'Yes!'"[28]

The membership of the newly named district has now broadened to fit its name. Moving beyond its original composition of immigrants from Latin America, it now has not only a wider diversity of members but also Brazilians, African-Americans, and Haitians in the pipeline to become ministers.

While the district conducts business in a bilingual mode now—always including Spanish—it can see a more diverse future coming. "We have a clear mission to reach everybody in our district," said González. He explained, "We are multicultural now. We need to move into intercultural, and then become transcultural. That's got to be the way we go. This is the beginning. We're already multicultural, because we're recognizing the culture of everybody."[29]

The roots of the church's multicultural perspective began with the diversity of Latin American nationalities the churches had begun to reach when they operated exclusively in Spanish. "Even among Hispanics," said González, "there is a diversity of culture, in terms of both ideas and language." But that diversity grows increasingly wider now. Already, ten of the churches conduct services exclusively in English.

As the diversity of the immigrant churches grows, the Assemblies of God denomination in the United States experiences broader and deeper renewal. In a way similar to what the Assemblies of God has seen, independent (non-denominational) churches have also proliferated among immigrants. Such churches logically tend to pursue a strategy of self-sufficiency, having no predetermined partners to interfere with their work by offering desirable aid and its usual partner, undesirable outsider authority.

ROMAN CATHOLICS AND IMMIGRATION

Lest anyone get the idea that immigrants only choose Evangelical churches, take a look at the Roman Catholic Church. With 78 million faithful members, the Roman Catholic Church stands firm as America's largest religious organization, making up almost a quarter of the national population. Immigration has always provided a large percentage of Roman Catholic Church membership in the United States! Centuries before the Mexican-American War, Spanish missionaries had settled in the Southwest.[30] Long before the Louisiana Purchase, Acadian French immigrants had settled in the Mississippi Delta. The original founding of Catholic Maryland, the annexation of the Mexican Southwest, and the influx of Irish immigrants in the 1830s, Italians in 1880s, and Polish in the late 1800s built and sustained a strong base of Catholics across America.

Just like Mainline Protestant denominations began to decline in the mid-1960s, Catholics began abandoning the church. The Pew Religious Landscape Survey reports:

> While those Americans who are unaffiliated with any particular religion have seen the greatest growth in numbers as a result of changes in affiliation, Catholicism has experienced the greatest net losses as a result of affiliation changes. While nearly one-in-three Americans (31 percent) were raised in the Catholic faith, today fewer than one-in-four (24 percent) describe themselves as Catholic.[31]

Statistics can present truth and also distort it, and despite a doubling of the U.S. population since 1960, Roman Catholics have managed to maintain a stable percentage of that population at around 23 to 24 percent. How did they manage to accomplish a feat like that? Immigration.

According to the Secretariat of the United States Conference of Catholic Bishops, 71 percent of all growth in the American Catholic population since 1960 has been due to Hispanics alone![32] This Hispanic portion of Catholic growth does not take into account massive Catholic immigration from other parts of the world such as the Philippine Islands and several African nations. The Pew study reported that while Protestants outnumber Catholics by more than two to one in America, almost the reverse holds among immigrants: "Among the foreign-born adult population, Catholics outnumber Protestants by nearly a two-to-one margin (46 percent Catholic vs. 24 percent Protestant)."[33] Immigrants currently make up about 30 percent of American Catholicism, with 22.2 million Catholics born outside the United States.[34]

Now think into the future. Birthrates in the U.S. have declined dramatically in the last fifty years and "dipped in 2011 to the lowest ever recorded."[35] The birthrate of immigrants stood much higher than that of the native U.S. population. According to Pew, "The 2010 birth rate for foreign-born women (87.8 [per 1,000 women]) was nearly 50 percent higher than the rate for U.S.-born women (58.9)."[36] Based on those birthrates—and the virtual certainty that immigrants will continue to come to the United States in future years from majority-Catholic nations—the Catholic faith has a bright future in America!

Already, today's immigrants from Latin America, the Philippines, and Africa keep parishes open and even thriving. In 2014, Hispanics made up almost half of all Catholics under age forty, with 54 percent of young Catholics being non-white. And in a 2013 cover story article entitled "The Latino Reformation," *Time* magazine has recently reported that 30 percent of Catholic immigrants to America convert to Pentecostalism, an Evangelical Protestant movement, after arriving. This phenomenon promises Protestant churches a share in the bonanza of Catholic immigration to the United States in the future.[37]

> Today's immigrants from Latin America, the Philippines, and Africa keep parishes open and even thriving.

IMMIGRATION AND THE FUTURE
OF AMERICAN FAITH

In contemporary American politics, especially among conservatives, a rising xenophobia has blinded many Christians to the spiritual effect of immigration on the United States. Undoubtedly, the material already presented here may have created discomfort and cognitive dissonance for some readers. "What benefit," some might ask, "could possibly come from millions of 'illegal aliens' storming over the borders of our country?" That question deserves an answer, and this book will offer it. In short, the arrival of millions of new immigrants to America in our time virtually guarantees a strong future for Christianity and other religions in America's future!

Faith in America will continue in the future, as immigrants restore and enhance the historic majority composed of diverse forms of Christianity. Even America's moribund Mainline Protestant churches will reap new members as the nation's robust free market for religion offers its wide variety of religious goods and services to meet emerging demands. The diversity of source nations for American immigrants will guarantee that America will continue to provide a sanctuary of religious freedom for other faiths as well.

> The arrival of millions of new immigrants to America in our time virtually guarantees a strong future for Christianity and other religions in America's future!

Immigrants have already begun to restore America's faith across the board. The main story, however, in immigration to America, centers on Christians.

Eminent sociologists of religion Roger Finke and Rodney Stark noted that "from 1965 to 2000 over 23 million immigrants arrived in the United States and . . . the vast majority of the new immigrants involved in religion are forming Protestant and Catholic congregations."[38] This flood of Christian immigrants not only carried people who were Christians before they came to America but also many converts who come to Christian faith after immigrating. Fink and Stark stated, "A study of Chicago Koreans found that 52 percent were affiliated with Christian churches before emigration and half of the remainder join Christian churches after arriving in the United States."[39] Anecdotal and participant observation evidence from Latino Evangelical congregations suggests that between 50 and 80 percent of all members have converted since coming to the United States, and the same pattern of Christian immigration and church planting, resulting in the conversion of other immigrants, holds true in Chinese, Filipino, assorted African and Caribbean nationalities, and other ethnic groups as well.

The positive, winning mindset of Christian immigrants in today's America does not spring only from the evangelistic success they see in their churches but also from the burgeoning global revival of Christianity.[40] Consider the state of Christianity around the world today. According to Pew Research, Christianity ranks as the world's largest religion. It numbers around 2.18 billion adherents, having almost quadrupled in size over the last one hundred years from about 600 million in 1910 to almost 2.2 billion in 2010.[41] Islam has about 1.62 billion adherents,[42] and Hinduism, a little less than 1.03 billion,[43] so Christianity is 35 percent larger than the second largest religion, and nearly as large as the second and third largest religions put together.

Around the world, Christianity has exploded with growth in the recent past. As renowned religion scholar Philip Jenkins has described in *The Next Christendom*, Christians in the Global South now outnumber Christians in the West. According to unofficial sources, the Chinese government estimates a Christian population of 130 million in China—up from 1 million in 1970![44] According to eminent sociologist Peter Berger, "The most reliable source for religious demography" estimates Chinese Christians to number 120 million.[45] Counting Christians in China presents a challenge since the great majority of them meet in illegal house churches. If the current growth continues, the number of Christians in China may reach 220 million by the year 2050.[46] Chinese church growth represents the greatest revival/awakening in the history of Christianity.

The worldwide revival has sparked church growth in South Korea also, where Christians now outnumber Buddhists and 29.3 percent of the population has affiliated with churches.[47] In Vietnam, the U.S. Department of State reported estimates in 2006 that "the growth of Protestant believers has been as much as 600 percent over the past decade, despite government restrictions on proselytizing activities," with churches reporting 1.6 million Protestants in that country.[48]

While North Africa remains a Muslim stronghold, Sub-Saharan Africa has joined the world Christian revival in dramatic fashion. According to *Christianity Today*, "In the twentieth century, the Christian population in Africa exploded from an estimated eight or nine million in 1900 (8 to 9 percent) to some 335 million in 2000 (45 percent)."[49] The Vatican reports, "In Africa, between 1978 and 2007, the number of Catholics grew from 55 million to

146 million," and a recent study by the Pew Forum on Religion and Public Life counts the continent's Catholic population at more than 175 million.[50] According to the World Christian Database, "Pentecostals today represent 12 percent, or about 107 million, of Africa's population" and the total number of Christians "grew to an estimated 400 million, making up 46 percent of the population."[51] The numbers expand too fast to count!

While Catholicism grows dramatically in Africa, it has shrunk to some degree in Latin America, where Pentecostalism continues to advance rapidly. Citing 2005 figures from the World Christian Database, Pew Research reports that

> Pentecostals represent 13 percent, or about 75 million, of Latin America's population of nearly 560 million. Charismatic members of non-Pentecostal denominations, who in Latin America are overwhelmingly Catholic, number an additional 80 million or so, or 15 percent of the population. As recently as 1970, Pentecostals and charismatics combined represented no more than 4 percent of the region's population.[52]

Despite centuries of post-Enlightenment claims that Christianity would fade away in the modern world, it continues to thrive in a way that ridicules secularist projections of its demise. Rather than opting for a modern, cerebral, de-supernaturalized faith like the one prescribed by liberal theologians and adopted by many rapidly disappearing Mainline Protestant churches, postmodern Christians choose Evangelical and Charismatic Catholic churches. As immigrants from countries like Brazil, where Pentecostals and

Charismatics make up 34 percent of the population, Guatemala (40 percent), and the Philippines (40 percent) come to America, they bring their high-octane faith with a positive expectation of missional success.[53]

A recent report from Pew Research states that "seven-in-ten evangelical leaders who live in the Global South (71 percent) expect that five years from now the state of evangelicalism in their countries will be better than it is today." In contrast, most Evangelical leaders in the Global North expect things to either remain the same (21 percent) or get worse (33 percent).[54]

The secularist europhilic elites who dominate traditional communications media have a strong motivation to give Christians the impression that faith has begun a long descent into oblivion around the world. A blindered look at post-Christian Europe confirms their narrative. But the New Pilgrims come to America from the context of hot Christian advance in their native lands, and they think America's religious future is bright. Samuel Rodríguez, a widely recognized leader of the Hispanic Christian movement in the United States, recently said:

> We are not drinking the proverbial Kool-Aid that Christianity is in decline, that this is the last hour of the Christian global narrative . . . We are not drinking the Kool-Aid. As a matter of fact, we have a very strong sense of optimism . . . we do believe the best is yet to come.[55]

Christian immigrants and their pastors have brought that same expectation of growth and expansion to America, and along with the new converts reached through the new churches they have planted, they intend to change America. Unlike those who want to change America to make it look like post-Christian Europe, Christian immigrants mean to turn America back to its historic identity, to make America a shining city on a hill for the world so that the world may see the glory of God. They are the New Pilgrims, and someday their descendants will proudly declare, "I'm a descendant of the New Pilgrims who came to America at the beginning of the twenty-first century and restored the faith of America."

2

WHY PILGRIMS?

The Essential Link between Christianity and Migration

M any may wonder, "Sure, lots of Christian immigrants come to America, but does that justify calling them the New Pilgrims? How can they compare to the legendary William Bradford, Miles Standish, and the other Pilgrims who signed the Mayflower Compact as they arrived in America with such high ideals of liberty, self-government, and Christian example?" In fact, the most prominent leaders among the New Pilgrims compare quite impressively with those Mayflower leaders, as the stories in following chapters will illustrate. But before looking at individual stories, consider the following good reasons to see today's Christian immigrants to America as pilgrims.

First, consider the definition of the word *pilgrim*. According to *Dictionary.com*, a pilgrim "journeys, especially a long distance, to some sacred place as an act of religious devotion." The word also refers to "a traveler or wanderer, especially in a foreign place" or even "a newcomer to a region or place, especially to the western U.S."[1] Christian immigrants certainly fit the second and third definitions of pilgrim, but do Christian immigrants see their journey to America as ending in a "sacred place"? Do they travel as an act of religious devotion?

Years ago I attended a national church meeting in El Salvador. A group of men announced to the leaders that they would leave the following day to cross the Rio Grande (without authorization) into the United States. So the whole crowd of thousands gathered around them and commissioned them as *misioneros mojados* or "wet missionaries." The entire group saw their sojourn as sacred, and many thousands of others continue to receive formal commissioning from their churches for their often arduous and hazardous travel to the United States every year. At the end of the journey, they often tell amazing stories of divine providence and care along the way, casting the entire experience in terms of pilgrimage.

> Christians around the world feel a holy zeal to give something back to America, and those pilgrims arrive daily on a mission from God.

Why would Christian immigrants from around the world see the United States as a sacred place to which they would begin a pilgrimage? It rises from the fact that people around the world see the United States as the paradigmatic Christian nation. Over the last century, the great majority of missionaries sent out around the world came from America. With the idealized zeal that only an expatriate can muster, American missionaries often presented their homeland as the prime example for all customs, culture, and practices. In the eyes of many

Christians around the world, the powerful American church could spare its best people as missionaries to reach the nations; it also possessed seemingly inexhaustible financial and strategic resources for the development of Christian institutions overseas; it enjoyed religious freedom and a roaring economy because of the biblical principles the nation was founded upon.[2] In addition, the story has made the circuit for years that Christianity in America has begun to decline and needs missionaries.

In the New Testament, the Apostle Paul travelled throughout the ancient Roman world taking up an offering for the saints in Jerusalem. He based his appeal to believers on the concept that they had a sacred obligation to the Jerusalem church that had sent out missionaries to proclaim the gospel to them. In a similar way, Christians around the world feel a holy zeal to give something back to America, and those pilgrims arrive daily on our shores, airports, desert sands, and riverbanks to take up the task. In their hearts, they come on a mission from God.

IMMIGRANT MISSIONARIES

The sense of mission felt by many immigrants finds illustration in Edgardo Montano's story. He grew up in poverty as a child in El Salvador, and his parents lacked the resources to send him to school until his pastor, an American missionary named John Bueno, procured an American sponsor to pay his school fees at the private Christian school operated by his church. After graduating from high school, he attended the national university of El Salvador for three years, where he majored in chemical engineering and began to sympathize with the Marxist guerrilla movement that had arisen to fight social injustice in his country.

The more Montano drank from the guerrilla wells, the more he came to resent the United States, seeing it as responsible for the poverty and oppression suffered by his people. Cognitive dissonance between the discourse of his peers on one hand and the American generosity he had received to fund his studies came to a head when the name of his pastor and benefactor, John Bueno, showed up on a hit list of "enemies of the Salvadoran people." America might be the source of economic inequality in Latin America, but Montano knew that John Bueno had acted heroically for twenty years in funding the education of thousands of Salvadoran children. Rather than cooperate with a movement determined to assassinate his pastor, he dropped out of the university and entered a Bible institute to study for ministry.

As a seminary student, Montano sat under the teaching of American missionaries and felt his own call to follow in their footsteps. After a successful experience as a missionary to Panama, he returned to his country, where he planted a vibrant church and worked with missionaries on national projects. Many trips to the United States during the ensuing years built in him a love for the country and the beginnings of a sense of calling to minister to the burgeoning population of Latinos there.

In 2010, he had the opportunity to attend a church conference in Anchorage, Alaska, where he learned that a tiny handful of Spanish-speaking churches struggled to reach thirty-six thousand Latino immigrants with the gospel. Dramatic need and intense calling led him to leave a strong middle-class church in San Salvador and a comfortable salary to accept a less-lucrative missionary appointment to Alaska, where he currently pastors a growing start-up church.

"I'm facing the greatest challenge of my life as a minister," Montano explained. "I accepted it because in Alaska, it's possible to do a pioneer work, like the Apostle Paul said, not building on someone else's foundation."[3] His gratitude to American missionaries did not send him to Alaska, but he recognizes,

If it had not been for the missionary work realized in El Salvador by American missionaries, my family might not have ever known the gospel. But thanks to a missionary who came to us in 1956, my family has had the gospel for five generations. Now the roles have switched, because when I found out about the need in the United States, and having the preparation, the anointing, and the call to take it there, I feel an inescapable commitment to give back to Americans what I received by their graces.[4]

He realizes his whole life has been a pilgrimage with Christ. "Like the Pilgrims that came to America in the beginning," he said, "I have come to stay. I plan to finish the rest of my ministerial life here. I'm not planning to go home. I want to establish a legacy for a new generation of ministers, leaving footprints for them to follow in their own pilgrimage."[5]

CHRISTIAN LIFE AS A PILGRIMAGE

It should not surprise Christians that their immigrant brothers and sisters see themselves as pilgrims, since Christians have considered their entire lives a pilgrimage from the very beginnings of the faith. For centuries, the best-selling Christian book besides the Bible was *The Pilgrim's Progress*, an allegory of the Christian life that portrays the challenges and temptations Christians face in the world on their way to Heaven. Before *The Pilgrim's Progress*, Dante's *Divine Comedy* transfixed Christian readers with its story of the soul's journey to God after death, describing as well the many kinds of snares people negotiate throughout the pilgrimage of their lives. Christians have long understood their faith walk as a pilgrimage and every Christian as a pilgrim.

The New Testament itself sets the basis for a Christian worldview of life as a pilgrimage, especially in Chapters 11 and 12 of the book of Hebrews. Hebrews 12:1–2 states,

> And let us run with perseverance the race marked out for us, fixing our eyes on Jesus, the pioneer and perfecter of faith. For the joy set before him he endured the cross, scorning its shame, and sat down at the right hand of the throne of God.

The anonymous author of Hebrews sees the Christian life as a "race marked out for us." He describes the role of Jesus as "the pioneer and perfecter of faith."

The word translated "pioneer" in this verse—the King James Version translates the word as "author"—offers an enlightening insight. The original Greek word, *archegos*, does not translate effectively as a single word in English. It carries the connotation of a pioneer, author, leader, trailblazer, scout, or prince, but it also has a special technical usage referring to the leader of a band of pilgrims and pioneers who would leave Greece to establish a new colony.[6] The *archegos* had already visited the destination beforehand and knew the way there. The *archegos* held the responsibility of guiding the pilgrims to their new home, protecting them from any natural or supernatural enemies they would encounter along the way, and helping them to establish Greek culture and the worship of their gods in their new place. In terms of Christian life, the word refers to Jesus as the leader of a group of pilgrims who have decided to leave their former home and follow Him to colonize a new, heavenly land where they will establish for eternity the worship of their God.

Chapter 11 of Hebrews sets the context for the summative declaration in Hebrews 12:2. In the list of Old Testament heroes of faith, the author singles out Abraham as a pilgrim called by God to leave his former home and go to the place God would show him:

> By faith Abraham, when called to go to a place he would later receive as his inheritance, obeyed and went, even though he did not know where he was going. By faith he made his home in the promised land like a stranger in a foreign country; he lived in tents, as did Isaac and Jacob, who were heirs with him of the same promise. For he was looking forward to the city with foundations, whose architect and builder is God.[7]

The story of Abraham and his heirs goes on to describe them as foreigners in the earth:

> All these people were still living by faith when they died. They did not receive the things promised; they only saw them and welcomed them from a distance, *admitting that they were foreigners and strangers on earth*. People who

say such things show that they are looking for a country of their own. If they had been thinking of the country they had left, they would have had opportunity to return. Instead, they were longing for a better country—a heavenly one. Therefore God is not ashamed to be called their God, for he has prepared a city for them.[8]

The rest of the chapter describes God's Old Testament pilgrims, who suffered incredible trials on their pilgrimage to the City of God.

Verse 38 declares, "The world was not worthy of them." The text goes on to explain, "These were all commended for their faith, yet none of them received what had been promised, since God had planned something better for us so that only together with us would they be made perfect."[9] In the verses that immediately follow, Jesus appears as the leader, the pioneer, the trailblazer—the *archegos*—who has gone before us, who has defeated His enemies, and who will establish His people in the eternal worship of God. Every Christian, every Old Testament believer, every follower of God's revelation in the history of the world has a part in that band of colonizers, immigrants, and pilgrims Christ will lead to victory.

The Christian concept of believers as pilgrims and strangers in the world finds powerful expression in the old American spiritual "The Wayfaring Stranger":

> I'm just a poor wayfaring stranger
> traveling through this world of woe.
> Yet there's no sickness, toil nor danger
> in that bright land to which I go.

I'm going there to see my father.
I'm going there no more to roam.
I'm just a-going over Jordan.
I'm just a-going over home.[10]

American churches have hardly sung these lyrics over the past forty years. They no longer resonate with most Christians who enjoy the privilege of native-born American citizenship.

It is true that books on near-death experiences of Heaven or Hell sell millions of copies to those who have lost loved ones to death and have begun to consider the matter of eternity.[11] Nevertheless, life in the world has treated today's American Christians well, and while they would rather go to Heaven than to Hell, they often do not pay much attention to the concept of the afterlife until they get close to experiencing it—either through the death of friends and family or through threats to their personal health.

Slaves in pre–Civil War America certainly understood the song. The migrant workers, coal miners, and mill hands of the Dust Bowl era and the Great Depression totally identified with the concept of Christians as pilgrims and strangers in this world. Immigrants who cross our borders without legal authorization also get it. They believe they do not enter the country as mere "immigrants" but rather as pilgrims of God.

THE ROLE OF MIGRATION IN GOD'S MISSION

A careful reading of the whole Bible reveals that human pilgrimage and migration play a crucial role not only conceptually in the Christian life but also in the fulfillment of God's mission in the world. From Genesis to Revelation, the Bible tells the stories of

God's people on the move. When Christians discover the role of immigration in God's plan of salvation, they see today's immigrants in a whole new light.

God's will for humanity begins with the very first words pronounced by God to humans, reported in Genesis 1:28. In the creation story, God creates the heavens and the earth by the power of His word. Light and darkness, dry ground and oceans, green plants and all kinds of animals follow—all summoned into being by the power of God's word. Finally, God says, "Let us make mankind in our image, in our likeness."[12]

At that point in the narrative of Genesis 1, a major change occurs. Up until then the Hebrew text has moved along in sober prose, but when God decrees the creation of humanity, the story bursts out into poetry—just like it does in classic American musical theater. When the drama gets to a high point, somebody breaks out singing. The greatness of the moment, when God created people in the divine image to rule and serve the Creation as God's regents, causes the narrator to break out into song:

> When Christians discover the role of immigration in God's plan of salvation, they see today's immigrants in a whole new light.

So God created mankind in his own image,
in the image of God he created them;
male and female he created them.[13]

The action pauses briefly for these melodic verses of celebration, but then the story gets right back down to business. Delighted with the new human creatures, God pronounces the first words of blessing on them.

Recent research conducted by the Gallup Organization on the subject of human well-being has revealed that people need a sense of purpose more than any other single factor in order to flourish.[14] Accordingly, the Bible presents God's very first words to humans as a blessing that includes a command, giving humanity a mission to fulfill:

God blessed them and said to them, "Be fruitful and increase in number; fill the earth and subdue it. Rule over the fish in the sea and the birds in the sky and over every living creature that moves on the ground."[15]

In this mission statement for humanity, Genesis lays out a triple mandate based on three fundamental characteristics of human nature people naturally long to fulfill: reproduction, migration, and dominion.

This triple mandate from God would ensure that human beings would flourish on the earth, increasing greatly in number (with over seven billion currently inhabiting the earth), spreading out to every corner of the planet (driven by their innate wanderlust to explore the whole world and even the moon and outer space), and establishing a habitat in the earth (by taking control over their environment and establishing a secure way of life). By the same inexorable word by which God called the heavens and the earth, light and darkness, seas and dry land, plants and animals into being, Genesis sets out a template for human nature and instincts to guarantee the success of God's mission on earth.

The book of Revelation envisions the endgame of the biblical description of God's mission. In John the Revelator's vision of the end of time, he describes a great heavenly multitude "that no one could count, from every nation, tribe, people and language, standing before the throne and before the Lamb . . . And they cried out in a loud voice: 'Salvation belongs to our God, who sits on the throne, and to the Lamb.'"[16]

That scenario reveals the success of humanity's mission. Reproduction has brought uncounted sons and daughters into life to receive God's love and salvation. Migration has brought on the full flowering of human diversity, creating dazzling beauty through diversity in race, language, culture, and nationality. All dominion has been yielded back to Christ, who sits on the throne of the universe as the guarantor of salvation for the human race. God's mission stands completed, to the benefit of redeemed humanity.

> Abraham becomes God's immigrant and nomad, moving from country to country to find God's promised land.

The Bible not only declares the beginning and the final scenario of divine mission but also chronicles how God used migration to move the plan of salvation forward. The story begins with Adam and Eve, whose sin results in their exile from the Garden of Eden.[17] Cain becomes the first fugitive after murdering his brother.[18] As the peoples of the earth wander and scatter, and as evil becomes rampant in the earth, Noah's household becomes the first family of refugees, fleeing from a natural disaster. After their rescue, God repeats the human mission statement, enjoining them to "be fruitful and increase in number and fill the earth."[19]

Genesis will continue to describe virtually every category of human migration.[20] After Genesis 10 describes the dispersion of the earth's peoples, the people of Babel in Chapter 11 disobey the mission by building a great city and high tower, "so that we may make a name for ourselves; otherwise we will be scattered over the face of the whole earth."[21] In response, God reasserts the migration mandate by increasing their diversity through confusing their language and forcing them to scatter.

The story then moves on to Abraham, the pivotal figure of the Old Testament and the patriarch of three of the world's great religions—Judaism, Christianity, and Islam. Although Abraham's father had already immigrated westward from Ur of the Chaldeans to the land of Haran, God calls Abraham to move further on to Canaan.

> Go from your country, your people, and your father's household to the land I will show you. I will make you into a great nation, and I will bless you; I will make your name great, and you will be a blessing. I will bless those who bless you, and whoever curses you I will curse; and all peoples on earth will be blessed through you.[22]

In the chapters that follow, Abraham becomes God's immigrant and nomad, moving from country to country to find God's promised land (as the book of Hebrews describes later in the New Testament).

Along the way, the flawed hero participates as both a victim and a perpetrator in many of the same struggles and ethical dilemmas faced by today's immigrants—getting deported from Egypt for lying about his marital status;[23] serving in the military of a foreign country;[24] taking ugly advantage of Hagar, an Egyptian victim of human trafficking, as a sexual slave in his household;[25] getting deported from Gerar for the same lie he had told in Egypt;[26] and sending his servant to Haran to get a bride for his son Isaac (a practice akin to the arranged marriages so common among East Indian immigrants today).[27]

The immigration stories continue with Abraham's son Isaac and his grandson Jacob, who live as nomads moving from country to country and experience a series of migratory misadventures including intermarriage, deportation, refugee status, deceptive labor practices, and even entrepreneurial success as foreign investors.[28] The book of Genesis ends with the story of Joseph, a victim of human trafficking, who serves as a labor slave in Egypt until his God-given wisdom saves the known world from famine and results in the migration of Jacob's descendants to Egypt.

After Joseph's death, the Egyptians reduce the Hebrew immigrants to slavery, and they suffer hundreds of years under Egyptian oppression—a story not unfamiliar to immigrants throughout world history who labor in ignominy as slaves and semi-slaves in harsh and ill-paid stoop labor to guarantee cheap food prices to native populations. In more recent centuries, African slaves and their African-American descendants under the oppression of Jim Crow laws found comfort and inspiration in the story of these Hebrews and their triumphant exodus, just as European colonizers around the globe during the Age of Discovery took motivation from the stories of Joshua's conquest of the Holy Land after Israel's generation of wilderness wandering.[29]

The early story of Israel's time in the Holy Land traces the efforts of the Hebrews to establish themselves as an independent nation in Canaan, and it finds its high-water mark in the success of Ruth, a Moabite immigrant to Israel, whose grandson David becomes Israel's greatest king. But Israel's Golden Age lasted for even less time than its captivity in Egypt, ending in the scattering (and virtual end) of the northern tribes and the Babylonian captivity of the surviving Jews from the southern kingdom. Many of the great Old Testament prophets lived as immigrants and foreign captives—notably Jeremiah, Ezekiel, Daniel, Esther, Ezra, Nehemiah, and others. The return of the exiles to Israel continued the saga of Old Testament migration in service to the call of Abraham and, only partially successful, resulted in massive migration out of Israel to Egypt and to the entire Greek world in the famous Jewish Diaspora.

As Hebrews 11 describes, all of this migration of God's people represented service (whether voluntarily or by obligation) to Israel's calling to be a light to the nations.[30] Wherever the people of God migrated, the story of Israel's God and Savior travelled with them. Stories like the visit of the Queen of Sheba, the healing of the Syrian captain Naaman, the evangelization of Babylon's Nebuchadnezzar, and others chronicle the success of God's migrants in preparing the way for New Testament mission around the known world after the coming of Jesus.

When the New Testament era dawns, the family of Abraham (the Wandering Aramaen, as Jews confessed on a daily basis) gives birth to Jesus.[31] The story of Jesus continues with the arrival of magi who arrive from Persia, the place of Israel's former captivity, as evidence of Israel's effective witness to the glories of God. After they arrive to worship the newborn King of the Jews, the narrative shifts to the flight of Jesus' family to Egypt as political refugees, escaping Herod's plot to kill the new King after learning of His birth through the report of the magi. Jesus' own stature as a refugee child in a foreign land has often provided inspiration to Christians to demonstrate special care to refugees and immigrants.

> With that command Jesus made every Christian in the world a potential immigrant and a spiritual pilgrim.

The life, death, and resurrection of Jesus, of course, set the message in concrete for the future of God's mission as the New Testament spells it out. Humanity had no way of rescuing itself from estrangement from God by its own efforts, and Christ's death on the Cross for the sins of humanity provided the way to reconciliation with God. "Whoever believes and is baptized," Jesus said in Mark 16:16, "will be saved." Just before moving on to the right hand of God and the throne, Jesus gave His disciples a final command known as the Great Commission, which calls upon every Christian to:

> Go and make disciples of all nations, baptizing them in the name of the Father and of the Son and of the Holy Spirit, and teaching them to obey everything I have commanded you. And surely I am with you always, to the very end of the age.[32]

With that command Jesus made every Christian in the world a potential immigrant and a spiritual pilgrim.

The rest of the New Testament, especially the book of Acts, tells the story of how Christians—both missional migrants and specially appointed missionaries called apostles—carried the good news from Jerusalem to the far corners of their world. Many of the New Testament books constitute letters to God's immigrants and their converts in places around the Roman world. Take a look at any of the epistles and look for immigrants. Look in Romans 16 at the impressive list of immigrants Paul salutes. The Bible is a book to immigrants, for immigrants, about immigrants in service to every nation in the world.

MISSIONAL MIGRANTS

An example of a missional migrant is Jesús De Paz. The phrase *high-octane* perfectly describes this pastor of *Comunidad Cristiana Latina Iglesia Rio de Vida*, also known as River of Life Foursquare Church in Wenatchee, Washington. Known as the "Apple Capital of the World," the region around Wenatchee produces 60 percent of the apples sold in the United States—over 100 million forty-pound boxes of apples[33]—on "more than 175,000 acres of apple orchards . . . nestled in the eastern foothills of the picturesque Cascade Mountains."[34] Latin Americans have migrated to Eastern Washington for many decades to work in the booming agricultural industries that sprang up with improved irrigation in the twentieth century, and they now constitute a majority of the population in many of the towns and counties throughout the area.

Jesús De Paz came to Washington from El Salvador as a fifteen-year-old in 1972, brought to America on a legal work visa by a relative who worked as an engineer. But the relationship did not go well, and Jesús soon left his relative's custody, losing his legal status but gaining independence to live life his own way. He went to work in the apple, pear, and cherry orchards to support himself, and his talents would quickly ensure his promotion. Within two years, he had become the manager of a large orchard, with responsibilities over all the workers and the technical operation of the orchards.

In 1975 everything changed. He met the other Jesús and surrendered his life to Christ. "I found the Lord," he said, "and I started to share what God had done in my heart, right away, within a month of getting saved."[35] Full of zeal and blessed with a natural talent for leadership, he quickly led many others to Christianity. In 1976 he felt led to go back to El Salvador to preach to his friends and relatives, and when he found he could not return to the United States without getting his papers in order, his employer helped him obtain legal status and become a United States citizen. Since that time, he has brought his whole family to America—his parents, five brothers, three sisters, and other relatives also.

As De Paz led more and more immigrants to Christ, their fledgling church brought in a number of pastors from Central America and other places to tend them. But none of the pastors stayed for long. "I always got left doing the work—the Lord's work."[36] So De Paz, who had become an effective preacher, assumed the pastorate in 1982, and the church prospered further. After twenty years in the orchards, he would walk away from his well-paid secular position to pastor the church on a full-time basis. The results of his ministry reflect the high energy of his work:

The work started growing. We started the Bible institute, we started to have men and women ready to go and pastor, and we sent them out. And we've been planting churches since that day until now. We have planted more than a thousand churches in Mexico, Central America—Nicaragua, Guatemala, El Salvador, the majority in Honduras—and quite a few here in the United States. And that has been a blessing, what we've occupied ourselves in.[37]

In the United States alone, the workers, raised up by De Paz through his congregation and Bible institute, have planted fifty-two churches.

While the church has provided some temporary financial support for its daughter churches in the United States, the workers sent to other countries have generally made their own way financially, following the model De Paz himself set as a bi-vocational pastor, working hard in both agricultural and mission fields. Limitless in his energy and powerful in his passion, Pastor Jesús has preached in countries all over the world, including churches on five different continents. His approach to combining physical and spiritual work finds expression in the church's ownership of several orchards and fields, which not only provide work for people but also profits and foodstuffs for the vigorous social outreach of the church.

Although attendance suffered when the church recently moved to a new location, about five hundred people now attend the mother church, which offers multiple services in Spanish and English to immigrants representing twelve to fifteen nations at any given time. About forty white Americans attend the church because of the excitement generated by its high-energy worship.

Pastor Jesús explained, "The church exists exclusively to preach a message of consolation, hope, and healing to the community, and every time we plant a new church, we always ask God to show us the next location."[38]

"*¡Mira lo que ha hecho Dios!*—Look what God has done!" exclaimed De Paz. "Not only did God bring us here and save us, but he has carried us to five continents to preach!"[39] Not every immigrant pastor has his level of talent for leadership and ministry, but the same work ethic, positive outlook, godly enthusiasm, personal charisma, and fruitful evangelism have made an appearance across America as the immigrant Christian movement has spread.

Whether Christians preach the gospel in their homeland or carry it to the ends of the earth as missionaries, they "go." This sacred mission should convert their whole lives into a pilgrimage—a sacred journey to a holy place. The "end of the age" would bring about the fullness of the Kingdom of God, the inheritance of eternal life for God's people, and the gathering of the great multitude of Revelation 7:9–10. Christian non-pilgrims do not exist. Just like American Christians may appropriately see their lives as a pilgrimage to Heaven, in which they carry out a calling to spread the gospel to everyone as they go, immigrant Christians interpret their journey to the United States as part of that holy pilgrimage—one in which God has shown mighty deliverance and power to save.

3

THE NEW PILGRIMS SPEAK

Recently the headlines of the *Seattle Times* declared a vision for America's future. The lead article celebrated, "Retail pot to get rolling Tuesday," explaining why it took several months for legalization of marijuana to result in retail sales.[1] At the bottom of the front page, another story bore the headline, "Coming to U.S. for baby—and womb to carry it." The article went on to explain how *American liberalism has surpassed that of more conservative Europe* in legalizing the hire of women's bodies for childbearing, especially for homosexual couples like Joān and Paulo from Portugal. The article obliquely mentioned that critics of the practice "sometimes draw an analogy to prostitution, another subject that raises debate over whether making money off a woman's body represents empowerment or exploitation."[2]

Across the country at the mother ship of liberal journalism, the *New York Times*, columnist Maureen Dowd asked, "Who Do We Think We Are?" and quoted Republican pollster Frank Luntz as saying, "The Fourth of July was always a celebration of American exceptionalism . . . Now it's a commiseration of American disappointment." She noted, "For the first time perhaps, hope is not as much a characteristic of American feelings."[3] Neither the right nor the left can celebrate what America has become.

The long culture wars, pressed aggressively on American society from the left, have borne the fruit of confusion and division in what founders conceived as the "United" States of America.[4] Fundamentalist Christians know better than anyone how reluctantly they took up the battle after years of cultural isolation, deeply conflicted about the morality of getting involved in politics. Yet despite the unquestionable victories of the left, Dowd—a high-ranking liberal cultural warrior—seemed almost to lament the left's success in dividing the country:

> Sadly, we see ourselves as a people who can never understand one another. We've given up on the notion that we can cohere, even though the founders forged America by holding together people with deep differences.[5]

Dowd recognizes immediately that immigrants currently pay the price for American division:

> A nation of immigrants watched over by the Statue of Liberty—with a government unable to pass immigration reform despite majority support—sees protesters take to the streets to keep Hispanic children trying to cross the border from being housed in their communities.[6]

America's Pilgrim founders would not approve of the tragic irony of the situation. It seems almost no one in today's America sees the country in the terms taught us by our Puritan forefather John Winthrop, as a shining "city on a hill."

Like some seventy-five or more generations of Christians before them, today's Christian immigrants clearly qualify as pilgrims. But they also deserve comparison with the Plymouth Pilgrims of 1620. Can they help us bring about a renewal of American unity and purpose? If they cannot, the culture wars will soon succeed in irreparably destroying the America our Pilgrim forebears bequeathed to us. The good news brought by the New Pilgrims not only offers a renewal of America's faith but also hope for an end to the culture wars that have paralyzed her politics.

> The standoff between the right and the left, offers challenge enough, but the introduction of immigrants as a third element to the standoff converts it into a Mexican standoff.

The standoff between the right and the left, the stubborn donkeys and the never-forgetting elephants, offers challenge enough, but the introduction of immigrants as a third element to the standoff converts it into a Mexican standoff. *Wikipedia* explains:

A *Mexican standoff* is most precisely a confrontation among three opponents armed with guns. The tactics for such a confrontation are substantially different from those for a duel, where the first to shoot has the advantage. In a confrontation among three mutually hostile participants, the first to shoot is at a tactical disadvantage. If opponent A shoots opponent B, then while so occupied, opponent C can shoot A, thus winning the conflict. Since it is the second opponent to shoot that has the advantage, no one wants to go first.[7]

Today's crisis of culture in America will never resolve itself. The right and the left will never back off from each other. They will need a third, non-political force to help them break the impasse. The New Pilgrims make up that third force. Nobody needs to shoot first in the immigration standoff. Even as we speak, the third force offers a peaceful way forward.

Samuel Rodríguez, president of the National Hispanic Christian Leadership Conference, calls the third way "the Lamb's Agenda."[8] America will win its future, he says, neither by the victory of the Democratic Donkey or the Republican Elephant but rather by following the Lamb. But before considering the Lamb's Agenda, let's go back to seventeenth-century Massachusetts.

THE PILGRIMS' DREAM

Most Americans have a vague memory of the real identity of the Pilgrims that landed at Plymouth Rock. Some people may be able to name Miles Standish and William Bradford as early leaders among them, but almost no one can quote anything they said or wrote. Some know that 41 passengers among the 101 souls on board the *Mayflower*, all adult men, signed a document called the Mayflower Compact, modestly committing themselves to live under the Rule of Law. The text of the covenant, in modern language, reads:

We, whose names are underwritten . . . Having undertaken, for the Glory of God, and advancements of the

Christian faith and honor of our King and Country, a voyage to plant the first colony in the Northern parts of Virginia, do by these presents, solemnly and mutually, in the presence of God, and one another, covenant and combine ourselves together into a civil body politic; for our better ordering, and preservation and furtherance of the ends aforesaid; and by virtue hereof to enact, constitute, and frame, such just and equal laws, ordinances, acts, constitutions, and offices, from time to time, as shall be thought most meet and convenient for the general good of the colony; unto which we promise all due submission and obedience.[9]

The agreement stands as a landmark in the formation of American government, but its modesty surprises those who may have an exalted view of the Pilgrims' vision for a Christian nation. Their modest experiment met with equally modest success, and William Bradford would not only serve as author of the Compact and governor of the colony but would also go on to write the first histories of the colony, complete with his reminiscence of the Pilgrims' mission and zeal and his disappointments with the results of their work.

The quote most regularly recognized by Americans as belonging to the Pilgrims actually came from a later arrival to Massachusetts who represented a slightly different religious group—John Winthrop, the Puritan governor who arrived in Massachusetts ten years later. Like Bradford, Winthrop wrote a sermon aboard ship (the *Arbella* in 1630) in which he famously envisioned the Puritan mission in America:

Now the only way to avoid this shipwreck, and to provide for our posterity, is to follow the counsel of Micah, to do justly, to love mercy, to walk humbly with our God. For this end, we must be knit together, in this work, as one man. We must entertain each other in brotherly affection. We must be willing to abridge ourselves of our superfluities, for the supply of others' necessities. We must uphold a familiar commerce together . . . We must delight in each other; make others' conditions our own; . . . always having before our eyes our commission and community in the work, as members of the same body . . . The Lord will be our God, and . . . we shall find that the God of Israel is among us . . . for we must consider that we shall be as a city upon a hill. The eyes of all people are upon us. So that if we shall deal falsely with our God in this work we have undertaken, and so cause Him to withdraw His present help from us, we shall be made a story and a by-word through the world . . . We shall shame the faces of many of God's worthy servants, and cause their prayers to be turned into curses upon us till we be consumed out of the good land whither we are going.[10]

Winthrop, like the Pilgrims before him, envisioned an America where righteousness and justice dwelt together. Not only would people enjoy freedom; they would do so in a state of submission to God.

Notice what the vision lacks: it includes none of the rugged individualism that would characterize later visions of America. Neither does it include any celebration of pot use or prostitution.

People would live together in a society of common interest, with love for one another, with commerce together, with concern for the needs of others, and sharing of their goods in times of need. "We must be willing to abridge ourselves of our superfluities, for the supply of others' necessities," Winthrop wrote. Not only would Americans serve one another in his vision, they would also serve the God of Israel.

Winthrop includes both Republican and Democratic values, without the extreme dimensions of either. Winthrop would have abhorred the current state of affairs in America—in which one extreme argues for radical personal freedom to pollute the nation's righteousness with legalized drugs and prostitution while the other extreme combats mercy by blocking the path of government buses trying to move recently arrived children, immigrating without the supervision and protection of any adult, to safe places where they can receive decent nutrition, medical care, and rest.[11]

> Winthrop's vision of America as a shining city on a hill set the template for American patriotism for three hundred years.

Winthrop's vision of America as a shining city on a hill—following up on the vision of Bradford and the Pilgrims with even greater eloquence—set the template for American patriotism for three hundred years. While the Massachusetts colony may have converted rapidly into a non-church-going group of rough and rowdy pioneers, the call to righteousness and justice made by the early Massachusetts settlers has endured as the expectation of our national destiny. Every American until recently knew that America stood as a beacon of goodness for the rest of the world. The idea of American Exceptionalism emanates from Winthrop's vision. America's destiny depended on shining the light of justice and freedom and goodness. "America is great," states a national proverb celebrated by politicians from Bill Clinton to Pat Buchanan, "because she is good, and if America ever ceases to be good, America will cease to be great."[12]

Almost four hundred years later, the world still watches us— and streams to us. Can today's immigrants renew the vision of goodness that made us great? Do they have the moral vision to reestablish America's dual heritage of righteousness and justice? Do they have eloquent leaders capable of stirring the hearts of future fellow citizens with beautiful ideals and values? Can they leave behind them a heritage that will one day result in people proudly tracing their ancestry back to the New Pilgrims of the early twenty-first century, who restored America's faith and steered it away from the impasse of the culture wars?

I offer Samuel Rodríguez as Exhibit A.

A NEW JOHN WINTHROP

Born to a Puerto Rican family in Newark, New Jersey, and raised in the "little town of Bethlehem (Pennsylvania)," some might argue that Rodríguez does not count as an immigrant since he enjoys natural citizenship. Furthermore, Puerto Ricans have enjoyed full U.S. citizenship since 1917, so Rodríguez's parents and grandparents have held the same American citizenship he treasures. Anyone listening to Rodríguez for any time at all will notice his absolute American patriotism. As part of his commitment to America, Rodríguez stands in total solidarity with immigrants. I have watched him address a group of American college presidents in English, where I noted that he was the most eloquent English-speaker in the room. But I have also watched him preach in Spanish with equal poise and power. Like the children of immigrants since the beginning of America, he is a multicultural person, able to transcend cultural barriers because of his own multicultural self.

The New Pilgrims, as I have described immigrants in this book, include more than just the first generation that moves to American territory. They include the children and sometimes the grandchildren and even later descendants of immigrants—everyone who stands close enough to the immigrant generation to continue speaking its language, preserving its customs and cuisines, or feeling its marginalization. Full assimilation to the dominant American culture can take one or two generations, and even more when poverty or racism or well-meaning multicultural separatism colludes to slow it down. Rodríguez has no mixed loyalties. He stands for God and America by standing with immigrants. And he has a vision for the future. Listen to it:

Envision.

Envision a village or town or suburb or city anywhere in North America on a lazy, late Sunday morning in May. Envision, too, the signs of God's simple glories in full bloom, each flower opening to the skies, every blade of grass reaching for the heavens, every child's face turned upward in a smile.

Envision a golf course this Sunday morning, lavish and well tended but with no one on it, a bountiful Wal-Mart with no one in it, a thriving outlet mall with no one hurrying through it.

Envision the bright and shiny new hospital, whose skeleton ER crew treats the occasional bee sting or broken ankle or fainting spell, but who are not at all weary from early Sunday shooting victims or ODs, those sad afflictions of yesteryear, now as obsolete as STDs or HPV or HIV.

Envision the old state prison on the outskirts of town, the concertina wire recycled, the fences pulled down, the cells restructured into classrooms for the new community college where the one-time correctional officers learn altogether different career skills—the local police will not need new officers for years.

Envision Main Street, quiet now on a Sunday morning, except for the odd bakery or convenience store, but soon to be bustling with families—the tattoo parlors closed for lack of business, the pawn shops shuttered, the strip clubs faded into memory, the old abortion clinic now a memorial in much the spirit of the Holocaust Museum.

Now envision the real action. You can hear it, sense it, feel the vibration bleeding through the walls of one church after another all over town—in the section that used to be called a ghetto, in the quarter once known as the "barrio," in the community previously gated.

Listen to the pulse from Evangelical churches to be sure but also from more-established Christian churches and the Catholic churches. Hear it, too, in the old mainline Protestant churches that have shaken out the cobwebs, stopped preaching about yesterday's news, and unapologetically renewed their relationship with Jesus.

Envision aisle after aisle of all these churches, filled with children, and every child well dressed and well behaved, with a loving mother and father. Envision these intact, prayerful, God-centered families freely sharing their time and treasures with those less fortunate. Envision them, through their generosity, consigning those faceless, family-busting welfare bureaucracies to the history books.

Envision the faces of the people in these churches so lively, so filled with joy in the Lord, so brimming with hope, and so stunningly diverse, that phrases like "black church" or "Latino church" or "white church" have lost all cultural meaning.

Envision the spirit of these Kingdom-culture, Bible-believing Christians as they reach up to the Lord and out to their fellow man, as they sing and pray and praise God without embarrassment, without fear of ridicule, without having to brace themselves for some new battle in a culture war they did not start.

Now, remember the day when these Christian soldiers, armed with the Truth and inspired by Christ, gentle as a Lamb and roaring like the Lion, marched onward and won those battles, not with revenge in mind, but reconciliation, not by imposing a religion, but by proposing a relationship. Remember how the Holy Spirit penetrated some very hard hearts, until finally even the most impenetrable skeptics had to concede that life now in the spiritual present was tangibly better than in our materialist past, and emotionally so much richer.

Now celebrate the life made real by the Third Great

Awakening and the path God has laid out before us to save this great nation. If we have the character and courage to follow that path, what you are envisioning and celebrating and thanking God for is our very future as a church and as a nation as we follow the agenda of the Lamb.[13]

I have both seen the thrill and sensed the incredulity as *Hermano Sami* prophesies this future at churches. From my writer's armchair now, I imagine the cringing of extreme culture warriors on the right and the left, a few offended by the disappearance of their racially segregated church and others stinging from the thought that they need a man to help them raise their children. Some recoil from the notion that "illegals" could teach righteousness to the nation. Others imagine that Rodríguez would impose the harmony he envisions by force of violence, bristling at the mention of Christian "soldiers," even as he has made it clear that he sees God accomplishing it by the winning of hearts and minds and their voluntary assimilation to godly living.

A group remains that does not cringe. From Heaven's great cloud of witnesses, Pilgrim forebears pump their once-calloused fists and shout, "Yessssss!"

CAN THESE THINGS HAPPEN?

The most congenial Christian readers will ask, "Can these wonderful things really occur?" Surely the utopia Rodríguez describes can never become real. Surely America has already gone too far into decline. The answer to their question recalls Winthrop's unrealistic vision of the city on a hill—it never saw perfect fulfillment. Dare we put our hopes in dreams of something we think will never come to pass?

I often remember a stanza from my favorite patriotic song, "America the Beautiful." After mentioning how the "stern, impassion'd stress" of pilgrim feet beat a "thoroughfare for freedom. . . across the wilderness," it continues:

> O Beautiful for patriot dream
> That sees beyond the years
> Thine alabaster cities gleam,
> Undimmed by human tears![14]

Rooted in Winthrop's vision of a shining city on a hill, the songwriter Katharine Lee Bates imagined an America akin to the description of Heaven in Revelation 21:4, where God "will wipe every tear from their eyes. There will be no more death or mourning or crying or pain, for the old order of things has passed away."

But tears remain across America, where children go to bed hungry for a father's love, confused teenagers mar their skin in self-loathing, addicts crave dosages only crime can afford, convicts rot in prisons, former college students struggle despairingly under mountains of debt, sexual slaves walk despicable streets, and immigrant children sit on buses watching people shout and scream and spit at them. Tears still dim the gleam of our cities.

And so the question stands: Did America fail? If we did not achieve a tearless society, did we waste the efforts of a dozen generations in seeking to achieve it? Only the basest fool would claim that we have. By setting our sights on Heaven—by trying to achieve the very best—we built alabaster cities from shore to shore. We established universities and research laboratories. We invented modern medicine. We exported democracy around the world by force of our ideals rather than by our military. Our military has spilled precious American blood to deliver other nations from the scourge of fascism and the chains of communism. Police and fire personnel have served and protected the dreams of their neighbors. Our commerce and culture have succeeded in inspiring people around the globe to want something better than they have. As the Irish musician Bono has said, "America is an idea . . . That's how we see you around the world, as one of the greatest ideas in human history."[15]

> Our commerce and culture have succeeded in inspiring people around the globe to want something better than they have.

Inspired by its best ideals, America funded the post–World War II development of the world and created a rising standard of living all over the planet. Never in human history has infant mortality fallen so low, literacy risen so high, life expectancy stretched so long, and illness shrunk so short.[16] In virtually every measure, human well-being has reached its highest point ever during our lifetime, and America played the leading role in achieving it. Had we not set out on a national campaign to build gleaming alabaster cities undimmed by human tears, we would never have created the reality we enjoy today.

Yet despite the many benefits we enjoy from our unprecedented standards of living, some would pretend that we have lost everything, either because conservatives won't play along with radical liberalism or because liberals refuse to go to church. I have seen both sides quoting Yeats' poem about the apocalypse as they moan: "Things fall apart, the center cannot hold, mere anarchy is loosed upon the world."[17] And as two extremes sit in their armchairs, bemoaning the end of all things, immigrants enter the scene to join with native-born doers to build a new and better world.

The idealism that shines in Rodríguez's vision for the future hardly suffers from its gleaming unreality. Precisely the opposite obtains: its unreality inspires us and calls us to strive to make it a reality. As the old saying goes, "Faint heart never won fair maid." In the same way, faint visions of spiritual mediocrity never drove persecuted Pilgrims across the ocean in the seventeenth century to carve America out of the wilderness. They never put wind in the sails of itinerant Great Awakening preachers who crossed the oceans, nor saddles under the Second Awakening circuit riders that planted churches across the prairies.

Nor did faint visions fund the citywide crusades of Finney and Moody and Sunday and Graham. Incoherent groanings of "It can't be done" would have required the gift of interpretation at Azusa Street for early Pentecostals, whose ears rang with the biblical slogan "'Not by might nor by power, but by my Spirit,' says the LORD of hosts"[18] and the motto "I can do all things through Christ who strengthens me."[19] A group of those Pentecostal pioneers pledged in 1914, "We commit ourselves and the Movement to Him for the greatest evangelism the world has ever seen."[20] As over five hundred million souls touched by the Pentecostal movement around the world can presently attest, their "mission impossible" has proven quite possible indeed.

Such a vision as Rodríguez outlines might actually cause an atheist to pray insincerely against it, but it can never elicit an "It can't be done" from any champion of faith. The Spirit of God blows where it wills, and Great Awakenings can always occur, especially where sin seems darkest. The preeminence of faith in 1950s America would have seemed impossible in 1776 or 1890 or 1928, even as it does in 2015. But those who do not believe that spiritual renewal can occur consign themselves to irrelevance in bringing it about.

WHEN THE AWAKENING COMES

Those who think the liberal dominance of the media will keep America from renewal have a twenty-year-old view of the media. The days when television and radio dominated that national conversation have long since ended. Today, social media rules the realm. The nation could turn back to God tomorrow and it might conceivably take years for the mainstream media to recognize it! At the same time, the ratings-driven nature of the media means that they would broadcast church services (like they used to do!) if the public appetite called for it. When the Awakening comes, the media will cover it. If they decide to mock it, they will consign themselves to the insignificant market niches that will irrelevantly applaud their petty behavior.

The vision of a new Great Awakening that Rodríguez preaches has enough constituents to bring it to pass with God's help. Today's Christian immigrants believe in it, and just as God honored past generations with spiritual breakthroughs, God will honor them.

THE AWAKENING AND OTHER RELIGIONS

How would such a Christian resurgence in America affect other religions, such as Islam, Hinduism, Buddhism, and Judaism?

History and current trends prove that many members of those religions and others will convert to Christianity in the context of a revival. In order to avoid such conversions, other religions will have to step up their game to meet the demands of America's highly competitive free market for religion. As a commercial for the U.S. Army once urged, you will have to "be all that you can be." As trends accompanying the puissant advance of Pentecostalism illustrate around the world over the past fifty years, other religions will borrow from what works for Christians, contributing to the similarity among American faiths and making America's almost universally shared faith, American Civil Religion, more popularly viable than ever before.

BEYOND THE IMPASSE

How will America get past our Mexican standoff? Rodríguez explains that the Lamb's Agenda resembles the Cross of Christ, with a vertical stroke and a horizontal stroke. The vertical stroke represents the relationship between a Holy God and sinful humanity, calling us to obey God in matters of righteousness. No nation will ever enjoy the blessings of liberty very long if it ignores God's standards of right moral behavior. The Religious Right emphasizes this dimension in its fight against abortion, pornography, drug use, prostitution, and other moral issues, just as it moves in a vertical dimension in its defense of religious freedom and the right to exercise faith freely in the public square. While these issues have horizontal dimensions also, the Religious Right deserves credit for seeing that they are primarily vertical—moral issues that begin as spiritual issues between people and God.

On the other hand, Rodríguez points out, the horizontal plane of the Cross reminds us of the social dimension of God's will for humanity, characterized by justice. When children face inequality of opportunity and access to basic needs because of the accident of their birth or the misbehavior of their parents, justice demands that society do something to address their situation. When people face mistreatment because of their race, ethnicity, socio-economic class, disabilities, marital status, sexual orientation, or religious convictions, society has work to do. Similarly, when the religious rights of people or their institutions suffer assault, society has a duty to defend their rights of conscience. In a land of plenty, no one should go hungry, suffer ignorance, or face exclusion. Laws must either promote justice or change to allow it. In this horizontal dimension, liberals have often excelled.

> The horizontal plane of the Cross reminds us of the social dimension of God's will for humanity, characterized by justice.

Justice and righteousness flow from God to humanity and they must flow horizontally among people as well. The Agenda of the Lamb insists on both righteousness and justice, bringing together—as Rodríguez always mentions—the values of the twentieth century's greatest religious leaders, Billy Graham and Martin Luther King Jr. For good measure, throw in Pope John Paul the Great, who also promoted both righteousness and justice. Include Mother Teresa, Mahatma Gandhi, the Dalai Lama, and other religious leaders who have stood at the intersection between divine righteousness and human justice.

Righteousness and justice frame the essential values of all the world's great faith traditions, and exalting righteousness and justice in the land provides a meeting place where liberals and conservatives can lay down their arms and come together for the common good. As immigrants become voters, they will vote for those candidates who promote both righteousness and justice. And although Rodríguez does not emphasize the point, the new generation of American youth—whether religious or secular—has a passion for justice that political parties will ignore to their own peril.

Lest anyone think that immigrants have no power in America today and cannot broker a peace between the donkey and the elephant, Rodríguez's résumé offers evidence. He has offered prayers at both the Democratic and Republican National Conventions and has served as a consultant and task force member for Presidents Bush and Obama. He received nominations for *Time* magazine's "100 Most Influential People in the World" in 2013[21] along with Wilfredo de Jesús, a Chicago pastor who works with Rodríguez as vice president of social justice for the National Hispanic Christian Leadership Conference (NHCLC).[22] CNN and Fox News Channel have called Rodríguez "the leader of the Hispanic Evangelical movement." NBC/ *Telemundo* recognized him as "America's most influential Latino Evangelical leader." The Black Christian News Network included him as one of the top "10 White & Brown MLKs of Our Time." The *San Francisco Chronicle* named him as a member of "the New Evangelical Leadership."[23] A wide variety of news media across the country have interviewed and featured him. And in case anyone suspects that "he jests at scars, that never felt a wound,"[24] he has experienced the acid of criticism from both the far left and the far right.[25]

And lest anyone think he stands alone as an eloquent

immigrant leader, consider Luis Cortés, president of Esperanza, or internationally famous evangelist Luis Palau. Moving beyond the Latino community, listen to Francis Chan, Ravi Zacharias, Bobby Jindal, Ted Cruz, or thousands more rising preachers, professionals, politicians, and media stars across the country who believe in and declare the revival of our nation's spirituality.

Much attention should also be on Gabriel Salguero, pastor of The Lamb's Church in New York City, whose rhetoric and brilliance rivals that of Rodríguez. Salguero serves as president of the National Latino Evangelical Coalition, which along with the NHCLC and Philadelphia-based Esperanza, constitutes one of the Big Three organizations that mobilize Evangelical Latinos in the United States. When I called to ask him to contribute to this book, he had just come out of a meeting with President Obama, whom he serves as an advisor on immigration. Salguero describes himself as "a living paradox":

> Often when [I'm] speaking to a new group of people, many assumptions are made depending on how I am introduced. If they lead with "Pentecostal" or "Nazarene" I'm pegged as a conservative Republican who has made up his mind about most things. If they lead with "Latino" and "Union Ph.D. student," the assumption is that I am a theological social liberal who has made up his mind about most things. Now I know I'm not the only one who, in searching to be a faithful disciple of Christ, eschews facile definitions too often used to divide and alienate.[26]

WHAT IF IT CANNOT BE REALIZED?

As I will explain further in Chapter 6, a Golden Age view of America's past Great Awakenings can lead Christians to over-estimate the potential fruits of revival. But as left-wing political researcher Frederick Clarkson notes, Rodríguez's vision for a new American Great Awakening does not need to succeed completely in order to have a telling effect:

> Grandiose visions, of course, like anything else, do not always turn out as planned. However, if . . . NHCLC, and the many other partner organizations find even a few million ideologically oriented new voters who can be engaged in the wider movement we broadly call the Christian Right, it could be, as Rodríguez suggests, a transformational moment in American history.[27]

Clarkson referred to political action on the part of conservative Latinos rather than to a vision for a Great Awakening. But just like the patriots' original vision of gleaming alabaster cities did not require full realization to change the world, the vision of virtuous, sin-free cities, towns, and villages does not have to come true fully in order to renew America's faith. By their very presence, millions of new immigrant Christians and the Americans they influence will bring "a transformational moment in American history"—a moment and a movement worthy of the label "the New Pilgrims."

4

WHY DO THEY COME?

Overwhelmingly, the migrational pattern of human beings in today's world moves from the Global South to the Global North. Southerners move north today because northerners went south to conquer five hundred years ago. With the discovery of a warm sea route to the Americas by Columbus in 1492 and the stunning revelations of indigenous wealth in the Global South, Europeans moved out "conquering and to conquer."[1] Spain and Portugal, but also France, England, and Holland, embraced massive migration quickly as the report of available riches travelled. The poverty of Europe in the sixteenth century held millions in feudal servitude and oppression, and the opportunity to leave weary Europe for a new world and a chance to prosper induced millions of Europeans to risk everything by migrating to the Americas and Africa over the following three hundred years.

Armed with innovative conveyances and weapons and, more effectively, ancient diseases, they made short work of conquering native populations in the Americas, even as many of the colonizers died in the fray. As Charles Mann conclusively demonstrates in *1491: New Revelations of the Americas Before Columbus,* the victory of the Europeans in North and South America had little to do with technological or educational superiority.[2] Their triumph rode on the back of their immunity to European diseases, to which they unwittingly (and sometimes purposefully) submitted the indigenous Americans.

European victory over southern peoples and the spread of colonialist fever throughout Europe would induce most of the nations of Western Europe to send settlers south. From 1492 to 1962— for half a millennium—Europeans conquered and ruled over large portions of the Global South, destroying indigenous governments, cultures, and civilizations, preaching a message of European superiority. Arguably, some elements of European culture did represent technological and other kinds of advance over some elements of local culture, but the cause of colonial domination requires conquerors to invalidate local culture completely in favor of the concept of Western superiority or, in more ugly terms, white supremacy. Even if one chooses to argue that Westernization of the world brought a net benefit, one should not underestimate the price paid by indigenous peoples.

Europeans flooded into the Global South in numbers that rival today's immigration from South to North. From 1800 to 1930 alone, some 85 million Europeans emigrated to the Americas, southern Africa, Australia, and Oceania.[3] Even so, colonies proved impossible to maintain, due to emerging patriotism among Creoles as well as opposition from indigenous peoples. America would rebel against England and gain independence. Spain and Portugal would spend themselves into oblivion in European wars and would lose control of virtually all their colonies over the course of the nineteenth century as Latin American Creoles followed the American example.

In the twentieth century after World War II, the nations of Europe spent themselves into a state from which they could no longer govern the world directly. In addition to economic troubles, the Indian independence movement led by Mahatma Gandhi brought great shame and embarrassment on the United Kingdom. The nobility of Gandhi's nonviolence against repressive colonial authorities provided a strong contradiction of the concept of Western moral superiority over the colonized peoples of the world. Resistance movements broke out all over the world, and by the 1960s, the Americans had yielded control of the Philippines, the French had given up control of their North African colonies, and the British had turned their colonies into a global Commonwealth of Nations.

Although America rose to great power during the last fifty years of the Colonialist Era, it did not follow the model of the great European empires in establishing its worldwide economic leadership. America had established a new approach to global hegemony that French Communists in the late 1940s dubbed "coca-colonization"—global influence through commerce rather than direct military domination.[4] While America had temporarily colonized the Philippine Islands and a few other small islands like Puerto Rico, Guam, and others, it had not set up a massive empire ruled by its armies, like previous powers had done. Some would argue that the forcible annexation of Hawaii offers a contradiction to this statement, but perhaps such a singular exception merely proves the rule. As a whole, America stood instead for ideals of freedom, sending its military around the globe during World War

II to liberate other nations and to invite all of humanity to share its ideals of democratic self-governance, free markets, technological advance, and personal freedom.

During the twentieth century, the nations of northern Europe and North America established a standard of living that no civilization in human history had ever enjoyed before. The rise of globalization after World War II, fueled by technological advances like almost instantaneous international airline travel, truly instantaneous global telecommunications, massively popular consumer products, the widespread use of refrigeration and air-conditioning, the glamor and glitz of Hollywood and American television, and eventually the Internet, would make the Western lifestyle known to almost every human being on the planet. In America, anyone could attain style, wealth, education, and power.

> America stood instead for ideals of freedom, sending its military around the globe during World War II to liberate other nations and to invite all of humanity to share its ideals.

The word went out to all the world. Children and teenagers around the globe would idolize America. People would grow up dreaming of personal freedom and economic opportunity. If you belonged to a persecuted religious minority, you could gain freedom of worship in America. If your political views subjected you to the threat of imprisonment or even death, you could find freedom of speech in America. If you desired a world-class education, America had almost all of the top one hundred universities in the world. If your country suffered intractable poverty and you had no opportunity to lift yourself out of starvation and squalor, America towered as the Land of Opportunity.

As a result, many of the world's most spiritual, most brilliant, most freedom-loving, and most economically ambitious people set out for America. The rigors of the journey kept lazy people back in the old country. As a matter of fact, studies of immigration have found that immigrants self-select for success. As economist Barry Chiswick of George Washington University has put it,

> One of the standard propositions in the migration literature is that migrants tend to be favorably "self-selected" for labor-market success. That is, economic migrants are described as tending on average to be more able, ambitious, aggressive, entrepreneurial, or otherwise more favorably selected than similar individuals who choose to remain in their place of origin.[5]

More able, more ambitious, more aggressive, more entrepreneurial—these characteristics explain another question many Americans ask about undocumented immigrants: Why don't they just get in line and wait like everyone else?

They don't wait because they can't wait. They have an ants-in-their-pants inability to stand still and tolerate endless oppression.

THE MEANING OF OPPORTUNITY

I asked Hilario Garza, a Mexican-American religious leader in Washington State, why people break American law to immigrate to the United States. He answered that they break the law because what they are leaving is a lot worse than any problems they may encounter here in the United States.[6]

I think people leave poverty, leave oppression, leave behind the lack of hope in their country, because there is no opportunity, and it doesn't matter what they may suffer along the way, even unto death, the opportunity afforded in America is greater than any sufferings that may be encountered along the way. People are responding to their need, the need to feed their families. So the moral need to feed their families is greater than any law they may be breaking. America means opportunity, hope, a better future. Not just for themselves, but more so, for their families. Because immigrants in my opinion aren't—how can I say this carefully— aren't individualists. What we do, we do for family.

The word is opportunity.

ECONOMIC IMMIGRANTS AND FREEDOM SEEKERS

Some people might see economic immigrants in a different category than they see immigrants who come to America to gain freedom of speech or freedom of religion. But such a distinction lacks any warrant in American history. In 1941 President Franklin Delano Roosevelt—famous for his Good Neighbor policy toward Latin America—delivered a speech called "The Four Freedoms." In the middle of World War II but before America's entry into it, Roosevelt sought to define the values that the United States should defend all over the world: freedom of speech, freedom of worship, freedom from want, and freedom from fear. The first two freedoms permit individuals to *define* themselves; the others *defend* them from threats.[7]

Many immigrants come to the United States in search of freedom of speech, because the land of their birth has failed to guarantee that basic human freedom. Others come because they long to worship God according to their own convictions. In many cases, when they can prove that they suffer the threat of persecution for their faith or their political beliefs, they receive the support of the American authorities. But when they come to "the Land of the Free and the Home of the Brave" to escape from want and fear, they do not receive the same hospitality and deference.

Immigrating to gain opportunity relates directly to the question of freedom. What does it matter if a society offers you freedom of thought and speech but does not offer the freedom to survive or to thrive? In Nobel Prize–winning novelist Gabriel García Marquez's famous novella, *El Coronel No Tiene Quién le Escriba* (*No One Writes to the Colonel*), the starving wife of the protagonist protests, "*La ilusión no se come*" (A dream can't be eaten), to which the Colonel lamely responds, "*No se come, pero alimenta*" (It can't be eaten, but it does nourish).[8] Undoubtedly, millions of malnourished, would-be immigrants remain behind with daydreams of a better life, but immigrants have the courage and drive to get up and brave the risks to make their dreams come true—even if those dreams seem somewhat pedestrian to established Americans, and even if the dream goes no further than three square meals a day for their family.

As a child, I once asked my uncle LeRoy why he never came home to Jasper, Alabama, after moving to Denver, Colorado. He had left Alabama as a young man, fleeing the dusty, coal mine poverty he had survived during the Great Depression. (My grandfather didn't survive it and died of black lung disease.) His answer made a great impact on me. He said, "I got used to sleeping between sheets and eating three meals a day." A generation of people around the world has watched Americans living in relative luxury on television and in the movies, and millions of them dream of sleeping between sheets and eating three meals a day. They understand that without opportunity, freedom means nothing.

The Land of the Free will always serve as the natural Home of the Brave. No one else really deserves to live there. Freedom without courage loses all legitimacy. In most countries of the world, getting a visa to come to America means getting your name drawn from among thousands of entries into a visa lottery at the American Consulate. There is no line, but only a lottery. Does America really prefer immigrants who sit back—contentedly or otherwise—waiting for their names to rise up in a lottery magically, impossibly, rather than risk their lives to gain a chance at the American Dream? Which of the two kinds of immigrant stands a better chance to start a new business and contribute to the betterment of American society?

CHILD MIGRANTS

A recent issue that has created significant controversy in America involves tens of thousands of children who have risked their lives to leave Central America. They illegally hop a freight train at the Guatemala border and ride thousands of miles through Mexico to the American border, where they engage a smuggler to take them across a desert into the United States. The 2009 documentary film *Which Way Home* presents a compelling record of the perilous journeys of several Central American children.[9] Interviews with the children reveal their motivations for leaving their homes, but for the most part, the search for opportunity drives them, whether they seek the opportunity to work, to get an education, or to re-unite with their father or mother. Many of the children have lived on the streets since early childhood, and their precarious situation means they can no longer wait for something good to happen to them. They choose to take their destinies into their own hands.

Many wonder how the United States should respond to these children, with some choosing compassion and care while others insist on immediate deportations of the children. Interviews with children who have set out in hope and anticipation of a better life—risking their lives, witnessing or experiencing unspeakable atrocities, and spending time incarcerated at the border, only to wind up deported to where they started—offer heartbreaking stories of hopeless disillusion. They have watched some pay "the last full measure of devotion," as Lincoln once said, dying in the effort to gain a better life. Living in a state worse than death, they will try again. What do they have to lose? They cannot live without hope. They cannot live without opportunity.

OUR CHANGED VIEWS OF CHILDREN

Americans today cannot imagine a child traveling on his or her own the way Central American child migrants do. We have long since made child labor illegal, but anyone who has visited the Third World knows that street labor makes up a very important part of a child's life in much of the world. In contrast, today's American parents have become the most overprotective parents in history.[10] No one in their right mind would argue that children should migrate on their own in such conditions as we currently witness. I recently heard someone allege that after a year on the street, children regress to a feral state. But a century ago, such so-called feral children played an important role in the American imagination.

Who can forget the literary characters Tom Sawyer and Huckleberry Finn, American heroes brought to life by the pen of Mark Twain, who at tender ages explored dangerous Missouri caves in *The Adventures of Tom Sawyer* (1876), floated down hundreds of miles of river in *The Adventures of Huckleberry Finn* (1884), or travelled by balloon around the world in *Tom Sawyer Abroad* (1894)? Rudyard Kipling's novel *Kim* (1901) presented the abandoned child of a British soldier, who survives as a street child and travels all over India on train and on foot. In *The Jungle Book* (1894), Mowgli rules the forest after being raised by wolves. Edgar Rice Burroughs, just a century ago, enthralled American audiences with *Tarzan of the Apes* (1914) and its many sequels, in which another feral child turned hero. Author Horatio Alger Jr. (1832–1899) similarly inspired Americans with novels about impoverished boys who rose from humble backgrounds to lives of prosperity through hard work, determination, courage, and honesty.

> Today's American parents have become the most overprotective parents in history. No one in their right mind would argue that children should migrate on their own in such conditions as we currently witness.

Admittedly, such examples come from the world of fiction, but they rose out of the reality of America's frontier, in which children accomplished incredible things because their lives and futures depended on it. The life story of Christian philanthropist Clement

Stone, who made and gave away a tremendous fortune, stands as a real-life validation of the power of children. In 1908 at the age of six, he began to sell newspapers on the street in Chicago and by thirteen, owned his own newsstand. Left alone to manage for himself at that age, he went on to build an empire in the insurance industry.[11] Many other stories of adolescent immigrant success grace American history as well. Henry Ness came to America alone from Norway at the age of seventeen—running away from his mother's attempts to convert him to Christian faith. He thrived in business, but he eventually succumbed to his mother's prayers and became a Christian minister, founding Northwest University in the Seattle area, where I currently serve as president.

During my childhood, just fifty years ago, my mother would fix a sack lunch for my brother, Randy, and me, and we would leave home in the morning to seek adventures. Either on foot through the woods or on our bikes in the street, we would range for miles with nothing but a mixed-breed collie dog to protect us. Such wanderings began when we were preschool children. As long as we got home for supper, Mom never saw any reason to raise an alarm. Our parents bought us a library of children's books that we read early in our lives, featuring child heroes like Tom Sawyer, and as we grew into teenagers we bought every single volume of the Hardy Boys, including both the original volumes and contemporary rewrites of the original titles.

Through a combination of literary experience and real copycat adventures in play, we learned to believe that children had amazing capabilities, and we saw ourselves as woodsmen and explorers in the manner of our television heroes, Daniel Boone and Davy Crockett. We thought everything was possible. We thought we had an obligation to go places no one had ever gone before and fantasized that our daily wanderings might take us to some new and undiscovered place. To this day we both live lives of adventure that fit our inner natures. Randy sought adventure in a military career, in an active outdoor life, and in his creative arts business. I seek my adventures in collegiate life, in global missionary travels, in marathon running, and in a project to visit all fifty-nine U.S. national parks with my wife, Kathleen.

I do not argue with the current American view of children as weak, defenseless, and in need of constant protection. Children are indeed vulnerable, and I have watched my three daughters like a hawk. I do argue, however, that today's migrant children, if given a chance to pursue the American Dream, have an extremely high chance of success in achieving the American Dream. I understand the argument that deporting them may discourage future child migrants from risking their lives. But surely the American mission does not find dignified expression in the task of discouraging desperate children around the world. Those who have come here in search of the Land of Opportunity—the Land of the Free and the Home of the Brave—have certainly proven their merit to occupy the land.

Who could possibly make a stronger claim to deserving a place in that home? Does America, or does America not, still send out its light to the tired, huddled masses of the world who yearn to be free?

5

WHY CHRISTIAN IMMIGRANTS JUSTIFY BREAKING IMMIGRATION LAWS

If Christian immigrants come to America as holy pilgrims, why do they break American law by crossing the borders without legal permission? That question haunts many Christians in America who see immigrants as morally deficient, even as criminal, for their decision to become "illegal aliens." In today's English, this phrase brings to mind images of hostile extraterrestrials that would invade the planet and kill us all.[1] It dehumanizes undocumented immigrants and makes their very personhood illegal. I remember hearing, as a child in the 1960s, public service announcements aired on television and set to creepy music, reminding all who were not citizens or nationals of the United States who lived within U.S. borders to "go to the local post office and register their alien status with the government."[2] Those messages taught many children to fear foreigners living in our country, creating a sense of suspicion that persists in many people to this day. Despite its long history of usage, we should discard the term. But the question deserves a straight answer: Undocumented immigrants break American law to enter our country because for years now, no legal way has existed for most of them to get a visa that would allow them to come to the United States. But before addressing that issue in detail, I believe fairness requires a more complex explanation of the ethics of immigration to the United States of America.

THE FOLLY OF LAWS AGAINST HUMAN NATURE

Christians have always known that they must obey the law of God above human laws.[3] From a biblical perspective, current American immigration law circumvents essential characteristics of God-given human nature as described in Genesis 1:28, where God dictates the first law or commandment to the human race: Be fruitful and multiply, fill the earth, and subdue it. Even outside the framework of the Bible, reproduction, migration, and dominion can be seen as forming part of human nature, and if so, laws to prohibit them have little chance of success. Efforts to stop human reproduction by force of law, such as the one-child policy in China, have proven disastrous, succeeding only by dint of massive forced abortions. Mothers have paid with the sorrow of lost children. Millions of baby girls have paid the cost of their very lives, millions of single men have paid the price of lifelong loneliness, and the future economic sustainability of the nation has come into question.[4]

Similarly, legal prohibition of migration has failed as well, as human beings instinctively move from low-opportunity environments to high-opportunity situations. For most of American history, sound public policy let supply and demand regulate the flow of immigration. During the heyday of immigration through

Ellis Island in New Jersey, healthy immigrants got a visa and a chance to earn their way, except for those deported as undesirables. To avoid what we now call human trafficking, unescorted women and children experienced detainment until a family member came to claim them, but those without family in America faced deportation, along with stowaways, alien seamen, anarchists, Bolsheviks, criminals, and those judged to be immoral. Approximately 20 percent of immigrants inspected at Ellis Island were temporarily detained, half for health reasons and half for legal reasons.[5]

In contrast, immigration has faced highly restrictive legal prohibition in the United States in recent years. Consequently, today's congressional stalemate between elephants who refuse to forget and donkeys who refuse to work has stymied principled reform and led to a state of utter chaos on the borders that fails to keep out disease, criminals, and even terrorists, exacerbating an otherwise manageable problem.

The dominion mandate, climate change, global warming, the hole in the ozone layer, plain old air pollution, and other environmental threats have led developed nations, hypocritically, to put pressure on governments in the equatorial regions of the planet to outlaw the cutting of rain forests for building materials, fuel, and new farmland. (All the while, they have shipped petroleum across the oceans to fuel their own economies.) But destitute people will build homes and take charge of their surroundings in

> Today's congressional stalemate between elephants who refuse to forget and donkeys who refuse to work has stymied principled reform and led to a state of utter chaos on the borders.

order to survive, regardless of what the law says. Forward-thinking economists and pundits constantly call on the world's governments to move past petroleum and coal mining and adopt sustainable energy sources, but so far, no country has outlawed petroleum production. Human instinct drives people to take control of their surroundings, mine their resources, and build homes, societies, and civilizations. The solution to our ecological problems will force us to do something more thoughtful than mere prohibition of survival.

While governments can and must regulate human behavior, laws designed to prohibit reproduction, migration, or dominion will fail because they fundamentally violate human nature. Wise government can find solutions to all of the problems related to reproduction, migration, and human dominion in our time, but public policy that ignores human nature will always fail.

Undocumented Christian immigrants to America know they have either entered the country illegally or overstayed legal visas, but they also feel a sense of divine right to be here. Very few immigrants could fully articulate the biblical basis for migration, but they report that God has walked beside them every step of the way from the country of their birth to the Land of Opportunity, the Promised Land of the American Dream. They feel they have a mission from God in this country, and that God has given "space for us to prosper in this land."[6] The Bible counsels them that, even if the people of the land reject them, they should "seek the peace and prosperity" of their new country and "pray to the LORD for it, because if it prospers, [they] too will prosper."[7]

LEX REX, THE RULE OF LAW

Fully understanding the essence of the immigrants' dilemma requires careful consideration of the nature of the Rule of Law. The concept of *Lex Rex* stands as the cornerstone of the American system of government. In 1644, the Scottish theologian Samuel Rutherford coined this Latin phrase, meaning "The law is King," in the book *Lex Rex, or The Law and the Prince*, one of history's most foundational treatises on limited government and constitutionalism.[8] Arguing on the basis of Deuteronomy 17 in the Bible, Rutherford insisted the king should not be above the law and a just society could not exist apart from the Rule of Law.

No discussion of the crucial issues at stake in the current debate—or perhaps we should say, the current incoherent crossfire rant—over immigration in America can avoid the issue of *Lex Rex*. About half the American population stands deeply disturbed over the undeniable fact that the twelve million or so undocumented immigrants in America today live here illegally. They cannot understand how anyone can justify any change in immigration policy that rewards lawbreaking. They know that without the Rule of Law, America has no future. In this latter belief, they have it totally right.

On the other hand, most immigrants in America—whether documented or undocumented—tend to see the whole question in terms of human rights. They ask themselves how half the people in America cannot see that the current legal structure is unfair, impractical, and un-American. Anyone who hasn't heard the horror stories of cruel mistreatment of defenseless people at the hands of heartless state authorities simply does not have enough immigrant friends. Most Americans have never heard about the human rights abuses that immigrants suffer in private prisons and holding areas, outsourced by the government to private companies with minimal official supervision.[9] Allegations of abuse include substandard food, lack of medical care, force-feeding and long solitary confinement of hunger strikers, detainment without bond or at exorbitant bond amounts, and being paid one dollar per day for full-time labor while being charged exaggerated prices for essential items.[10]

THE ROLE OF CULTURE

My experience living as an immigrant/missionary in Latin America taught me a lot about the role culture plays in the way people interpret these issues. For example, although I qualify as a "virtual native" speaker of Spanish and taught college classes in Spanish for over twenty years, I have never found anyone who can adequately translate the English phrase "Rule of Law" into Spanish. Although the words "*el dominio de la ley*" come close, no one uses that phrase. You won't find it in a Google search, and its words fail to express what Americans mean by the Rule of Law. The closest equivalent in Spanish is the phrase *estado de derecho*. Rather than speaking of the establishment of the Rule of Law, Spanish-speaking societies talk about achieving a "state of justice." In other words, they correctly see that the Rule of Law does not make injustice right.

Nazi Germany and the old Soviet Union zealously enforced the Rule of Law, but they did not have "a state of justice." Interestingly, Latin America has no law schools but rather *facultades de derecho* (faculties of legal justice or rights). Today's Latin American cultures understand that unless a society bases the Rule of Law on equal justice for all, *Lex Rex* becomes nothing more than another form of oppression. In the twentieth century, too many Latin American countries suffered the Rule of Law in cruel police states governed by murderous dictators from the right and left such as Trujillo, Batista, Somoza, Stroessner, Castro, Noriega, Pinochet, and others. The Rule of Law becomes toxic when monsters write the law. Unfortunately, precious few Latin American countries can truly boast of having achieved an *estado de derecho*, a fact that generates large numbers of refugees who come to America seeking justice, fairness, and equal treatment under law.

To the detriment of everyone—American-born citizens and immigrants alike—the United States has allowed an unfair, unjust code of laws to develop. When President Reagan and Congress succeeded in passing a general amnesty for undocumented immigrants in 1984, the Congress failed to create a system of guest worker visas that would have allowed immigrants to cross the border to provide agricultural and other service economy labor the American economy demanded. The economic growth that began under President Reagan after the end of the 1981–82 recession pushed unemployment levels to around, and sometimes below, the mark of full-employment, which economists generally consider to be 5 percent, and the Reagan recovery turned into a twenty-five-year boom.[11]

In order to harvest American crops and provide low-cost food to the American public, farmers had no choice but to employ the labor supply that showed up to work. Not enough American-born workers arrived, and the surging market for immigrant labor had no legal covering. So, the desperate need of agricultural labor sucked millions of illegal workers across our southern border. The result was the creation of an underclass of foreign workers with almost no guarantees for basic human rights as defined by both America and the United Nations. While many employers have treated immigrants very well, others have treated them cruelly.

The U.S. government took full advantage of the situation, refusing to give the workers legal status, forcing them into the shadows, and leaving them exposed to atrocious abuses. Deportations occurred in sufficient numbers to keep immigrants destabilized and vulnerable, with the Obama administration claiming to deport even more immigrants than Bush.[12] But government put little serious effort into controlling the flow of immigrants, because the economy needed them too badly for government to block their arrival.

Sometimes a nation does not respect its own laws enough to enforce them. At other times it will refuse to reform laws that no longer fulfill a valid function. One thinks of the ridiculous laws that still remain on the books across the United States that prohibit women drivers or demand that a person driving a car must send someone ahead on foot with flags to warn walkers.[13] When a nation will neither change nor enforce outdated laws, as we have done, it can hardly expect compliance with the law from people whose access to food, security, opportunity, and freedom force them to violate those laws. Who has respected the law less— undocumented immigrants or the American government itself?

You cannot spend a one-sided coin. Both sides of the coin are necessary. In general, but especially in the case of current immigration law, we cannot remain content merely to enforce unjust laws. As a matter of fact, no responsible national politician holding office in America has called for the mass deportation of undocumented immigrants, as our immigration laws would seem to require. They do not propose such a measure because they know our economy would have collapsed long ago without undocumented workers. Neither can we afford to emphasize rights apart from obedience to the law. To solve our current problems, we must address both justice and legality simultaneously—or at least in immediate succession—not achieving one while postponing the other.

The immigration morass we have created results precisely from our negligence of both law and justice. On one hand, we have depressed the growth of the native population for fifty years through lower birthrates, all the while operating in an economic system that requires population growth to maintain its economic advance. The Social Security system offers a prime example: we cannot support a rising population of seniors on a shrinking population of young people. At the same time, the globalization of our economy in the 1990s caused a massive increase in the number of highly skilled jobs in the country, making it unnecessary for many native-born Americans to take low-skilled, low-paying jobs. This once happy situation made increased immigration necessary, whether the law supported it or not.

> Sometimes a nation does not respect its own laws enough to enforce them. At other times it will refuse to reform laws that no longer fulfill a valid function.

I have always objected to the idea that Americans are lazy and unwilling to do low-skilled, low-paying jobs. Studies consistently prove that Americans work harder than the citizens of most other developed nations.[14] Americans love to work, but they very intelligently prefer to take better-paying jobs. If current unemployment levels do not improve soon or if unemployment benefits end, more Americans may feel driven to low-paying jobs. But even if Americans want to work in such jobs, they usually lack the skills to succeed in them. In any case, the lack of Americans showing up for low-wage employment made it necessary to increase our immigrant numbers to keep our society functioning over the past fifty years.

Unfortunately, lack of public understanding of our economic system and prejudice against foreigners gave rise to loud voices that induced our government leaders (both Republicans and Democrats) in the past half century to govern on the basis of invalid ideas about immigration. As a result Congress made no legal provisions for the mass entry of immigrants we have needed to supply our unskilled labor needs. Rather than creating a legal framework for providing the labor supply we needed, our country opted to tolerate the hiring of illegal workers. This solution offered a cheap way out of the political dilemma and absolved legislators from the duty to provide leadership. America benefitted financially, but paid a heavy price in terms of justice.

For example, if immigrants have no visas, they cannot receive Social Security numbers, and we don't have to pay them Social Security benefits. But despite this truth, most undocumented immigrants pay Social Security taxes for which they will never receive any benefit. In 2007, for example, 10.8 million workers paid a total of $90.4 billion in Social Security taxes under false names and numbers.[15] They don't show up at hospitals to receive medical attention unless they absolutely cannot avoid it, and they generally lie low instead of asserting their needs. This situation has cost us cheaply in money, but has cost us dearly in national dignity, eroding the state of justice in America.

On the other hand, undocumented immigrants consciously chose to break the law and wound up exposed to the ugly consequences of doing so. Part of dignified civil disobedience implies accepting the consequences of one's actions. Facing a catch-22 type of dilemma, immigrants had to choose between the hard consequences of breaking American law in order to survive and gain a measure of prosperity and the worse consequences of staying in their native countries and languishing in oppression. They chose to come here and serve us, picking our fruit, mowing our lawns, and building our houses without fully enjoying the fruits of a just and legal residence here. Even if they did freely choose to impale themselves on this horn of the dilemma, no American should be proud of the anguish they have suffered to our benefit.

I frequently tell undocumented immigrant friends to trust the American people. I tell them our people love justice, and once they become aware of the reality of immigration in our country, they will fix the laws. I want immigrants to love America, not to become embittered by their suffering. I hope that the information I will present in the following chapters will help Americans see immigrants in America in a new light, with both sides releasing any resentment they have felt toward each other. Immigrants pose no greater threat to America on average than our native-born citizens do, and in fact, they represent the most realistic hope for revival and awakening that we have seen in our lifetimes.

6

IMMIGRANTS AND REVIVAL
IN AMERICAN HISTORY

According to the logic of Genesis 1:28 and its mission statement for humanity, migration plays an important part in a biblical understanding of human flourishing and salvation. From the scattering of the early Jerusalem church in Acts 8:1 until the present, the migration of Christians has had a huge role in the spread of Christianity around the world and in its periodic revitalization. According to that text, "A severe persecution began against the church in Jerusalem, and *all except the apostles* were scattered throughout the countryside of Judea and Samaria" (NRSV, emphasis added). Note the irony: the apostles, or "sent ones," stayed in Jerusalem while everyone else went on the road. While the evangelization of the world has always involved sending missionaries to reach native-born populations around the world, the mass movements of Christian immigrants have played an important role as well—perhaps a role even greater than that of the official missionaries in many places.

Think, for example, of early Roman Catholic missions to the

Americas. While missionary priests had some success in converting local populations to the church, a mass migration of Spanish, Portuguese, and French Catholics provided a powerful base for the founding of new churches. The same thing holds true for English Protestant migrations to North America, Australia, New Zealand, and South Africa. Immigrants and their many children played the initial role in populating the new churches that missionary/immigrant pastors founded, although converts always joined them. Dutch Calvinists, German and Scandinavian Lutherans, and other Christians also carried their churches with them as they migrated around the world during the Colonial Age.

The list could go on and on with other nations and locales around the world, and more examples will follow soon. But before offering a more detailed historical analysis of the role of immigration in founding, growing, and revitalizing the church, an important piece of sociological theory needs introduction. According to Emile Durkheim, one of the founders of academic sociology, immigrants typically suffer a phenomenon he called *anomie*.[1] In the context of his analysis of the Industrial Revolution, Durkheim considered the massive immigration of workers to the United States. Cut off from their communities of origin and the norms and values they had traditionally held, immigrants found themselves struggling to survive, adapting more to individualism and flexibility, and navigating new ideas, pressures, and belief systems. The dissonance between their old values and the new ones adopted for survival created a sense of "normlessness" among them. Free from traditional restraints, immigrants often turned to crime, alcohol abuse, or other deviant behaviors. Christians often refer to this state of normless confusion as "lostness." Finke and Stark eloquently describe *anomie* as follows:

> The real basis of moral order is human relationships . . . People who have no relationships with family or close friends, or whose relationships are far away, are essentially alone all the time. They do not risk their attachments if they are detected in deviant behavior, because they have none to lose . . . In frontier areas, most people are deficient in attachments, and hence very high rates of deviant behavior exist.[2]

Such a situation among immigrants, as well as domestic migrants, exposes their need for the self-control that friends and faith offer, and it leaves them ripe for religious renewal or conversion.[3]

Popular culture continually tells the story of immigrant gangs in America, whether they be the Irish gangs of the mid-nineteenth century, the *Cosa Nostra* featured regularly in mafia movies, the African-American or Puerto Rican gangs in the movie *The Cross and the Switchblade*, or the Broadway play *West Side Story*. Almost certainly a movie is coming soon to a theatre near you about the *Mara Salvatrucha* or MS-13—Salvadoran gangs from Los Angeles that have spread around the country. The same phenomenon of lostness has broken out among immigrants throughout American history.

Far from the families that once loved and nourished them and the constraints of community and tradition, some immigrants descend into chaos. Christians in the home countries have always sent missionaries to minister the gospel to such immigrants and to plant new churches, and native-born Christians have helped as well. As churches bring converts to faith, lives change. As the numbers of converts expand, societies awaken. Discouraged Christians experience revival.

When such revitalization occurs on a societal scale, the phenomenon is known as an awakening, and church historians have identified multiple periods during American history that can be called "Great Awakenings." According to William McLoughlin, America has experienced five such awakenings, which he sees as "cultural transformations affecting all Americans." His analysis reflects the concept of *anomie*, noting that awakenings "begin in periods of cultural distortion and grave personal stress, when we lose faith in the legitimacy of our norms, the viability of our institutions, and the authority of our leaders in church and state."[4] Not only do such awakenings enliven churches and bring lost people into them, they also affect society through social reforms that renew entire nations.

> Such awakenings always move from religious piety to social reform. They result in economic lift and social mobility for the poorest Americans— often immigrants.

Along the same line, Nobel Prize–winning economist William Fogel has suggested that Great Awakenings usually last one hundred years and consist of three phases, each lasting a generation.[5] Such awakenings always move from religious piety to social reform. They result in economic lift and social mobility for the poorest Americans—often immigrants—and make a substantial contribution to social equality. Though such awakenings may appear otherworldly in some cases, they never remain at a merely religious level but provide concrete political, social, cultural, economic, and technological benefits to society.

The growing gap between rich and poor in America, Europe, and the rest of the world has become a signature issue for left and center-left politics, and even center-right politicians have picked up the rhetoric of inequality. A recent book by French economist Thomas Picketty, *Capital in the Twenty-First Century*, has given fresh impetus to the political call for greater economic justice.[6] Right and left may disagree about whether governments should impose confiscatory taxes on prodigious producers of wealth, but no credible political actor can openly suggest that greater generalized prosperity in society would present a bad situation (aside from arguments about environmental sustainability).

From my own point of view, it would seem that greater secularization in America and Europe has not contributed to greater equality but rather has coincided with wider polarization of rich and poor. In keeping with Fogel's analysis, I would argue that the solution to economic injustice starts with religious revival, not with political action. Virtuous political action can never succeed without virtuous citizens. No drug-, alcohol-, or entertainment-addicted nation in the history of the world has avoided economic ruin. As David Goldman has brilliantly demonstrated in *How Civilizations Die*, many wealthy nations have descended into sexual libertinism throughout world history, but no sexually licentious society has ever sustained economic prosperity or even a self-sustaining birthrate.[7] Contrary to the imaginations of popular singers, societies dedicated to living for the moment do not build stable futures. The only reasonable hope for a prosperous future in America arises from evidence of religious revival and moral renewal, and today's immigrants present the best hope for such an enlivening in America.[8]

THE HISTORY OF RELIGIOUS AWAKENINGS IN AMERICA

In spite of the fascinating analyses of McLoughlin and Fogel, not all historians agree that our national religious history in America fits into the neat frameworks of Great Awakenings, and the messiness of reality always confounds the interpretive frameworks imposed on it by scholars. Many historians and sociologists of religion deny that such awakenings exist at all.[9] The tradition of naming Great Awakenings tends to focus on Protestantism and utterly ignore Catholic growth. The concept also contributes to a fictitious "Golden Age" view of America's religious past that creates unreasonable expectations for what future revivals might bring. Nevertheless, while these recognized weaknesses serve as caveats, the framework of Great Awakenings has merit for organizing American history in a way that credibly connects America's high points in Christian zeal and church-planting success with renewal of our national faith and character.

Consideration of the role immigration has played in America's religious revivals—whether Christian, Jewish, or of other religions brought here by immigrants—will shed light on the role we can hope today's immigrants will play.

THE BIRTH OF AMERICAN CHRISTIANITY AND OUR FIRST GREAT AWAKENING

While many immigrants to America have experienced *anomie* over the past five centuries, it hardly characterized the experience of many of the earliest immigrants, like the *Mayflower* Pilgrims, who came precisely because of their religious convictions in a community of peers. Many of the original Baptists who settled in Rhode Island, Catholics in Maryland, and Quakers and German-speaking Mennonites in Pennsylvania came with strong faith. Scots-Irish Presbyterians moved inland to the Appalachian region, and large numbers of Irish Catholic indentured servants scattered across the colonies.[10] In western regions along the Mississippi River, French Catholics and their missionary leaders settled early, while Spanish Catholics explored and settled in the farther West.

Such iconic groups of pilgrims seeking religious freedom, however, represented a distinct minority among the populations that colonized America. In 1776, only 10 percent of the population of Rhode Island claimed Baptist affiliation; Catholics made up 3 percent of Maryland's people, and Pennsylvania's Quaker meetinghouses served 5 percent of its people.[11]

Contrary to the mythical "Golden Age" theory of American religiosity, in which people always imagine the "good old days" as far better than they were, America's past did not exemplify any sort of Christian paradise. Despite the high ideals of the Pilgrims, a rough and rowdy group settled the American colonies, and few people attended church at all. The actual facts of American history tell the story of rough frontiersmen and their women, tough soldiers, slavery, the Wild West, the Gay Nineties, the Roaring Twenties, and also of religious people leading increasing numbers of others to God over the centuries.

In the early eighteenth century, thousands of convicts would arrive in Georgia, a group that might reasonably lean toward *anomie* more than some others. Large numbers of African slaves also entered the colonies until the slave trade began to diminish in 1775. Dutch traders settled in New Amsterdam. Other German, French, and Scandinavian immigrants also populated the colonies. Despite the fact that few immigrants to America held to religion as closely as the leaders of the Pilgrims at Plymouth Rock, these immigrant groups populated America's earliest churches and gave Christianity its start on the new continent. The point stands irrefutable: without the immigration of Christians to America in our first two centuries, there would be no American Christianity as we have known it. It would not have existed at all, nor would it have taken on the wide-open pluralistic character that it has enjoyed ever since America invented the world's first free market for religion.[12]

> Without the immigration of Christians to America in our first two centuries, there would be no American Christianity as we have known it.

A century of immigration and settlement in America set the scene for what became known as the First Great Awakening. The social conditions of the frontier and the efforts of faithful Christians resulted in vigorous efforts at church planting to serve the burgeoning population growth and immigration from England, Wales, and Northern Ireland.[13] The introduction of slavery into the South called for evangelization of African-Americans as well, and a few missionaries, such as David Brainerd (Protestant) and Christian Priber (Catholic), made attempts to evangelize Native Americans.[14]

Historians generally agree that America's First Great Awakening began around 1730, most importantly led by several foreign evangelists who came as missionaries and immigrants, along with the

American-born minister Jonathan Edwards. The English missionary evangelist George Whitefield and the Scots-Irish Presbyterian immigrant William Tennent, along with his four sons, not only led revivals but also founded the Log College in New Jersey (now Princeton University) to train clergymen for the ministry on the frontier.[15]

Many thousands of Christians revitalized their faith and their passion for the work of the church during this period, and thousands of others, mostly immigrants and first-generation Americans, turned away from *anomie* and converted to faith for the first time. Native Americans and African-American slaves also converted to Christianity through the ministries of Tennant and others.

My own ancestor William Castleberry, a first-generation American, experienced conversion to Baptist faith in the 1750s. Together with the Reverend Samuel Newman, he planted some of the first Baptist churches in the South, migrating along the old Philadelphia Wagon Road from Pennsylvania to Georgia and leaving churches behind like a couple of spiritual Johnny Appleseeds.[16] The leadership of immigrants and their children (like the Tennents), along with foreign preachers (like Whitefield) and native-born pastors (like Jonathan Edwards), played an indispensable role in the First Great Awakening.

THE SECOND GREAT AWAKENING

Unfortunately, awakenings do not guarantee that everyone will convert or experience revival, and even the greatest revivals sputter and lose their fervency. By the latter decades of the eighteenth century, about 17 percent of the American population affiliated with a church.[17] Historians of revival have tended to see the cooldown of the First Great Awakening in dramatic, perhaps even over-dramatic fashion. According to the late J. Edwin Orr, one of the world's great authorities on the history of revival, "The last two decades of the eighteenth century were the darkest period, spiritually and morally, in the history of American Christianity."[18] He attributed the decline in Christianity to

> the unsettled state of society following a long-fought war and a revolution, the self assertive feelings which accompanied independence, the changing social conditions, the lure of the western frontier, the rugged individualism of the frontiersmen, [and] the break-up of family and church relations due to migration.[19]

Clearly, *anomie* had broken out among the international and domestic migrants who fanned out from the original colonies to the western frontier.

At the same time, a growing secularization weakened religious orthodoxy and practice in the Northeast. Orr further described the shocking situation of the nation's spiritual condition as follows:

> Not many people realize that in the wake of the American Revolution there was a moral slump. Drunkenness became epidemic . . . Profanity was of the most shocking kind . . . Women were afraid to go out at night for fear of assault. Bank robberies were a daily occurrence. What about the churches? The Methodists were losing more members than they were gaining. The Baptists said that they had their most wintry season. The Presbyterians

in general assembly deplored the ungodliness of the country . . . The Lutherans were so languishing they discussed uniting with Episcopalians who were even worse off. The Episcopal Bishop of New York . . . quit functioning . . . The Chief Justice of the United States, John Marshall, wrote . . . that the Church "was too far gone ever to be redeemed." Voltaire said, "Christianity will be forgotten in thirty years" and Tom Paine preached this cheerfully all over America . . . In case this is thought to be the hysteria of the moment, Kenneth Scott Latourette, the great church historian, wrote: "It seemed as if Christianity were about to be ushered out of the affairs of men."[20]

Orr drew special attention to the fact that Christians came together in concerted prayer for the nation, and by the turn of the nineteenth century, revival would come.

According to Mark Noll, the Second Great Awakening "was the most influential revival of Christianity in the History of the United States."[21] Beginning on the Kentucky frontier around 1801 with the Cane Ridge camp meetings, the Awakening owed a great deal to immigrants and slaves, as well as to internal migrants. Black and white preachers alike "fervently proclaimed the Good News" at the meetings, suspending the question of race.[22] The revival "embraced blacks, who eagerly participated [alongside whites] in the tumultuous exercises which became characteristic of frontier revivalism."[23] The electrifying meetings included "jerks, dancing, laughing, running, and 'the barking exercise.'"[24] Such revivals "proved to be a powerful instrument for accelerating the pace of slave conversions."[25]

The form of the meetings appealed to the vestiges of African culture among the involuntary immigrants (slaves), but it also "owed something to the Scottish observance of 'communion season.'"[26] In noting this Scottish influence, Noll acknowledges in an oblique way that the camp meetings included voluntary immigrants in their audiences: "If the pattern of intense evangelistic gatherings lasting several days originated in Scotland, it assumed an unusually powerful force in the backcountry where Scottish immigrants were only a part of a mobile population drawn from many sources."[27]

Despite the short shrift immigration has usually received in the standard histories of American revival, the influence of immigrants at the beginning of the Second Great Awakening on native-born Americans offers direct evidence to the idea that migration has played an important role in the revival of Christian faith in America.

Without the migrational aspect of American life during the period, the "most influential revival" in American history would not have materialized.

As a result of the meetings, Presbyterian churches proliferated, but Baptist and Methodist churches grew even faster throughout the South and the newly opened western frontier as "Methodist circuit riders and Baptist farmer-preachers fanned out . . . in unprecedented numbers."[28] The westward migration of Americans not only included immigrants but also turned previously settled Americans into migrants themselves. The social forces that accompany migration do not discriminate on the basis of the national identity of the people they influence but rather destabilize the lives and open the minds of migrants on an equal-opportunity basis. Leaving one's home and moving to a new place creates an enlivened awareness of the need for God and for godly neighbors.

Without the migrational aspect of American life during the period, the "most influential revival" in American history would not have materialized. By 1830, the immigrant-influenced churches founded during the Second Great Awakening enabled the Baptists and Methodists to replace Congregationalists and Presbyterians as the largest denominations in the whole United States.[29]

THE AWAKENING CONTINUES AND DIVERSIFIES

While immigrants from earlier history had an important role in the Second Great Awakening, immigration during the early years of the Second Great Awakening slowed in the United States because of the Napoleonic Wars in Europe and the illegalization of the African slave trade. New entries from the 1790s through the 1830s only averaged about sixty thousand per decade,[30] but as mid-century approached, a new wave of immigration would bring massive growth to American Catholicism.

Catholicism started early in North America, with missionaries arriving at the end of the fifteenth century. The first Catholic congregations in English North America emerged in 1630, when Lord Baltimore received a charter to found Maryland as a Catholic colony.[31] By 1830, about three hundred thousand Americans confessed Roman Catholic faith, but the mass immigration of Irish to America provoked by the potato famine meant that by 1860, the Catholic population would grow by a factor of 10. The national population had grown by a factor of only 2.5. Among the three million Catholics living in America at the beginning of the Civil War, about one million had emigrated from Ireland alone.[32]

To serve the exploding population of American Catholics, John Carroll, America's first Roman Catholic bishop, succeeded in recruiting large numbers of European priests and religious workers to cross the Atlantic.[33] Although many of Carroll's recruits were French, in time the Irish would begin to dominate the hierarchical offices of the American church. Across the country, Catholic priests adopted many of the revivalistic practices Protestants had used to such strong effect, building a solid ecclesial structure to welcome immigrants over the years to come.[34]

Between 1800 and 1920, over forty million immigrants would come to America, a substantial majority of whom were Roman Catholics from Ireland, Italy, Germany, Poland, and other Catholic nations.[35] Over 1 million Catholics emigrated from Germany alone over these years.[36] Shortly afterward, between 1880 and 1890, Italians would join them in large numbers, averaging over thirty thousand per year during the decade. By 1900, the numbers would grow to over sixty-five thousand per year, totaling 1.5 million.[37]

The increase of immigrants during the middle years of the nineteenth century not only brought stunning growth to American Catholicism but also a massive migration of German and Scandinavian Lutherans who populated America's Midwestern frontier in the middle years of the nineteenth century. The need for religion out on the frontier had not diminished since Pilgrims had landed in Massachusetts two hundred years earlier.

As Norwegian journalist Ole Much Raeder reported in 1847, "Spiritual needs do assert themselves even out here in the West, as soon as the first severe struggle with nature is over . . . Many a person who never has experienced the influence of religion in a thickly populated civilized country, learns to appreciate, out here in his loneliness, how deep an influence religion exerts upon the soul of a man."[38]

These needs resulted in the founding of churches throughout the Midwest, and by 1870, about 440,000 Lutherans attended American churches, compared to only 480,000 Congregationalist descendants of the original Pilgrims.[39]

ANOTHER AWAKENING

Even as massive waves of immigrants increased the diversity and geographic dispersion of Christianity in nineteenth-century America, another Awakening would dawn among the traditional Protestant Evangelical churches that flourished during the Second Great Awakening.[40] While church historians have argued over whether the emergence of the nineteenth-century Holiness movement constituted a Third Great Awakening, no one can deny the global impact this revival achieved, along with its successor, the Pentecostal movement, which now numbers more than half a billion participants, including Pentecostal and Charismatic Christians.[41]

The new Awakening began not long after the Second Great Awakening, as Charles Grandison Finney, a law student converted to faith, established a revivalistic career that spoke powerfully to the challenges of his times. His Rochester revival in 1830–31 got the nation's attention, and a series of urban revival meetings in Philadelphia, Boston, New York, and Great Britain increased his influence greatly. Many of those affected by his urban revivals would have been immigrants. Many of the Irish immigrants who came to America at that time professed Protestant faith or none at all, and such immigrants would certainly have joined churches planted because of the Finney revivals and their spin-offs.

The range of Finney's influence was massive, and historian Mark Noll considers him not only the crucial figure of the nineteenth century in white Evangelicalism but also one of the most important influences on American life in general during his time.[42] Finney's ministry had two major impacts on American Evangelicalism—an emphasis on social reform that would strongly affect the abolition of slavery and the later Temperance Movement; and a doctrine of spiritual empowerment known as "the baptism in the Holy Spirit." In Finney's preaching and theology, the two poles of biblical justice—social justice and personal righteousness—held together and would inspire both social reform and revival well into the twentieth century, directly touching the lives of countless urban immigrants in the Northeast.

> Two poles of biblical justice—social justice and personal righteousness—held together and would inspire both social reform and revival well into the twentieth century.

A list of important figures of the post–Civil War phase of the mid-century Awakening would include figures like Phoebe Palmer, Hannah Whitall Smith, Dwight L. Moody, Billy Sunday, and others—all white Americans. The advent of the Pentecostal movement would bring African-American Holiness preachers like William J. Seymour, the leader of the Azusa Street Revival, and C. H. Mason, founder of the Church of God in Christ, to the nation's attention as well. But for the purposes of this discussion, the question arises: What role did migration play in America's third round of religious awakening? While the Roman Catholic Church grew very large on immigrant entries during this time, the contributions of immigrants to Protestant growth do not appear as obvious. Nevertheless, migration played both a contributing role as well as a dependent role in the Third Protestant Awakening.

The transatlantic Higher Life movement had a very important role in shaping the piety that undergirded Protestant vitality in the Third Awakening. As Charles Finney began to preach the baptism in the Holy Spirit, the Reformed circles in which he moved came into closer contact and indeed overlapped with Wesleyan circles, bringing a widespread desire for personal holiness. Although the two circles had different doctrines about holiness, they cohered in a movement that embraced both circles. American-born women like Phoebe Palmer and Hannah Whitall Smith and the English-born immigrant Catherine Mumford Booth grew to prominence in America and the British Isles during the 1850s through their preaching and writing, not only in promoting a life of Spirit-filled holiness but also in promoting the role of women as leaders and preachers in Protestant churches.

The American Holiness movement grew throughout the nineteenth century, playing an important role in massive revival movements during the American Civil War (on both sides of the conflict). In the late 1860s the movement came together in huge national camp meetings, drawing ten thousand people to Vineland, New Jersey, and twenty-five thousand to Mannheim, Pennsylvania. Remarkable spiritual experiences and widespread coverage by the press fueled the movement to even greater prominence, and its leaders—especially the women—soon carried their message across the ocean to England, where they experienced equal success.

As the English wing of the Holiness movement prospered, it gave birth to the Keswick Convention in 1875—a ministry that has had great influence on Evangelical leaders from Dwight L. Moody to Billy Graham—and its influence continues to this day. Thousands of American Christians visited the Convention, where they heard such English luminaries as Frederick B. Meyer and Hudson Taylor (founder of the China Inland Mission); Irish missionary to India Amy Carmichael; Prussian prayer hero George Mueller; South African evangelist Andrew Murray; and others. This international mixing of influences inspired not only a greater interest in "entire sanctification" and "the Spirit-filled life" but also contributed to the fervor that would create the other great migrational aspect of the Awakening—the Missions movement.

THE MISSIONS MOVEMENT

Prior to 1870, the American Protestant churches had produced about two thousand missionaries, about 10 percent of whom worked among Native Americans.[43] An American Presbyterian pastor and leader in the Keswick Convention, A. T. Pierson, became the leading advocate of foreign missions, popularizing the writings of foreign missionaries like Hudson Taylor, F. B. Meyer, and George Mueller and provoking much zeal. As a result, the Student Volunteer movement was born in 1886 at Dwight L. Moody's popular summer conference at Northfield Mount Hermon School in Massachusetts, when 100 out of 251 students present signed a pledge stating: "We are willing and desirous, God permitting, to become foreign missionaries."[44]

Students at colleges all over the Northeast and around the nation soon became consumed with interest in foreign missions, especially at the Ivy League colleges. A group of 4 students from the Northfield Conference toured 167 colleges over the next academic year, collecting declarations from 2,200 young people who signed the missions pledge.[45] Interest continued at a high level until the outbreak of World War I, and between 1886 and 1920 the Student Volunteer movement recruited 8,742 missionaries for foreign service—about half of the total number of Evangelical Protestant missionaries sent out during that period.[46]

Foreign missionaries count as immigrants too, and even if immigrants did not play the largest role in producing the Third Awakening, they unquestionably represented one of its largest effects. On the one hand, thousands of Americans migrated into missions because of the Awakening, and on the other hand, those missionaries founded, assisted, and nurtured new Evangelical Protestant churches around the world—especially in Latin America—that would later send their members to America by the millions.

> Thousands of Americans migrated into missions because of the Awakening, and nurtured new Evangelical Protestant churches around the world—especially in Latin America.

THE PENTECOSTAL AWAKENING

One might say that America daisy-chains its Awakenings. Just as the Second and Third Awakenings came on the heels of (and can only be artificially separated from) previous revivals, a fourth movement grew directly out of the third. The Pentecostal movement resulted directly from the Holiness movement and represents a continuous renewal and dramatic extension and expansion of it.[47]

The Pentecostal movement began around the world in various places more or less simultaneously. The strong emphasis placed on baptism in the Holy Spirit by the Holiness movement inevitably led to a group of students doing a homework assignment in Topeka, Kansas, in 1901 to discover "the biblical evidence of the baptism in the Holy Spirit." That question, seeded by their professor Charles F. Parham, led them to study the book of Acts—the only book in the Bible that describes the experience of receiving the baptism in the Holy Spirit. The students concluded that every incidence of Spirit-baptism in Acts included "speaking in tongues," in which the recipients spoke in languages they had not naturally learned through the empowerment of the Holy Spirit. The students consequently laid hands on each other and prayed until they had received the same experience.

From Topeka, the phenomenon of speaking in tongues would spread out across the country. When a black man named William J. Seymour migrated to Los Angeles with the message in 1906, the Azusa Street Revival ensued. Led by a black man in the context of an originally black audience, the revival quickly attracted a wide variety of immigrants from Latin America and Asia who lived in Southern California as well as many white people. Reports of the revival in the nascent Pentecostal press would soon bring pilgrims from literally all around the world to receive the baptism in the Holy Spirit at a revival where "the color line was washed away in the Blood."[48]

Like the Cane Ridge Revival a hundred years before, the Azusa Street Revival suspended the question of race or ethnicity. Participants in similar outbreakings around the world came to Azusa Street for fellowship and instruction and spiritual experiences. From there not only would missionaries return to fields they had already worked, but new missionaries would experience a call to carry the Pentecostal message. The obvious symbolic value of the experience of speaking in unknown foreign languages and the way the experience and its doctrinal adjuncts appealed to primal human drives[49] made Pentecostalism "a religion made to travel, cosmopolitan both in its scope and outlook."[50]

In America, Pentecostalism would grow steadily until the late 1950s, when it would begin to spread into the historic Mainline Protestant churches. David DuPlessis, a South African immigrant to the United States, began to exert significant influence among Mainline Protestant leaders through his participation in the World Council of Churches (to the great consternation of most other Pentecostal leaders!). Through DuPlessis' work and that of many others, the Charismatic movement broke out in the traditional Protestant churches and, beginning in the 1960s, in the Roman Catholic Church. Today hundreds of millions of Charismatics around the world share the distinctive experiences of Pentecostalism, having earned the approval of several recent popes, including Pope Francis.[51]

According to the *World Christian Encyclopedia*, Pentecostal Christianity numbered 12 million adherents by 1970, but now "incorporates some 600 million worldwide in its various expressions, a fourth of all Christendom."[52] In America, C. H. Mason's

Church of God in Christ has grown to over 6 million adherents in the African-American community. The Assemblies of God denomination numbers over 3 million in the United States, with a total worldwide membership in excess of 67.5 million.[53] These American examples of Pentecostalism shared in the same explosive growth that occurred worldwide between 1970 and the present, a growth that both profited and suffered from the heyday of Pentecostal television ministries in the 1980s (Jimmy Swaggart, Jim Bakker, Oral Roberts, Rex Humbard) and in the following years (TBN, Joel Osteen, Benny Hinn, and many others).

Today, on the heels of the Fourth Awakening and in the penumbra of the worldwide Pentecostal mushroom of the last thirty years, immigrants from Latin America, Africa, and Asia stand ready to launch America's next Great Awakening.

7

THE NEW LATINO REFORMATION

My friend Javier Castillo sent me an email directly from Caserta, Italy, within moments of the end of his meeting with Pope Francis. Javier, a missionary to Spain who served with me on a church staff in Quito, Ecuador, had received an invitation through friends to attend the Pope's visit and actually spend time in the papal presence, where he had spoken to the pontiff and invited him to pray with him for Spain on a future occasion. In his native Spanish, the Holy Father graciously accepted, calling an aide to take down Javier's data and make future arrangements. The email percolated with excitement, pride, and a sense of spiritual victory.

At that meeting, Pope Francis made headlines around the world by apologizing for previous Roman Catholic treatment of Pentecostals:

"Among those who persecuted and denounced Pentecostals, almost as if they were crazy people trying to ruin the race, there were also Catholics," he said. "I am the pastor of Catholics, and I ask your forgiveness for those Catholic brothers and sisters who didn't know and were tempted by the devil."[1]

While Italian Evangelicals reacted to the Pope's words with caution and puzzlement, Latino Pentecostals widely celebrated this Pope from their own continent, the first man from the Americas to hold the office.[2]

Since his days as a bishop in Argentina, Jorge Bergoglio (aka Pope Francis) had sought out friendly relationships with leaders of the burgeoning Argentine Pentecostal movement. The pastor of the Evangelical church in Caserta, Giovanni Traettino, had first met Bergoglio in Buenos Aires, Argentina, in the late 1990s while working to foment relationships between Charismatic Catholics and Pentecostal Protestants.[3] As soon as the smoke rose declaring a pope from the Americas, the buzz began. Word about Bergoglio's friendship with Pentecostal leaders and their positive comments about his spirituality spread quickly among Pentecostals around Latin America and the United States.

Javier often participated in ecumenical efforts in Ecuador, and I accompanied him on several occasions to meet with Catholics and explore Christian unity, but the late 1990s seem like a century ago now. Among those Catholics "tempted by the devil" to persecute Pentecostals stood Pope John Paul the Great, who in 1992 responded to massive defections from Roman Catholicism to Pentecostal churches in Latin America by using "the phrase *lobos rapaces* (ravenous wolves) to refer to Pentecostal and Evangelical 'sects.'"[4] The faithful responded to the call, and on multiple occasions afterward, evangelism teams from the church I pastored in Ecuador faced the literal sticks and stones of Catholic mobs that rose up to drive the young *lobos* from their towns. On one occasion, only a sudden freak thunderstorm averted violence against our defenseless youth team in the town of Olmedo.

On another occasion in Carpuela, a lady who had led a mob of stick-wielding Catholics against our team in Chota showed up for medical treatment at our clinic the next day. Recognizing her as the ringleader of the previous day's mob, our pastor escorted her to the front of a hundred people in line to give her preferential treatment. The persecution never mattered to our teams. We always taught our people to forgive everything on the same day, and our young evangelists always retreated peacefully, glorying in the privilege of having faced persecution for Jesus' sake.

How the climate has changed! Today the Pope calls us his friends, and indeed we accept his friendship. Many of today's Latino Pentecostals genuinely like the Pope, returning his affection without the slightest intention of letting up in their efforts to reach the lost, regardless of their formal religious affiliation. To them, the task has nothing to do with proselytizing devout Catholics but rather with reaching people whose lives have withered because they do not know God. In the late 1990s, research conducted on behalf of the Latin American Catholic Bishops' Conference "found that 8,000 Latin Americans were deserting the Catholic Church for Evangelical Protestantism every day."[5] Two decades later, the conversions continue apace. In the United States, the share of Catholics among Hispanics fell from 67 percent to 55 percent in the four-year period between 2010 and 2013.[6]

In a *New York Times* editorial, Virginia Garrard-Burnett, a professor of history and religious studies at the University of Texas and a leading expert on Latin American religion, recognized that

"Pope Francis's election may be a good start" toward regaining the allegiance of Latin American Catholics."[7] She recommended three strategies for winning back converts, including encouragement of the Catholic Charismatic Renewal, reviving traditional Catholic pieties from the pre-Vatican II era, and advancing "neotraditional Catholic organizations, like Opus Dei"—only to recognize that "the problem with all of these options . . . is that they have been tried and found lacking."[8]

AMERICAN *EVANGÉLICOS*

The juggernaut of Evangelical growth in Latin America—especially in Pentecostal churches but including all other Evangelical expressions of Christianity—has come to America in full force. In a recent cover story entitled "The Latino Reformation," *Time* drew attention to the growth of Latino Protestant churches and the shift of many American Hispanics away from the Catholic Church. While Catholicism got started in Latin America before Martin Luther's Reformation in Germany and managed to fend it off for four hundred years, the Protestant Reformation now advances in full force.

> The juggernaut of Evangelical growth in Latin America— especially in Pentecostal churches but including all other Evangelical expressions of Christianity—has come to America in full force.

By no means do all *Evangélicos* in the United States belong to Pentecostal churches. *Time* reported that while the Assemblies of God counts about 2,500 churches, churches affiliated with the Southern Baptist Convention number 3,200.[9] The label on the church sign does not matter but rather what happens inside the churches, and Hispanic Evangelical churches present a decidedly pentecostalist tone regardless of their specific denominational affiliation, whether Mainline Protestant or Evangelical. The question at stake here involves the vitality of the churches and their potential for renewing faith in America. According to Pew Research,

> On average, Hispanic evangelicals—many of whom also identify as either Pentecostal or charismatic Protestants— not only report higher rates of church attendance than Hispanic Catholics but also tend to be more engaged in other religious activities, including Scripture reading, Bible study groups and sharing their faith.[10]

Precisely these practices and others drive vitality in churches, and will drive many Americans from a formal or nominal faith to a vibrant, revived, new expression of faith in the years to come.

LATINO LEADERS

Dr. Samuel Rodríguez figures prominently in the *Time* article, as does Wilfredo "Pastor Choco" de Jesús, the pastor of a Hispanic church numbering fifteen thousand members in Chicago. Both Pastor Choco (short for "chocolate") and Dr. Rodríguez are American-born Hispanics with master's degrees from excellent universities and highly refined skills that new immigrant pastors can only hope their children might someday wield in God's service. Yet other Latino immigrants have established themselves as stars in the American Evangelical scene. Peruvian-born evangelist Luis

Palau similarly reaches across all sectors of the American population and enjoys a worldwide following.

Pastor Erwin McManus, who received a very American name from his adoptive stepfather, came to the United States from El Salvador as "Irving Raphael Mesa Cardona." Going beyond mere assimilation to a position of cultural leadership, he has become one of the most influential pastors in the United States. He came to prominence as pastor of Mosaic Church in Los Angeles, which counts thousands of members at multiple sites involving people from approximately sixty nationalities in attendance. Educated at the University of North Carolina and at Southwestern Baptist Theological Seminary, he has established himself as a popular TED-talk speaker, and his creativity has spilled over into filmmaking and fashion design as well.[11]

Hardly alone in their ability to cross over from a minority identity to a leading role in mainstream American religion, such Hispanic leaders offer a picture of the future of American faith—creative, inclusive, vibrant, committed, and hip. Evangelical churches cater to youth, and they express strong spiritual commitment in sync with the latest cultural trends.[12] As Dartmouth College religion scholar Randall Balmer noted in *Time*, Latinos "see the move to Protestantism, particularly evangelicalism, as a form of upward mobility, and very often I think they associate Catholicism with what they left behind in Latin America . . . They want to start anew."[13]

COMPETING IN THE RELIGIOUS FREE MARKET

No religion in America gets to rest on the laurels of last year's achievements. The religious pluralism that American liberty fosters has a specific effect on its churches: they must compete with each other (and with other forces) for the attention and fidelity of the American public. Finke and Stark have pointed out that America shifted from a beginning in which "most people took no part in organized religion to a nation in which nearly two-thirds of American adults do" through a process of economic competition.[14] In assessing the whole of American religious history, they recognized that churches lost market share when they "rejected traditional doctrines and ceased to make serious demands on their followers." They forthrightly declared, "The churching of America was accomplished by aggressive churches committed to vivid otherworldliness."[15]

As *Time*'s Elizabeth Dias recognizes, Evangelical churches have struck the very note that Finke and Stark emphasize as crucial to organizational success in American religion:

> The *evangélico* boom is inextricably linked to the immigrant experience. *Evangélicos* are socially more conservative than Hispanics generally, but they are quicker to fight for social justice than their white brethren are. They are eager to believe in the miraculous but also much more willing to bend ecclesiastical rules to include women in church duties and invite other ethnic groups into their pews. The new churches are in many cases a deliberate departure from the countries and the faith their members left behind.[16]

Dias erred in her analysis only inasmuch as she failed to recognize that no ecclesiastical rules against female leadership exist to be bent in most Evangelical denominations and independent churches, a distinct advantage over the Roman Catholic Church for Hispanic women who have the calling and talent to serve as the head pastors of churches, whether large or small.

EVANGÉLICO RELIGIOUS CULTURE

Pentecostal and other Evangelical churches fit the description of "aggressive" and "otherworldly," but the adjectives "compassionate" and "effective at social uplift" fit just as well. Evangelicalism as a whole features a very strong commitment to evangelization as well as a strong doctrine of eternal life in Heaven, an eager expectation of the return of Christ, and the end of evil's reign over the earth. But at the same time, *Evangélicos* believe in and fervently preach earthly success, healing for the body, education and social mobility, and the concept of "redemption and lift." No churches have shown greater commitment to reaching out to drug addicts, prostitutes, gang members, and other victims of poverty, and *Evangélicos* delight in nothing more than testimonies of rising, as their American co-religionists sometimes say, from the "guttermost to the uttermost."

> *Evangélicos* delight in nothing more than testimonies of rising, as their American coreligionists sometimes say, from the "guttermost to the uttermost."

The global Pentecostal/Evangelical religious culture balances between two magnetic poles.[17] A radical eschatological hope pulls them from one side. They love to say they have read the book of Revelation, "and it says we win." They "know deep in their knower" that no matter how things go in this life, for better or for worse, they have a rock-solid eternal home in Heaven. From the other side, they feel the attraction toward success in this world, prosperity that emanates from a good God who loves them and wants the best for them. They send their children to school and on to university. They know their honest work ethic will bring improvement. Their positive confession of faith will defeat the negative forces—whether natural or supernatural—that have held them back. For freedom Christ has set them free.[18]

Americans—and immigrants in general—hold to an unwavering philosophy of pragmatism. They do not have the luxury of cerebral, decaffeinated religion. They like things that work, and Pentecostal Evangelicalism, a made-in-the-Americas faith, appeals powerfully to immigrants. Mainline Protestant churches and liberal Catholic ministries may offer the worldly pole of sanctuary for undocumented immigrants, social services, and other temporal benefits upon their entry to the country, but if those ministries do not offer the balance immigrants need from the pole of transcendent hope, immigrants quickly get pulled in by the magnetism of the *Evangélicos*.

BOTH *EVANGÉLICOS* AND ROMAN CATHOLICS NEEDED

America needs a strong, vibrant Roman Catholic Church, just like Latin America does. As I used to say in the culturally Catholic but minimally observant town of Carpuela, Ecuador, the pastoral needs of the town (and of Latin America and of the United States) cannot be met by the Roman Catholic Church alone. Not enough priests staff the churches to meet the people's pastoral needs. In Latin America, about equal numbers of Roman Catholic priests and Evangelical ministers serve the churches. In America, the shortage of priests presents a critical barrier to success among immigrants, whose needs loom large in the face of the *anomie* that complicates family and individual life. They need more than *attractional* churches ready to receive them. They need *missional* churches that will go out and bring them in.[19] The problem in the United States among Hispanic Catholics, according to *Time*, springs from the minimal levels of engagement with religious activities that they exhibit.[20] Immigrants require a religion that clicks on all cylinders, and if they don't find one, they will abandon faith altogether.

In fact, competition from the *Evangélicos* has proven to offer a healthy incentive to Roman Catholics in Latin America. According to David Briggs, executive director of the International Association of Religion Journalists, "In countries where a higher proportion of the population is Protestant, Catholics tend to attend more and be more likely to say that religion is important in their daily lives."[21] As the future unfolds, Protestants and Catholics may find a way to work harmoniously to bring more and more Christians in America into a vibrant relationship with God, in the same spirit of brotherhood that Pope Francis has placed on the table. In the meantime, on the Evangelical side of the Christian family table, the Latino Reformation has set out a sumptuous banquet, and it offers powerful nourishment for the renewal of American faith.

Leaders like Rodríguez believe in the possibility of a massive new awakening in America because of what they see happening in the churches. But the revival will not continue automatically. The Latino Reformation only tells half the story of defections from Roman Catholic faith among Hispanics. According to Pew

Research, about 18 percent of Hispanic Catholics become religiously unaffiliated—almost as many as turn to Protestantism (22 percent). Such former Catholics

> describe themselves as having no particular religion or say they are atheist or agnostic. This group exhibits much lower levels of religious observance and involvement than Hispanic Catholics. In this respect, unaffiliated Hispanics roughly resemble the religiously unaffiliated segment of the general public.[22]

America needs a strong Roman Catholic Church to do its part in preserving faith among Latinos and other immigrants.

The longer immigrant families stay in the United States, the more they tend to look like average Americans. As throughout the history of religion, from the Old Testament to the present day, "regression to the mean" happens. But that does not mean that an Awakening has not already begun in America's immigrant communities. Awakenings do not hinge on what the uninterested do and think. They happen when the faithful rise to new levels of devotion and witness—and that is exactly what the New Pilgrims have come to do.

8

RENEWING
THE CHURCHES

Christian immigrants in the United States engage American churches in several formats, including ethnic enclave churches, transitional bilingual churches, international churches, traditional churches, and neo-traditional churches. These categories represent various assimilation stages, approaches, or strategies, and each variety offers strengths that particular kinds of immigrants need. The overall structure provides a niche for everyone and an opportunity for all immigrants to strengthen and renew American faith.

ETHNIC ENCLAVE CHURCHES

Ethnic enclave churches serve as a haven for the culture and language of "the old country," offering deeply caring community and powerful relief for those struggling with the very difficult task of adjusting to a new country. As Finke and Stark have noted, such ethnic enclave churches represent nothing new but rather a long-standing American tradition. They state:

Regardless of the immigrant religion being studied, whether it is Christian or another world religion, a growing volume of research documents the remarkable similarities of the new immigrant congregations with those of the past . . . [The late eminent sociologist and Catholic priest Andrew] Greeley noted that the Catholic parishes of the early immigrants simultaneously preserved a distinctive religious and ethnic subculture as they assimilated immigrants into the larger culture.[1]

Such churches may or may not continue long-term in a state of ethnic homogeneity. Factors such as doctrine, racial makeup, and isolation play a part in their fates.

As *Plattdeutsch*-speaking Amish churches across the eastern Great Lakes region illustrate, ethnic enclave churches can last for centuries. The particular doctrines of the Amish promote isolation and non-assimilation, and their churches exist to ensure that the total assimilation of their community does not occur. African-American churches also present evidence for centuries of permanence in ethnic distinctness, although their homogeneity springs from centuries of racial prejudice against them and a continuing need for a community of refuge from an often inhospitable outside culture.

> The complaint often arises, "Why don't they just learn English and attend our church?" Strangely, I've never heard that comment offered by anyone who has actually mastered a foreign language.

Sadly, some all-white churches from a variety of denominations also persist due to racial prejudice. In contrast, many small town churches across Middle America would love to include more ethnic diversity but nevertheless continue to serve remarkably homogeneous populations of Germans or Scandinavians and haven't seen a new surname on the church rolls for a hundred years. Their homogeneity has not necessarily sprung from prejudice, but rather from the historical absence of other ethnic groups in their environment. Such places serve as the inspiration for Garrison Keillor's description of the Scandinavians and Germans of the fictional Lake Wobegon, "Where all the women are strong, all the men are good-looking, and all the children are above average."[2] As for both rural and urban Roman Catholic churches, the preponderance of Latino immigrants in recent years has pretty well guaranteed at least a partial ethnic diversification among their members, even in Lake Wobegon.

WHY WE NEED ETHNIC CHURCHES

Many American Christians opposed to immigration resent the congregating of immigrants into churches along ethnic and linguistic lines. The complaint often arises, "Why don't they just learn English and attend our church?" Strangely, I've never heard that comment offered by anyone who has actually mastered a foreign language and has any clue how much effort it takes to do so. The answer to this question, as noted above, must include the fact that since colonial days, immigrants have always sought refuge, fellowship, and the opportunity to worship among those who speak their first language.

In 1993 I returned to the United States after the first three years of my missionary career in Central America. My new job involved frequent travel throughout Latin America to establish a new college degree program through distance education, but I wanted to ensure that the Spanish-language skills of my young family would not slip during our years back in the United States. I had two little tow-headed girls who had not reached their fourth and second birthdays, but they could speak Spanish fluently.

Soon after we arrived, I took my three-year-old, Jessica, with me to visit a Hispanic church that met in the facilities of an English-speaking church in Fort Worth, Texas. In El Salvador and Costa Rica, where we had recently lived, my little girls would literally shut down governmental and business offices when I walked in with them, mobbed by women who had never seen such blonde hair and blue eyes up close. *"Es una muñequita!"*—a living doll—squealed the women at the main post office in San José, Costa Rica, literally shutting all twenty service windows—despite the long lines of customers who waited—and mobbing my baby Jessica. I wrongly expected she might get a similar, if toned down, reception in the Spanish church in Texas.

Similarly, I presumed I would receive a warm welcome in my own right. In El Salvador, if I wanted an invitation to preach, I merely needed to walk into a small church with a Bible in my hand. The presence of an American missionary usually brought a sense of honor to churches there, along with the possibility of financial help or other benefits. While I did not expect to receive an invitation to preach at the church in Texas, I assumed people would treat me with some degree of courtesy.

I walked into the church with Jessica, but no one came over to greet us. As a matter of fact, it seemed like they went out of their way to avoid us. We sat alone for ten minutes or more before the service, watching everyone around us greeting one another joyfully *in English*! But no one among the fifty or so congregants greeted us, despite all of my nodding and smiling. The service began, and after a few songs, the pastor stepped up and began to recognize visitors. He carefully presented each of the new people and asked them questions about themselves, but he clearly and very purposefully ignored Jessica and me, in spite of our conspicuousness. After the people interacted with all of the welcome guests, the singing resumed with everyone standing, and I carefully beat a retreat out of the side door. I knew the church did not want us there, and as we walked to our car, I thought about why.

One of the key elements to intercultural communications involves empathy—putting yourself in the other person's position and attempting to imagine their perspective. In just a few moments, I understood the reception we had received. No language barrier had separated us, as I could speak Spanish as well as anyone present, and they all spoke English to each other. I recognized a great cultural difference between Latinos living in their own country and Hispanics living in America long enough to prefer English as their interpersonal language but still preferring to worship in Spanish. In their own countries, they enjoyed a great sense of security, but in America, they were a *minority*. Because of my very brief experience as a minority among them, I immediately felt a sense of empathy with them.

In every other context of their lives, the members of the church answered to native-born Americans. In their jobs, in the marketplace, in government offices, and in almost all other social spheres, the dominant culture held sway. Only in their church did they enjoy the first place of leadership. Unlike the churches in El Salvador, the Hispanic congregation in Texas saw me as a threat to their autonomy and dignity. I would have to earn a place in their community by long, patient attendance before they would open up to me. I didn't resent their standoffishness, but I decided to move on and I determined never again to visit another immigrant church without first making a courtesy call to the pastor.

Since that strange occasion, I have preached in dozens of Hispanic churches in the United States, always well received and never seeing that kind of treatment again. The weird lack of hospitality I experienced in that strange setting does not characterize Latino churches in the United States at all. But the radical insecurity I experienced there gave me important insight into the immigrant church. Everyone wants a place where they stand on equal ground with everyone else, where their culture comes first, where people speak their language, where no one will treat them as "less than." Having such a place of retreat renews their energy for facing the task of interaction with, and even assimilation to, the dominant culture.

The Church Growth movement that became popular in the 1970s and '80s taught an idea called the "homogeneity principle." According to that theory, churches grow fastest when they reach out to a homogenous group of people. The rise of interest in diversity in the 1990s made that principle anathema in most Evangelical churches, and today most churches with a dominant-culture majority recognize that they need to reach out to a diverse crowd of people. The danger of adopting (or maintaining) a culturally biased ministry style and thus treating members of minority cultures unjustly—indeed unjustly depriving them of the gospel—constitutes a serious spiritual threat to the integrity of dominant-culture churches.

But churches in ethnic minority groups, and especially immigrant groups that have not yet mastered the English language, must deal with a different set of issues. In today's America, people who have mastered America's dominant culture and the English language have a significant power advantage over newcomers to America or monocultural members of ethnic minority groups. Ethnic-minority groups need a place to worship without having to resolve ethno-cultural conflicts as a prerequisite for coming to Christ or serving in church leadership.

In order for new immigrants to worship freely, they need to worship in their first language. If they want to exercise their spiritual gifts, they need an environment that empowers them to do so. The development of their unique sense of calling from God needs nurture from their own people group. Imagine trying to exercise even minimal leadership in a dominant-culture church without the ability to speak English. Further imagine the challenge a non-English-speaking pastor would face in attempting to plant a church to reach dominant-culture Americans. But since it historically takes a generation for adult immigrants to master English (and some adult immigrants never will), many immigrants would have no opportunity to develop preaching and other leadership skills if they did not have a church dominated by their ethnolinguistic group.

IMMIGRANT CHURCHES IN HISTORY

Once again, the segregation of new immigrants into churches founded specifically for their group has a long tradition in America (as well as in every other country). The German Mennonites who came to America in the 1680s (my ancestors Heinrich and Katrina Kesselberg among them) congregated in German-speaking churches. Like today's immigrants, my family's immigrant generation preferred the religious fellowship of their own kind, but their children all mastered English and converted to the Episcopal faith, except for my ancestor William, who married a Welsh girl and converted to the English Baptist church. Not all of those early immigrants assimilated to the dominant culture, and to this day, Amish and some Old Order Mennonites still worship in their antique German dialect across Pennsylvania and in other states.

As Jenna Josselitt records in *Parade of Faiths*, an important history of the impact of immigrants on the religions of America, Catholic immigrants in the middle years of the 1800s and afterward, "whether they lived in the city or on a farm . . . preferred to worship in their mother tongue and among their own kind . . . [and] strongly preferred that their priests be of the same ethnic background as themselves."[3] As a result, a diverse system of Catholic parishes emerged, "each with its own set of priests, parochial schools, and literature in this parallel universe."[4] That same truth found illustration in every wave of immigrants to America, whether they belonged to churches, synagogues, mosques, temples, or other houses of worship.

In my own church, the Assemblies of God, from the very beginning of the denomination's history in 1914, ethnically and linguistically distinct congregations in America led to the formation of parallel jurisdictions for Italians, Germans, Hispanics, Koreans, Chinese, Brazilians, Portuguese, Filipinos, Vietnamese,

Fijians, Samoans, Slavs, and other groups. Organization among ethnic lines did not begin with this generation of immigrants, but has always existed. As Finke and Stark have noted:

> The new immigrant congregations continue to do the same [thing immigrant churches have always done]. Congregations teach the younger generations to speak English. They hold worship services in the native tongue and promote traditional rituals as they assist members in getting citizenship, jobs, and training. Whether the congregation was German at the end of the nineteenth century or Chinese at the dawn of the twenty-first, the immigrant congregations seek to reproduce portions of the old culture as they assimilate members into the new.[5]

The value of ethnically homogeneous immigrant churches to American society has proven itself over and over again throughout our history.

TRANSITIONAL BILINGUAL CHURCHES

Bethel Spanish Church in Othello, Washington, nicely illustrates what usually happens over time to Evangelical churches that begin as ethnic enclave churches in America. The history of the church began in the late 1950s when a group of Pentecostal believers, mainly from a church in a small village named San Benito in the state of Nuevo Leon, Mexico, migrated north for the seasonal opportunity to work on the farms surrounding Othello. In early 1963, they had officially started a Spanish-speaking church, together with other migrant workers who had settled in Othello.

For decades, the church and its people prospered, achieving the American dream for themselves. Through the years, a large number of the Mexican attendees, who would not transfer their church membership for fear of losing their spiritual heritage, kept sending generous portions of their income back to the mother church in Mexico. Accordingly, the San Benito members held this local congregation as a branch church in America. The pastorate of the prosperous American church became a highly desirable placement for Mexican pastors, and even more so as family growth enlarged the church.

The biggest problem with such churches arises as children become teenagers. Like all children raised in America, the teenagers of these churches speak English as their preferred language and assimilate to American ways of doing things. This development makes it very difficult for churches to keep their young people engaged.

Like many other Latino churches, the Othello church eventually split when members who wanted to focus on their American identity broke away from those who wanted to keep doing things more traditionally. The new church began to do everything in both Spanish and English.[6] Young people took up places of leadership and service, especially in terms of the music of the church, which always made room for the styles of music preferred by the young. As a result, the youth of Bethel Spanish Church (notice the English name for a Spanish church) tended to remain in church as they grew up, got married, and had kids of their own. The church continues to thrive, exhibiting a lively, vibrant worship style that not only results in faithful young members but also a continuous stream of new religious vocations and college students preparing for ministry and for the practice of other professions, usually conceived in terms of a divine calling.

Centro de Vida in Tacoma, Washington, represents another outstanding example of a transitional bilingual church. The pastor of the church, Roberto Tejada, perceived a call to come to the United States as a missionary while living in his native Peru. When an opportunity to start a Spanish-speaking church embedded in an English-speaking megachurch presented itself, he came to the United States legally on an R-1 Visa, a special religious worker visa authorized by the Department of State.

Tejada brought highly sharpened pastoral skills, a generous love of people, and unusually sensitive spirituality to an almost ideal context—a guaranteed salary, start-up resources, and stunning church facilities in a city full of unchurched Latinos. But he also brought a wife and two children whose aptitude matched his own. As his two daughters grew up in the church as teenagers, they devoted themselves to the ministry of the church. Beautiful, bursting with charisma, well educated, completely bilingual, musically gifted, and blazing with religious conviction, Tejada's daughters ensured a flourishing youth culture in the church. Together, the whole family succeeded in establishing a church with an average Sunday attendance of 1,600 (representing a total adherence of perhaps 4,500) within the still larger Life Center Church that serves as their host.

Like other churches of this type, converts make up about 75 percent of the members of *Centro de Vida*. Hispanic pastors interviewed for this study typically reported that 75 to 80 percent of their members are new converts, a fact consistent with the data presented by *Time* in its Latino Reformation issue. Everything the church does attracts new converts. The bilingual services not only ensure that children and adolescents understand the proceedings, they also make the church more attractive to English-speaking spouses of members. Such churches appeal strongly to immigrants with a moderate-to-high desire to assimilate to English culture, and such immigrants often intermarry with native-born Americans or English-speaking immigrants of another ethnicity. As a result, the church broadens its ministry beyond the original audience of Hispanics and includes Americans from a wide variety of racial and ethnic groups.

Latinos have long referred to themselves as *"la raza cósmica"* (the cosmic race), a term coined by the Mexican philosopher and politician José Vasconcelos Calderón. Made up from the mixture of the indigenous and the immigrant—both voluntary and involuntary—from Africa, Europe, the Middle East, and Asia—Latinos defy the false and oversimplified American definition of race, and they find it easy to mix with other groups. As Samuel Rodríguez has said, "We Latinos will marry anybody, because we think every human being is beautiful."[7]

Intermarriage offers far more than an assimilation strategy, and people who want to assimilate to another culture naturally understand the old phrase, *"Vive la difference."* Human diversity has been "endowed by its Creator" with an undeniable beauty that assimilating immigrants see more clearly than perhaps anyone else. When Latino immigrants marry native-born Americans (as well as immigrants from other ethnic groups), they tend to take their new spouses with them to church. On the spouse's side, the same exotic ethnic mystique that they love in their marriage partner gets played out on a community level in their vibrant, Latino churches. The same phenomenon works in Brazilian, Slavic, Romanian, Korean, pan-African, Chinese, pan-Asian, and all other immigrant churches.

Such churches serve as magnets to the future of ethnicity in America, a nation that has never shared a single, common ethnic origin. As America achieves a minority-majority around 2043 and continues to intermarry over decades and centuries, the day will come when most Americans will have an ancestor who fought in the Revolution, one who witnessed the Conquest of Mexico by Cortez, one who suffered pre–Civil War slavery, and another who cleared customs on Ellis Island. *Time* first announced "the browning of America" in 1990, and events since then have only made the emerging interracial American ethnicity more certain.[8] Bilingual and international churches renew America's faith even as they speed the dawning of its future and create a context in which it can shine.

> Human diversity has been "endowed by its Creator" with an undeniable beauty that assimilating immigrants see more clearly than perhaps anyone else.

INTERNATIONAL CHURCHES

When Varun Laohaprasit graduated from medical school in Bangkok, Thailand, he never expected to become the pastor of an international church in the United States. He began to practice his profession, but shortly afterward, began helping Southern Baptist missionaries from America plant a church in Thailand. The people respected him as a doctor, and as he translated for the missionaries, he found that he loved ministering to the spiritual needs of people as well as their physical needs. Still, he never thought he would become a pastor. His dream of further medical studies led him to seek a medical residency in the United States, and as a top candidate, he secured a position at the University of Washington, one of America's highest-ranking medical schools.

After completing his residency, the brilliant foreigner qualified for a seven-year specialty program in neurosurgery. But throughout his time as a resident, he continued to share his faith with people, especially Thai students and immigrants he met in the Seattle area. "The first thing I did," he remembers, "was to try to evangelize Thai students, because I spoke Thai. I'm not a pastor. I didn't have a church."[9] He noticed that his converts, Thai students and local Thai residents of Seattle, had trouble fitting into American churches because of the language barrier and also cultural differences, but he didn't know what to do about it. "I just left them alone and didn't do anything much because I couldn't force people to go to church," he says.[10] As he continued to explain,

> A couple of years later, God began to speak to me that He wanted me to start a church, which I rejected. I said no, because I could not do it. I'm not a Bible school graduate. I'm too busy with my training. But eventually I responded to say yes. "God, if You want me to do it, I'll do it."[11]

So Laohaprasit started New Life International Church in the basement of his home and continued to evangelize students, friends, and immigrants in the Seattle area. Immigrants made up all of the early membership of the church. "Because I didn't know how to reach out to Americans," he explained, "we reached immigrants."[12]

As the church grew, a few native-born Americans began to attend along with their Thai or Laotian husbands or wives. Other non-immigrant Americans would soon join them. When Dr. Laohaprasit's house became too small to accommodate the crowd, the church moved on to a classroom at Seattle Pacific University, then to a nursing home, then to a hotel. "We moved to hotels, like a gypsy, from hotel to hotel, and then we rented an office space."[13] Eventually the church bought a building that would hold 250 people on Mercer Island, an upscale neighborhood on Seattle's east side. Although the congregation still owns the building on Mercer Island, growth soon forced them to move again. They found a building with a meeting room for 400 people in Enatai, an upper-class neighborhood of adjacent Bellevue. "We bought it at the bottom of the market," beams Dr. Laohaprasit.[14]

Including children, about four hundred people currently attend the church. According to the pastor, the church features a very mixed ethnic composition. A Spanish-speaking congregation meets on Sunday afternoon and a Thai-Laotian congregation also has its own meeting in the afternoon. "Laotian people understand Thai," he explains, "but we don't understand Laotian. Laotian people watch Thai movies, so they understand."[15]

The main service operates in English. "The morning service is really mixed," he says. The core congregation consists of Thai immigrants, but "it's English-speaking, with a lot of Chinese, some Iranians, some Indonesians, Malaysians, Koreans, Japanese, Latinos—we have so many nationalities in the church. We have some Africans from Kenya also."[16] Of course, a number of white Americans attend the church as well, whether they have married immigrant spouses or come for the pastor's fervent preaching or the church's vibrant community life. A white businessman I know recently began to attend the church after he sought a second opinion from Dr. Laohaprasit for his inoperable brain tumor. The doctor confirmed the presence of the tumor with X-rays, and then offered the only available treatment: prayer for divine healing. When the tumor disappeared on subsequent X-rays, my friend and his family found a new church home.

> Immigrant churches with highly talented leaders see a burgeoning future for Christianity in America and around the world.

I first became aware of Dr. Laohaprasit and his church seven years ago through a different white American businessman I met at a public lecture for the Discovery Institute, a Seattle-based think tank that focuses on Intelligent Design Cosmology. The highly educated man and his family attend the church because of its intense spirituality. I took down the pastor's name and followed up by contacting him and inviting him to lunch. Later, I visited the church and observed its high-octane brand of Pentecostal worship.

As the story of Pastor Jesús de Paz in Chapter 2 powerfully illustrated, immigrant churches with highly talented leaders see a burgeoning future for Christianity in America and around the world, and their size and vision usually result in church-planting efforts reminiscent of past Great Awakenings in America. Laohaprasit described his own church planting efforts as follows:

> Our church has already planted many churches in Thailand—about 40 to 50 churches—and we are still building a new church in Thailand every quarter. Also we

planted a church in Los Angeles and in San Diego. Now we just got a call from a Laotian group to start a church in Illinois. All of them are immigrant churches, started by Thai pastors or leaders, but ultimately international.[17]

Virtually by definition, international churches have expansive world views that fuel a spectacular vision for growth, and they naturally play it out in dramatic ways. Annual missionary budgets in international churches can exceed $1 million, not only in America but also in international megachurches located in world-class cities around the globe, such as the International English Service Church in Jakarta, Indonesia; Calvary Church in Kuala Lumpur, Malaysia; or Victory Family Centre in Singapore.

I recently preached at Word of Life International Church in Springfield, Virginia, where about two thousand immigrants and native-born Americans worship together under the leadership of Wendel Cover, an eighty-year-old white pastor. The church features members from 120 different nations, with about a third of its members coming from Africa, a third from Latin America, and another third from Asia—with a good mix of native-born Americans as well. The church's large sanctuary features flags from all the nations around the world where the church sponsors missionaries, including virtually every member nation of the United Nations. The missionary budget of the church never drops below the $1 million per year mark.

The church began as a white congregation and grew large before a number of factors combined to make it an ethnically diverse group. First, the demographics of the Washington, D.C., suburbs changed as immigrants began to flow into more affordable neighborhoods like Springfield. Second, the congregation's identity as an Assemblies of God church drew a few immigrants who had attended AG churches in their home country. Third, the pastor's passion for world missions and his genuine love for people of all races attracted an ever-increasing percentage of immigrants. Finally, the evangelistic focus of the pastor's ministry together with the zeal of the Christian immigrants who came to the church have resulted in many conversions among the compatriots of the diverse membership.

Such international churches, led by immigrants or by native-born Americans, represent a common type of Evangelical congregation in urban areas around the United States. The Reverend Dr. Martin Luther King Jr. once famously declared Sunday morning "the most segregated hour in America."[18] That maxim holds true in some places for reasons that hurt, as well as for reasons that help. But a visit to a church in a city near you, like Mosaic Church in Los Angeles, City Church in Seattle, Lakewood Church in Houston, Muldoon Community Church in Anchorage, Brooklyn Tabernacle or The Lamb's Church in New York City (which worships in English, Spanish, and Mandarin Chinese) will often afford a look at some of the most ethnically diverse mixtures of people in the world.[19] Christians in such churches frequently say in an outburst of joy, as if they had been the first people ever to think it up, that "this place looks more like Heaven than any place on earth."

TRADITIONAL CHURCHES

In contrast to immigrants in Evangelical churches, Roman Catholic immigrants tend not to establish ethnic enclave congregations. The structure and polity of Roman Catholicism requires the assistance of a priest in order for congregations to operate effectively. Consequently, Catholic immigrants must generally join established parishes, which typically set up foreign-language meetings for them. As mentioned earlier, the influx of immigrants in Catholic churches has had a major role in renewing the membership of the Church.

To a lesser degree, Mainline Protestant churches have also profited from the influx of immigrants into their churches. One of the main ways in which immigrants help to renew the historic churches involves providing an opportunity for ethical activism around the issue of immigration policy. Across the board, Protestant churches have issued statements urging biblically consistent ethics with regard to immigrants.[20] Many liberal churches have gotten involved in the Sanctuary movement, trying to help immigrants avoid deportation and offering legal assistance. As a result, liberal churches have seen modest additions from immigrants in their regular congregations as well as in new churches planted.

Another way in which traditional churches have engaged immigrants has to do with their church buildings. Across America, liberal churches, as well as Evangelical ones, have shown remarkable hospitality to immigrant congregations that have needed a place to worship. Whether they have lent their buildings, rented them at modest prices, or accommodated immigrant churches at reasonable rates, they have shared their facilities generously.

Often the denominational identity of the immigrant churches has differed from that of their hosts, and their theological positions often represent polar opposites, especially on issues such as acceptance of homosexuality as a moral alternative. Sometimes, the guest churches surreptitiously hold pre-service prayer meetings before their afternoon services to cleanse the building of any spiritual influence from the sparsely attended morning worship of their hosts. At the same time, cognitive dissonance does enter the picture, while conservative immigrant churches deeply appreciate their hosts, even as they regard them with spiritual suspicion.

The successor denomination of the Plymouth Pilgrims, Congregationalist churches that, along with their partners from mergers, now bear the name United Church of Christ (UCC), have experienced catastrophic losses of membership from their traditional constituency. They have nevertheless seen modest replacements from immigration. Over the last six decades, the percentage of new churches planted by immigrants and minorities has increased from about 15 to 80 percent. In other words, even as many churches that once served white populations have now closed, immigrant and minority pastors lead the vast majority of new churches being planted.[21]

The Presbyterian Church in the USA (PCUSA), by its own admission, is "mostly white, and therefore, not very diverse."[22] White members make up 91.3 percent of the total membership, but immigrants nevertheless figure in the church's statistics, primarily led by immigrants from South Korea, where Presbyterians conducted phenomenally successful missionary efforts in the early 1900s. The PCUSA currently includes about five hundred Korean congregations, and Asians currently make up 2.7 percent of U.S. membership.[23] Hispanics now compose 1.5 percent of the denomination's total membership, while Africans (not African-Americans, but immigrants) total .5 percent, with Middle Eastern Presbyterians (.1 percent) also figuring among the members.[24]

Mennonite churches have always demonstrated a special

concern for social justice, and perhaps no other branch of Christianity has paid more attention to the situation of immigrants in the United States. They have shown an extremely warm welcome to Latino immigrants, who have planted numerous Mennonite churches in the United States. As a result, they have seen steady growth. In 1955, only 185 Hispanic members attended Mennonite churches, and by 1970, the total stood at 490. By 2001, the Hispanic Mennonite Church encompassed about 134 congregations in the United States and Canada, with a membership of 4,191.[25] According to Rafael Falcón, by 2009 the number of Hispanic Mennonites had grown to 8,171—a doubling of the number from less than a decade earlier.[26] Other ethnic groups fed by immigration included thirty-nine Asian-American churches with 2,159 members and thirty Eastern European churches with 8,890 members.[27] Falcón points out, "These statistics are more significant when compared with the less than one percent annual growth rate of the North American Mennonite Church in general."[28] Currently, "nearly 20 percent of Mennonites in the United States are Hispanic, African- American or Asian."[29]

Lutherans have also gained new members through immigration. The Evangelical Lutheran Church in America (ELCA), the nation's fifth-largest denomination with a total of 4.5 million members,[30] reports a total of 255 congregations of "African Descent" with 49,000 people; 147 Latino ministries, and about 22,000 members of Asian and Pacific Islander descent.[31] The denomination remains about 97 percent white. Missouri Synod Lutherans, which hold more conservative doctrinal positions than the ELCA, have also begun to see modest growth from immigration, though remaining 95 percent white.[32]

CONSERVATIVE EVANGELICAL IMMIGRANT GROWTH

As already noted throughout this story, the more conservative traditional churches in the United States have seen the biggest influx of immigrants. Churches of Christ, for example, a significant group of about 13,000 congregations in the United States and a total of 1.9 million members in 2008, counted 240 Spanish-speaking congregations with about 10,000 members.[33] The number of Evangelical denominations and independent churches is large and their statistics do not always account for the growing ethnic diversity of their membership and congregations. But one of their biggest stories involves America's largest Protestant denomination, the Southern Baptist Convention.

Despite the fact that Southern Baptists have seen five consecutive years of declining membership overall, they have seen an increasing number of churches, largely due to the founding of immigrant churches.[34] Naturally, start-up churches have fewer members than mature churches, but the new immigrant churches offer hope for a turnaround in membership statistics. The Southern Baptists have seen a 66 percent increase in ethnic churches since 1998. As of 2011, over 10,000 out of a total 50,768 Southern Baptist churches had predominantly non-white congregations![35]

A Korean Southern Baptist pastor, Joseph Lee of Lawrenceville, Georgia, said, "It's clear that Southern Baptists have been multiethnic and are becoming an even more multi-ethnic convention of churches. The trend is gaining speed week by week. For example, the ethnic churches grew from zero to more than half of the total number of churches in our county in the past 10 years."[36] Not all of the expanding ethnic diversity among Southern Baptists comes from immigrants, as the largest increase in non-white congregations within the SBC from 1998 to 2011 stemmed from an 82.7 percent increase in the number of African-American congregations.[37] Hispanic and Asian churches grew by 63 and 55 percent, respectively.[38]

Currently, the Southern Baptist Convention includes 220 Filipino-American congregations among its Asian-American churches, and the various nationalities expect to grow quickly.[39] Chinese Southern Baptists recently set a church-planting goal of 600 churches by 2020.[40] Korean Southern Baptists have set a goal to increase their churches from 735 to 1,000 within five years.[41] As already mentioned, Latino Southern Baptist churches already number 3,200 in the United States and have every reason to continue experiencing rapid growth.

Like the Assemblies of God, Southern Baptists have excelled in global missionary efforts, deploying the largest overseas missionary force of any Protestant denomination. Those efforts keep coming back to bless them at home and offer a much more diverse future to a church that traditionally appealed almost exclusively to whites in the southern United States.

NEOTRADITIONAL CHURCHES

As traditional Mainline Protestant churches adopted increasingly liberal doctrinal stances in the 1960s, they moved further and further from biblical and traditional sexual morality, distressing many members who tried to remain faithful to the churches their ancestors had founded, where their faith had grown as children. With the rise of the Protestant Charismatic movement in the 1970s, literally millions of Mainline Protestant church members made their way into Pentecostal and independent Charismatic congregations. At the same time, millions of biblically orthodox Christians remained in their denominations after experiencing a Charismatic or Evangelical renewal of their faith. Overseas members of the same churches often did not experience the liberalization of doctrine and morality common in the American churches. A visit to the oldest Congregationalist church in Hawaii, on the Big Island at Kailua Kona, nicely illustrates the vibrant charismatic identity of many Mainline Protestant churches outside the U.S. mainland.

No issue has divided Mainline Protestant Christians the way the ordination of practicing homosexuals and the consecration of homosexual marriages currently does. While the pro-life movement and other culture war issues caused division among Mainline members and churches, the homosexuality issue has led not only to the loss of members but now to the loss of whole congregations. As congregations leave their more liberal denominations, they have begun to form new denominations that carry on the traditions of the sixteenth-century reformers.

One of the most vibrant religious movements in America today features one of America's oldest religious traditions—Anglicanism. The ordination of the first openly homosexual bishop by the Episcopal Church in 2003 led a number of churches to withdraw and reorganize as "Anglican" churches. The churches splintered into various organizations, which have largely coalesced into a new denomination, the Anglican Church in North America (ACNA). The story of these churches presents an interesting twist on the issue of how immigrants (and foreigners) are renewing America's faith. One of America's oldest churches, Falls Church Anglican, leads once again as the flagship of America's new Anglican movement.

Algonquian-speaking citizens of the Powhatan chiefdom originally inhabited the area around Falls Church, Virginia, but their lives would change radically after they received a visit from a group of English immigrants led by John Smith in 1608.[42] Over a hundred years later in 1733, English settlers would build a wooden church, giving the town of Falls Church its name.[43] Wealthy Virginia planters like George Mason and his family became vestrymen of the church, including George Washington himself, and in 1763, George Washington and George William Fairfax accepted appointment as church wardens with the responsibility of contracting for a new building.[44] Colonel James Wren designed a new brick building in 1767, and in 1769 the new church became the seat of the Church of England's Fairfax Parish.[45]

The Revolutionary War, however, would spell the disestablishment of the Church of England in Virginia in 1777 and by 1789, the church would stand abandoned until 1836, when an Episcopal congregation remodeled the building and resumed services there.[46] The life of the church suffered similar interruption during the Civil War, becoming a horse stable for occupying Union troops. But normal services resumed after 1875 and the church has remained active ever since.

Never immune to the ebbs and flows of the larger spiritual situation of the country and of Episcopalians themselves, the congregation suffered decline in the 1970s as the Episcopal Church in general adopted liberal theology. By 1979, the congregation at Falls Church had dwindled and had gone without the leadership of a rector for a full two years. Desperate for a transformational leader, the church invited John Yates, the rector of a thriving church in Pennsylvania, to visit as a candidate. "When I visited them,"

Yates later recalled, "I was bowled over by the tremendous need. There were few people, almost no children. Everything seemed dry, dead. Sunday attendance had steadily decreased all through the seventies."[47] Nevertheless, after six weeks of agonizing about the decision, Yates agreed to accept the church's call for him to lead.

Under Yates, a Charismatic and Evangelical Episcopalian, the church grew explosively and steadily, to the point that by 2006, it had expanded the original, Colonial Era facilities to accommodate a congregation of no less than four thousand fired-up members and adherents. The church stood as incontrovertible evidence that Episcopal churches could buck the tide of ebbing membership. But the installation of the openly gay bishop Gene Robinson in 2003 found a way to "controvert" the church's example. Committed to biblical morality, but unwilling to give up their commitment to the worldwide Anglican Communion, Yates led his church, together with other conservative Episcopal churches in the United States, to seek the covering of a Nigerian Anglican bishop.

One of the most established churches in America has once again taken up a pilgrim identity, "living in tents" so to speak.

When Falls Church voted to split from the Episcopal denomination, "only 27 of the nearly 2,800 members remained united with the Episcopal Church after the vote."[48] The 27 Episcopalians moved across the street to meet at a friendly Presbyterian church and promptly filed suit, along with the national denomination, to gain control of the original church building. Although Falls Church Anglican, as the larger church became called, won the initial court battles, they eventually lost at the Virginia Supreme Court in 2014 and turned their historic facilities over to the tiny group of "continuing Episcopalians."

After losing the final court battle to keep their historic church home, Yates reflected:

> Our congregation of 4,000 must begin again, finding a new home and place of worship . . . In a sense, this will be like starting all over again. There is a teaching in the New Testament: When you are at your weakest you actually are at your strongest. In weakness we are forced to trust in God. We know that where God leads us is a good place.[49]

And so one of the most established churches in America has once again taken up a pilgrim identity, "living in tents" so to speak. While the notable founders of the church, like George Washington, once held African slaves, the church humbly sought out the authority of a Nigerian bishop during its time of crisis.[50] Its mostly white membership includes a small but noticeable group of immigrants from Anglican places around the world.

THE NEW ANGLICAN MOVEMENT

A movement of orthodox Anglicans, made up of a large variety of different organizations, rose up quickly after the Episcopal Church ordained Robinson. Martyn Minns, the rector of Truro Church in Fairfax, which has had a sister-church relationship with the Falls Church since colonial days, accepted election as a Missionary Bishop under the authority of the Anglican archbishop of Nigeria in August 2006, and whole dioceses around the United States pulled out of the Episcopal Church and shifted their loyalty to Anglican archbishops in Rwanda, Kenya, and South America.

By 2008, most of the new Anglican organizations had come together under the banner of the Anglican Church of North America and its archbishop to form a new Anglican Province. Although the new communion has become independent of its African archbishops and does not enjoy official recognition from the archbishop of Canterbury, it received formal recognition on April 16, 2009, from the Global Anglican Future Conference and its member archbishops, which represent 70 percent of all Anglicans around the globe. ACNA currently counts over 100,000 members in nearly 1,000 congregations across the United States and Canada.[51] The battle over whether to include them in the Worldwide Anglican Communion will roil until either the whole organization splits over issues of biblical orthodoxy and morality or until ACNA enjoys full membership.

Discerning the immigrant contribution to the Anglican movement presents a challenge, aside from the obvious fact that several immigrant bishops lead dioceses attached to ACNA. Like the Falls Church, most of the churches in the movement have a majority of white members. Anglicanism/Episcopalianism in the United States has historically stood as a bastion of English culture in the Land of the Melting Pot. But the worldwide Anglican movement no longer has a white majority. While the British Empire has come to an end, the sun still never sets on Anglican worshippers around the world.

The spectacular success of Anglican churches in Africa and in other places around the world where the British Empire seeded it makes the Worldwide Anglican Communion, which operates under the covering of the archbishop of Canterbury, the world's third-largest Christian organization, with around 77 million adherents. The Roman Catholic Church leads with 1.2 billion adherents, followed by the Russian Orthodox Church with 150 million. The Assemblies of God World Fellowship now stands as the fourth largest, with 67.5 million adherents.[52]

The new Anglican churches unquestionably preserve many traditional aspects of historic Anglicanism, especially liturgy based in the Book of Common Prayer. But they also drink deeply from the Charismatic Renewal that began among Episcopal churches in 1962 when the Reverend Dennis Bennett announced to his congregation that he had received the baptism in the Holy Spirit and had spoken in tongues. Thousands of Episcopalians followed him, and thousands of Evangelical young people—fascinated with the classical Anglican liturgy and encouraged by the Charismatic movement's biblical orthodoxy and vital New Testament spirituality—set out on "the Canterbury Trail."[53] As former American Charismatic Episcopalians coalesce in the new Anglican churches, originally under the authority of African bishops and now under their own official province, Charismatic Anglican immigrants from around the world now have a place to land in America.

As more Anglicans immigrate to the United States, Anglican churches will continue to grow, but attracting existing Anglicans does not satisfy their sense of evangelistic mission. Keenly aware of the importance of reaching immigrants in the United States, former Archbishop Robert Duncan of the Anglican Church in North America said in 2009, "Immigrants are bringing unprecedented life and growth to the Church. In our own family, we have seen the rapid growth of ¡Caminemos Juntos!, which already includes over 60 Hispanic congregations."[54] To take advantage of the opportunities for ministry presented by undocumented immigrants, Duncan launched the Anglican Immigrant Initiative, a move to "start 30 legal aid centers around the United States that lead to new church plants."[55]

Mainline churches across the spectrum will struggle to keep immigrant congregations in their folds as the immigrant churches grow and gain greater economic resources. While educating the leaders of these churches in Mainline seminaries will undoubtedly liberalize some immigrant clergy and their American-born followers, the history of the last one hundred years suggests that immigrant churches will not respond well to their leadership and such clergy will migrate over to native-born congregations. The immigrant laity generally wants a fully biblical and spiritually vibrant expression of their faith, and their loyalty to Jesus and the Bible will trump their loyalty to the liberal churches that have helped them establish their presence in America. The more immigrant churches proliferate, the greater temptation they will face to form ethnic denominations that carry on the doctrinal and moral traditions that Mainline churches gradually abandoned over the course of the last century. Their mission is to renew America's faith, and if they find they cannot renew the faith of their American host denominations, they will find new ones where they can set their own course.

9

RENEWING FAMILY VALUES

Ilona Trofimovich does not look like an immigrant. With her fair skin, blonde hair, and perfect, Northwest-accented English, she fits the profile of America's traditional majority racial group, the Northern European "white" person. Born in America soon after her parents came from Ukraine as religious refugees, she grew up speaking Russian as her first language, always living in the tension between American culture and its highly individualistic values and the strong family values of her Ukrainian home culture. While her family experienced far more prosperity in America than they had known in Ukraine, they did not have the resources to send her to college. The ambitious Ilona knew that in order to make the most of American opportunity, she would have to make her own way through college.

Through a scholarship program that focuses on leaders at urban high schools in Tacoma and other Northwest cities, Ilona earned a full-need scholarship at Northwest University in Kirkland, Washington. With all of her educational costs covered, she focused on doing what got her to college—studying hard and leading other students. In the classroom, she majored in education and planned to become a teacher, but as she rose through the ranks of student government, she gained increased confidence as a leader and came to understand that she really wanted to focus on educational governance and policy. In her senior year, she won election as the student body president, kept her grades stellar, and applied for graduate schools. Her classmates recognized her speaking skills by choosing her as the student speaker for commencement, and at about the same time, she got accepted into a master's degree program in educational policy at a prestigious Ivy League university.

At commencement, Ilona announced that she would turn down the opportunity to earn an Ivy League degree and forgo the pursuit of a career shaping national educational policy in Washington, D.C., in order to attend the University of Washington and stay close to the people who had nourished her and shaped her identity. Recognizing the "sacrifice my parents made to move our family to America" and the "faith community where I was free to loudly proclaim my faith in Jesus—something I never take for granted because of my family's religious persecution in the USSR," she boldly concluded:

The choice lay between a dream opportunity and a dream community. Our society has a clear answer—pick the opportunity. Everywhere and all around, young people are hounded by innumerable opportunities. "Go do something with your life," society tells us. "Achieve greatness. Start a business; go to the prestigious graduate school; travel the world; teach overseas; dream up a non-profit that helps disadvantaged children in Africa. Be bold and daring and adventurous" . . . Instead, what God spoke to

me was that it was just as good, just as right, to pick my
dream community.[1]

Ilona did not renounce her dreams of transforming the world
nor her drive for personal achievement, but she would allow her
family and her community to shape the pursuits created by her
ambition to succeed. "As I weighed my East Coast/West Coast
options, God revealed the desires of my heart. It turns out that
more than opportunity, I desire community."[2]

The experience of tension between personal ambition and
community loyalty has affected immigrants in America since the
beginning of the country. First of all, the yearning for personal liberty
that gave birth to America's Declaration of Independence and
to the U.S. Constitution flowed out of the same European *zeitgeist*
that produced the radical individualism of Descartes' dictum,
"I think, therefore I am" and John Locke's individualist concept
of freedom reflected in his insistence
that the Creator has endowed humans
with natural rights to "life, liberty, and
the pursuit of property." Since human
beings cannot really survive without
community, these individualist creeds
necessarily enter into tension with the
realities of family and community life.

Beyond the individualist leaning of
America's founding ideology, imagine
the choices created by the American
continent itself. When the Pilgrims landed in Massachusetts in
1620, the whole continent lay open. Sparsely populated by Native

> When the Pilgrims
> landed in Massachusetts
> in 1620, the whole
> continent lay open.
> The richest land in the
> world beckoned any who
> would move to claim it.

Americans and minimally governed by colonial powers whether British, French, or Spanish, the richest land in the world beckoned any who would move to claim it. Unlike Ilona, whose opportunity would tempt her back to the East, most Americans in the early years faced the temptation to "go west, young man, and grow with the country." According to Josiah Bushnell Grinnell, that *phrase célèbre* originally came to him from Horace Greeley, whom he alleged to have said (*contra* Greeley's denial), "Go West, young man, go West. There is health in the country, and room away from our crowds of idlers and imbeciles."[3] Pursuing opportunity came to epitomize the highest American priority for many people, and those who eschewed it seemed like "idlers and imbeciles." The frontiers always attracted single men first, but women and families inevitably came to join them.

Out of the call of frontier and opportunity arose a spirit of what Herbert Hoover called "rugged individualism."[4] According to that belief, people should pursue their own goals and desires above those of the social group or community. Accordingly, each person should be self-reliant and not depend on others for the provision of their needs. This American emphasis on the worth and importance of the individual and individual goals, desires, and proclivities not only serves as the basis for some values of Republican and libertarian politics but also for progressivism, existentialism, feminism, anarchism, and other isms that place a priority on the development and expression of the self above community norms and traditions.[5]

At the heart of all American politics lies a tension between the individual self and the community. Republicans live in the tension between individual responsibility for economic well-being and traditional family and moral values. Democrats assert the welfare state and community responsibility on one hand while insisting on freedom for radical self-expression in terms of identity and morality on the other hand. While the two parties stand ideologically opposed, both of them take an essentially *liberal* stance—that is, commitment to individual freedom/liberation in one way or another. The ideological differences between the two emerge from the kinds of personal freedom and responsibility to others they emphasize.

Should individuals be self-reliant? Should the community take responsibility for the failures of individuals? Should only innocent victims enjoy the mercy and support of communities? Should families take care of their own? Should people let traditional morality guide their actions and values? These questions profoundly shape our politics as well as our personal choices, and they certainly affect families and other units of society.

While Herbert Hoover, the American president at the outbreak of the Great Depression, believed in rugged individualism and traditional family values, his successor, Franklin Delano Roosevelt, believed in the responsibility of government to protect individuals from forces beyond their control. The dire circumstances of the Great Depression and World War II allowed Roosevelt and the Democratic Party to effect changes in American society that would contribute dramatically to a sea change in American family values.

In 1935 Roosevelt led the American Congress in passing the Social Security Act to provide benefits to retirees and the unemployed, as well as other needy Americans. Very few Americans have ever complained about receiving a pension from the government, especially those who have contributed to the fund through the payroll tax. But no legislation in all of American history has had a larger effect on family values and structures.

Before the passage of the Social Security Act, American families tended to be multigenerational. After retiring from active work, grandparents tended to move in with their children (or the opposite) in order to receive their care. This system not only sustained relationships between parents and their offspring but also facilitated relationships with grandchildren. Aunts and uncles would visit their parents at the homes of their siblings, bringing their children along with them. Cousins played together there and knew each other as intimate friends. Families might include dozens of people, since earlier childbearing made it possible for four generations to know each other, along with first cousins once removed and second cousins and their families.

> Social Security, along with one of its provisions—aid to families with dependent children, commonly known as welfare—also affected the nuclear family.

Before Social Security, no government funding existed to finance a move to senior living, nursing homes, or other kinds of "old folks' homes," as people used to say. People lived with their families, and only the gravely misfortunate ever left them to reside in the dreaded old folks' homes. When Social Security came along, older people no longer had to depend on their adult children for care. Rising American rugged individualism made seniors loath to be a burden on their children. Parents did not have to treat their children with undue deference, since they would not be dependent on them in later years. Children, on the other hand, felt less pressure to tolerate their parents, since they bore less moral and societal obligation to care for them in their old age. Relationships became easier to discard. Retirees began to move into retirement communities rather than live with their adult children, sometimes moving to the Sun Belt states or even other countries for lower costs of living and better weather. The fabric of the American family began to fray.

In 1949, a relatively new sociological term entered the American vocabulary—the "nuclear family."[6] In contrast to the "extended family" described above, composed of grandparents, parents, children, uncles, aunts, and cousins, the nuclear family included only a father and mother, along with the children born to them. As grandparents became independent through Social Security and the roaring post–World War II economy, the nuclear family became the primary American definition of the word *family*.

Social Security, along with one of its provisions—Aid to Families with Dependent Children, commonly known as welfare—also affected the nuclear family. Before government took on the responsibility to care for elderly wives, most husbands felt a moral responsibility to stay with their wives and children. While many factors, including the Sexual Revolution, contributed to rising divorce rates in the 1960s, Social Security and welfare certainly increased the freedom of men to leave their wives and children without subjecting them to starvation. What emerged from the consequent weakening of the nuclear family? The single-parent family, blended families, and increasingly now, alternative families. The United States Census Bureau summed it up concisely in 2012:

> Families and living arrangements in the United States have changed over time . . . As a result, it is difficult to talk about a single kind of family or one predominant living arrangement in the United States.[7]

All of these new types of family definitions feature varying degrees of stability, and such families may shift wildly in composition over the course of a childhood or a lifetime.

My own family experienced a set of circumstances well known in America. During the 1980s, my parents in Alabama suffered a painful divorce. Both remarried, and my father moved to another state. My brother went to college and married a girl from out of state, as I did. My sister came to live with me temporarily in New Jersey, where she married. My brother joined the military and lived around the world before settling in South Carolina; my career took me to foreign countries and distant states; and my sister and her husband moved back to Alabama.

Job opportunities allowed all of us to pursue our dreams, and our parents' divorce gave us less and less of another opportunity— that of being together frequently. Our parents died young, and soon, our distant living places made it hard to spend any time together. We all made our own way in the world and won great benefits, at the cost of our children really knowing their grandparents, uncles, aunts, and cousins. We all have stable nuclear families. Many Americans have experienced the kind of disruption and dispersion my extended family has seen, but sadly, many have not enjoyed as much success in maintaining nuclear families in the process.

In too many cases, the nuclear family has proven to be far more fragile than some may have expected. Hollywood presentations of romantic love conquering all, pop music notions of the loving couple against the world, and the universally overestimated power of sexual attraction to hold a couple together all suggested that a couple only needed love to succeed in marriage. In retrospect, it appears obvious that a couple needs more than emotions to make a marriage work, and a vibrant extended family and commitment to the needs of others rather than to one's own basest drives and urges provides an essential element for marital success. The rugged individuals of the earlier days may have made for stable (if not always the warmest) marital partners, but the considerably softened-up, sex-crazed existentialists of the post–World War II era have experienced a totally different outcome from their kind of individualism.

Individualism may seem like the natural human default mode for postmodern America and Europe, but the majority of the world's cultures place far less importance on the individual self than Americans do. According to anthropologist Geert Hofstede, a majority of the world's cultures are collectivistic rather than individualistic.[8] In collectivist societies, people draw their sense of identity from their community rather than from their own personal choices. For example, the so-called Japanese Management Style originated in the Japanese cultural tendency for individual workers to look to the best interests of their group rather than their personal benefit. Asian cultures in general are well known for their collectivist approach to identity.

Alan Roland, a prominent American psychoanalyst, conducted extensive research into the concept of the self in India and Japan.[9] Roland concluded Indians and Japanese develop the familial self. Such a vision of the self, based on the authority of parents and

grandparents and the time-tested traditions of communities, provides a marked contrast to the Western vision of the individualized
self. Think of Tevya's song "Tradition" in the movie *Fiddler on the
Roof* for a powerful pop culture description of this tension or perhaps of Fotoula Portokalos' dilemma in *My Big Fat Greek Wedding*.

The American attitude toward individualism and collectivism
found stark expression in the television series *Star Trek: The Next
Generation*. In contrast to the highly individualistic crew of the
starship *Enterprise*, an evil menace called the Borg Collective presented a totally collectivist approach to identity. Borg citizens were
known by names such as "1 of 9," a designation that indicated
that they made up part of a team that worked together in a society
that took all its ideas from a central-
ized consciousness. As the incredibly
powerful Borg took over an individualistic society or group of people, its
invaders would drone, "We are Borg.
You will be assimilated. Resistance is
futile."[10]

Some interpreters might read
the Borg as a presentation of contemporary socialist societies like the
moribund Soviet Union or the more
successful but nevertheless undemo-
cratic communist China. On the other hand, other observers might
see the concept as a multiculturalist critique of America's melting pot philosophy toward immigrants. When announcing their
conquests, the Borg Collectives usually stated, "We will add your
biological and technological distinctiveness to our own. Your

> When announcing their conquests, the Borg Collectives usually stated, "We will add your biological and technological distinctiveness to our own. Your culture will adapt to service us."

culture will adapt to service us."[11] The two perspectives neatly emphasize the individualist approaches of the right and left, but in either case, the Borg clearly qualifies as a dread enemy. *TV Guide* ranked the Borg fourth among the "Nastiest Villains of All Time."[12]

The portrayal of all the earth's cultures, as well as those of almost all other (fictitious) life forms in the universe, as American-style individualists making up an effective crew on a starship betrays remarkable hubris in the face of the indisputable fact that most of the earth's people do not share America's view of the self. As a full-fledged, patriotic American exceptionalist, I chuckle as I write these words, wondering why the rest of the world does not share Western values of individual autonomy and self-determination. Nevertheless, the advance of globalization and an increasingly individualistic global urban culture does suggest that Western individualism has appeal.

Approaches to the self, whether individualistic or collectivistic, should not be hardened and treated as unchangeable destiny for any society. Roland recognized that when Indian and Japanese people encounter Western individualistic culture, they typically develop an expanding self that combines elements of collectivist and individualist approaches. In a comparative study of Chinese and American students, the researchers Parker, Haytko, and Hermans recently found that while Chinese are increasingly adopting a more individualistic identity, Americans seem to be moving toward a more collectivist approach. They observe,

> As world cultures become less isolated, change is undoubtedly going to take place. It may be a mistake therefore, to automatically assume that Eastern cultures are going to

remain collective and that Western cultures will remain more individualized in nature.[13]

As Christian immigrants from highly collectivist cultures in Latin America, Brazil, Sub-Saharan Africa, and Southern and Eastern Asia move to the United States, they bring values that have already begun to transform family and societal values in America, even as immigrant families experience conflict between the value systems of their old and new countries.

IMMIGRANT FAMILIES

The extended family thrives among today's Christian immigrants, and Mexican-American families present a representative paradigm. According to Hilario Garza, the Mexican-American family will have an influence in renewing family values in America:

I think we will benefit American family values. I think that we will influence mother, father, and children roles within the family. To us, family is important not just up to the age of 18. I heard someone on the radio the other day, a very influential person on radio, who happens to deal a lot with finances, and he said, "At the age of 18, my parents kicked me out, and I was on my own." But then he said, "You Hispanics are different. If it was up to me I'd tell you, 'Kick the kids out and don't feed grandma anymore.' But you guys work with a different mentality." You see, to us they're important. We'll feed them until the day they die. And children are important. They don't become independent when they turn 18. They become independent when they get married. And then still, when they're married, we belong to each other . . . That's what America used to be. It used to be family oriented.[14]

In Garza's view, "The immigrant church brings back the importance of family, the importance of community. I think it brings back the importance of God in the family and the community, and the importance of God for personal life."

The composition of the Mexican-American family includes a lot more people than typical American nuclear families. According to Garza, his family includes

> my wife, my children, my grandchildren, my parents, and my in-laws. Cousins are included, as they come together through the structure of who we're all related to, all the way to third and fourth cousins . . . When we mention family, we'll call someone uncle or aunt all the way up to the 6th generation. Friends are part of the family too, and as they become part of the family they are treated like one of our boys. And they are dealt with as if they were my children. Period. That's just the way we are.[15]

At my daughter Jodie's recent wedding to Roberto Valdez, a Mexican-born child of immigrants, members who posed for the Valdez family picture outnumbered the Castleberrys by a margin of five to one. Ask immigrants how many people belong to their family, and you will get a similar story.

In such embracing families, Garza noted there can be no such thing as a truly "single" mother. Among native-born Americans, the percentage of births out of wedlock in the Hispanic community doubles that of the white population (50 percent versus 24 percent), and 42 percent of children born to Hispanic immigrants enter the world without the benefit of wedlock.[16] Almost half of Hispanic mothers may lack a husband, but whether they are Catholic or Evangelical, their families tend to surround them with care, with grandparents to help with child care and brothers or uncles or family friends to provide male influence. According to Samuel Rodriguez, the family and the church says, "We've got you covered!"

> Immigrant families have a lot to teach native-born families about what an extended family looks like.

Immigrant families have a lot to teach native-born families about what an extended family looks like. The American household gets increasingly more complicated, and the example immigrants offer comes at an opportune time, as "boomerang kids" now return home after college, postponing marriage until twenty-eight or thirty and sometimes spending months or years in unemployment or under-employment after graduating from college.[17] American parents currently joke or even complain about their kids not leaving the home, but a better attitude stands close at hand.

A TROPHY FAMILY

The love of extended families among immigrants and their children stands out in a story told to me by Dr. Isaac Canales, a first-generation American born in East Los Angeles to Mexican immigrant parents. As he told me his story, I remembered the movie *Born in East L.A.*, starring the Mexican-American comedian

Cheech Marin.[18] The protagonist of the movie, the American-born Rudy Robles, gets caught up in a raid at a factory without any identification and gets deported to Mexico as an undocumented worker. Ironically, he can speak German fluently from having served with the American military in Europe, but he cannot speak Spanish and suffers a series of misadventures before he manages to cross the border illegally in order to recover his legal identity.

I had to suppress a chuckle as I compared the movie character with the incredibly accomplished Dr. Canales. Like most immigrant Christians, his parents had believed in the value of higher education and encouraged him to go to Vanguard University, a private liberal arts college in Southern California. After graduating summa cum laude, he continued his education with a master of divinity degree from Harvard University and a PhD from Fuller Theological Seminary in Pasadena, where he would later rise to the rank of dean of the School of Theology. He currently serves as senior pastor of the Mission Ebenezer Family Church, in Carson, California—a dynamic urban ministry, touching over three thousand people per week.[19]

Dr. Canales' career transcends any sort of minority identity, and he receives high-profile speaking invitations from all over the world in both Spanish and English church contexts. He represents the ultimate success story as the child of penniless immigrant parents, fully assimilated to American identity without the least estrangement from his rich immigrant background. His large extended family reflects powerful hope for the future of the American family.

The family story he told me begins in his childhood, when he fought off a case of poliomyelitis.

When I was two and half years old, I had polio and was in Los Angeles Children's Hospital for six months during the epidemic of the 1950s, before the Salk vaccine was developed. My pastor father and my mother fasted and prayed for a long time that the doctors would at least let him go in and see me. I was in quarantine with other children. I remember it even though I was less than three years old. They let him come in and he prayed for me, a nice Pentecostal prayer, in tongues, and I stood up in the bed! They let him take me home, but the polio returned and severely affected my right arm. At age eleven they performed two surgeries to give me 30 percent movement in the arm that I'd never had use of before. My arm remained atrophied at the bicep, so I always got picked last for any ball games. They would sit me on the bench during the game, afraid I'd get hurt. I did learn to catch a baseball with my left hand, take off the glove, and then throw the ball in.[20]

Years later, Dr. Canales and his Pennsylvania Dutch wife, Ritha Brubaker, had three healthy boys. The boys not only shared their parents' high intelligence and love of learning, but also prodigious athletic talent. Dr. Canales reminisced,

We brought up the boys to be loving and respectful—which is very much a part of our Mexican culture as well as my wife's German culture—that children should respect their parents and grandparents. So even though my kids are bilingual and bicultural, they were brought up with good family values, the love of God, a strong family bond.

It's only logical as a result that they all grew up to finish high school and go on to college. The highest honor they could pay their parents was to bring their athletic and academic trophies home. My garage is full of all of their trophies from age four onward. If their children want to see any of the trophies, they come over to Papa and Mama's house.[21]

Did they ever bring home trophies! Most importantly, they all got academic and athletic scholarships to play collegiate sports. The oldest son, Joshua, played baseball and was drafted by the Oakland A's right out of high school, but opted to go to college instead. He won a Southeastern Conference Championship ring for baseball at the University of Florida, and then transferred to UCLA so his father could come to his games. After finishing college, he joined the Los Angeles Dodgers organization, advancing to the Triple A level before joining the big leagues with the Houston Astros. Later, while attending an African-American church, he was "slain in the Spirit" and fell to the floor speaking in tongues for the first time. As he lay on the floor, he knew God had called him to the ministry, and after finishing a seminary degree at Fuller, he now serves on his father's staff at Mission Ebenezer.

David, the second born, not only excelled at football, but would draw up the plays on a transparent clipboard beginning in his peewee football days—a natural coach. He played quarterback as a player-coach in high school and set a state record for tackles playing defense as a safety in the California State High School Championships. Recruited around the country, he chose to stay close to home and played quarterback at Azusa Pacific University.

After a stint as a high school coach, he joined Pete Carroll's staff at the University of Southern California before following him to Seattle as assistant quarterbacks coach for the Seahawks.

Isaac's third son, Jacob, after receiving visits from Yale, Georgetown, Dartmouth, and Penn State, chose to play for the University of Pennsylvania because they would allow him to follow his dream to be a dual-sport athlete. In baseball he shined and became the freshman MVP, and his football team won the Ivy League Championship, so he got a NCAA Division 1 Conference Championship ring. Isaac remembers a phone call from Jacob, in which he said,

> "Daddy, I'm headed to practice, and I need to make the team. Could you say a prayer for me?" So I prayed and specifically asked God to let him hit the ball hard. When he got there, the practice was almost over and the weakest group was hitting. They put him last in the line. When he came up to bat, he hit the ball out of the park, close to the Schuylkill River. He hit three straight home runs. The team captain said, "Nobody in any group all day long has hit the ball out of the park."[22]

Obviously, Jacob made the team.

Isaac pursued his career hard and achieved spectacular success as an academic leader and as a pastor. It strains credulity to believe that he rose to the level of dean at the most prestigious Evangelical seminary in the world, while also building an urban megachurch. Virtually no one excels to that level in both academia and ministry, as the two activities tend to militate against each other. But the facts remain. He went on to serve as president of Latin American Bible Institute in La Puente after his career at Fuller.

Unquestionably successful in his career, he never let his family down along the way. In his heart's divisions, the kids always came in first place.

> They were just wonderful kids, so when I put them in baseball, basketball, football, and soccer, through the seasonal cycle, I kind of lived vicariously through their athletic prowess. I never missed a game. I got them whatever they needed to excel in sports, and also in academics. They all got athletic scholarships.[23]

In contrast, the typical American family has lived out the song "Cat's in the Cradle" since World War II as fathers (and often mothers) put their individual careers and pursuits above the interests of their kids as a cultural norm.

Whenever the boys won a championship ring, they brought it home to Papa. "My kids know the story. They've seen my [polio-afflicted] arm all their lives. They decided that since Papa never got to play sports, they would win the championships for him." While he never asked them for their championship rings, they always brought them home and gave them to Papa, "out of their own hearts."[24]

The glories of a large extended family meant even more championships for the little boy who never got to play. Joshua met a Nigerian immigrant (and California State High School champion track athlete) named Olabunmi at UCLA at an Athletes-in-Action Bible study. "As they shared a Bible," Isaac recounts, "he thought she was the most gorgeous thing on earth; she looked like a princess!" They married, and as Olabunmi adopted the family and its traditions, she proudly gave her NCAA track championship ring to Papa.

Like Hilario Garza's family, the Canales family includes many cousins. Isaac's nephew Kevin Nicholson, a member of the Central Missouri State University Hall of Fame, won an NCAA Football Championship ring, which he gave to Papa. "He calls me Papa," Dr. Canales said with familial pride. "They all call me Papa."

Dr. Canales kept the rings in a special box in his home, including a gold NCAA watch. In 2013 thieves broke into the house and stole the box, but shortly afterward, David's friend and colleague Russell Wilson would lead the Seahawks to the NFL Championship in Super Bowl XLVIII. David called Papa from Seattle to ask, "Papa, what's your finger size?" A few months later, David brought home his Super Bowl ring. As he gave the ring to his father at home, he said, "All the rings you lost are consolidated into this one ring."

> Nothing outweighs the glory of a family full of love and the presence of God. That outcome stands as the target for today's Christian immigrant families.

As impressive as a heavy Super Bowl ring can seem, nothing outweighs the glory of a family full of love and the presence of God. That outcome stands as the target for today's Christian immigrant families. As Ilona Trofimovich taught the Northwest University community, *ideal community trumps ideal opportunity.*

THE DOUBLE HELIX OF SOCIETY

According to Mary Eberstadt, a research fellow at Stanford University's Hoover Institution, family and religion constitute "the double helix of society," each dependent on the strength of the other for successful reproduction.[25] In Eberstadt's view, the true story of *How the West Really Lost God* begins not with an abandonment of religion but rather a rejection of the priority of families. America cannot survive the decline of the family, nor can the family survive the loss of faith. The existence of exceptional atheist families does not disprove the fact that no society, on the whole, can thrive without faith.[26]

Founding father John Adams, our second president, warned the nation in 1798 saying, "We have no government armed with power capable of contending with human passions unbridled by morality and religion . . . Our Constitution was made only for a moral and religious people. It is wholly inadequate to the government of any other."[27] Just as the nation cannot survive without faith, faith cannot survive without the family nor the family without faith. A radically individualist nation, in which everyone follows his or her unbridled passions and urges, will soon descend into hellish chaos.

CHURCHES AS SURROGATE FAMILIES

In the case of Christians immigrating without their families—usually as forerunners or as temporary workers—the immigrant church steps in to make up any deficit the family may leave. The same truth holds with reference to lonely converts who come to church in search of friends who will understand them. It extends to native-born spouses who intermarry with immigrants and find themselves embraced by the warmest community they have ever encountered. Attending an immigrant church service involves a serious commitment of time. Rather than limiting themselves to a "clock orientation," they operate under an "event orientation."[28] Typical church services involve far more than just singing and listening to a sermon. The community celebrates every person's victory, every birthday, and every achievement. They mourn every tragedy, share every suffering, and comfort every sorrow. Every immigrant church constitutes a massive extended family in which everyone has the attention of someone.

Readers familiar with America's churches in the past will recognize, and perhaps pine for, what we have lost through stagnant church isolation and megachurch anonymity. Immigrants and their churches offer a living memory of America's past values. As immigrants and their adult children and grandchildren make up an increasing percentage of the American population, their family and ecclesial collectivism will take America back to the future.

The New Pilgrims have determined to save the American family by submitting it once again to the worship of God. They are renewing the model of the Church as a surrogate family as well. Many of them believe God has sent them here for that very purpose.

10

RENEWING THE ECONOMY

Pedro Celis had never touched a computer and didn't even know how to turn one on. But he instantly developed a passionate interest in computers when he found out that Laura, a beautiful girl in his high school class in Monterrey, Mexico, liked computers. Pedro went to the library, checked out all the books on computer science, and began to learn how to code. It gave him a guaranteed topic of interest to engage Laura in conversation, and it worked. They have now enjoyed thirty-four years of successful marriage, having raised four kids to successful adulthood.[1]

Pedro and Laura both went to the prestigious Monterrey Institute of Technology to study computer engineering, and then on to the University of Waterloo in Canada to pursue master's and doctoral degrees in computer science. While Laura chose to devote herself to raising their four children instead of finishing her PhD, Pedro went on to a phenomenally successful career in academia and in software development. As one of the first twelve distinguished engineers at Microsoft, he was the chief technology officer for the development of the SQL Server. He also had a big impact in the development of the Bing search engine and personally holds over fifteen U.S. patents. In 2003, President George W. Bush appointed Pedro to the President's Information Technology Advisory Committee (PITAC), which advises the president on how to keep the United States at the forefront of information technology innovation in the world.[2]

As naturalized American citizens, Pedro and Laura excel in love for their adopted country. Devout Christians, they have been generous philanthropists, serving on the board of directors of Stronger Families, a non-profit organization founded by former Seahawk quarterback Jeff Kemp.[3] That organization works to support marriages, especially in military and first responder families. They have also worked in the for-profit sector to create opportunity for others in the immigrant community through their work in founding Plaza Bank in Seattle, which specializes in serving the needs of Latino businesses and individuals.[4] They have invested in many Latino businesses, such as *Tú Decides/You Decide*, a bilingual newspaper, and the Latino Business, Consumer and Career Expo, which sponsors trade shows and fashion events that bring together Latino entrepreneurs and their customers.

> American companies like Apple and Microsoft constantly have to lobby Congress to make a place for the thousands of workers they need but cannot hire.

Pedro's leadership also includes political activity. In 2014, he ran for Congress as a Republican and waged a strong, though ultimately unsuccessful, campaign against the incumbent Democrat in his district. He first got involved in politics in 2001, when he founded the Washington State chapter of the Republican National Hispanic Assembly, which he served as chairman for four years.[5] He also served as the national chairman of the organization for two years.

When Americans think about immigrants, they do not tend to think about people like Pedro and Laura Celis. They think of the farm laborers and service workers they may run into on a daily basis, who gladly take jobs most Americans do not want. But as Pedro knows better than most people, maintaining our dominance in information technology depends on attracting a steady stream of the world's most promising young computer scientists to study in our universities and work in our computer industry. Every year, eighty-five thousand high-tech workers come to the United States to take jobs Americans can't do because not enough of our native-born students choose to pursue the rigorous education the jobs require.

In fact, only eighty-five thousand people can possibly come, because our laws limit H1-B visas to that number.[6] In 2012, the supply of visas only lasted ten weeks, and American companies like Apple and Microsoft constantly have to lobby Congress to make a place for the thousands of workers they need but cannot hire. Nevertheless, for foreign students who earn advanced technological degrees in America and face deportation due to a lack of visas, good news waits for them just across the border. Canada makes it very easy for them to come and give their country a competitive advantage over the United States. In many cases, Americans paid for the education the foreign students received, but Canada, India, and China will reap the benefits of our investment.

RENEWING THE DEMAND SIDE
OF THE AMERICAN ECONOMY

While most immigrants work at the lower end of the pay scale rather than under Bill Gates' personal supervision, immigrants as a class have an important role in renewing America's economy. Not just the millionaire software developers but also ordinary manual laborers have literally saved America's economy from disaster.

The first way they accomplished such an incredible feat required nothing more than coming to America. By coming, they increased America's labor supply—allowing us to produce more— and they also expanded America's consumer base—increasing the demand for consumer goods. Since the days of Adam Smith, father of capitalist economics, economists have understood that economies need a growing population. According to economist Thomas Picketty, "Population growth typically drives about half of all economic growth."[7] When the economy does not grow, it shrinks. When the economic output shrinks for two consecutive quarters, economists say the economy has entered a recession. When a recession continues for an extended period of time, factory orders decline, housing starts get cancelled, businesses fail, unemployment rises, and economists say that the economy has entered a depression.

In fact the United States has suffered a steep decline in total fertility rate in the last sixty years, from a high of about 3.6 in 1961 to a low of about 1.7 in the mid-1970s—when the Supreme Court legalized abortion and permitted the prevention of some 57 million American births. Since that time, the average fertility rate among American-born women has stood below the replacement level of 2.1.[8] Since American immigrants generally have a total fertility rate of about 3.0, they have played a major role in keeping America's total fertility rate near the replacement level.[9]

According to Justin Fox, executive editor of the *Harvard Business Review*, the U.S. economy in recent years "has grown a bit faster than those of other developed economies, but that's purely because of population growth."[10] And immigrants and their children have contributed about 60 percent of the population growth that has kept the United States' economy growing.[11] The question arises: If a growing economy needs a growing population and if America's population would have grown much more slowly over the last fifty years without the higher birthrates of immigrants and their children, what would have happened to America's economy during the last two recessions without more than sixty million consumers—forty million immigrants and over twenty million children of immigrants—who currently live in the United States?[12] We very well might have entered a depression.

If that had happened, the worldwide economy would have followed us into depression. It is possible that the people who left their own countries to come to America as immigrants have saved the American economy from grave hardship, and in doing so, saved the world economy from utter calamity. Next Christmas, when you go to Walmart or the mall, take a look around you and notice the immigrants. If they had not come to America, what percentage of holiday sales would not occur? How would that affect jobs across the American economy?

RENEWING THE SUPPLY SIDE

For a consumer economy to work, two sides have to cooperate. One side, the consumer, brings demand to the table, and as I mentioned, sixty million American consumers—more than one out of every five Americans—came to us by courtesy of immigration. The other side of consumer economics, the supply side, provides goods for consumers to buy. Workers make the supply side possible.

Immigrants touch virtually every product sold in American supermarkets, especially those foodstuffs that have to be picked by hand. Immigrant truckers also play an important role in getting goods to market, and immigrant labor has become even more important in recent years as there has been a huge shortage of available drivers due to difficult working conditions and low wages.[13] In 2014, a total of thirty thousand trucking jobs went unfilled.[14]

> Without immigrant labor, the price of American groceries would have risen sharply in our lifetimes, and the supply of items on the shelf would not have grown.

Without immigrant labor, the price of American groceries would have risen sharply in our lifetimes, and the supply of items on the shelf would not have grown. Compare today's grocery stores to the ones you grew up with. I remember going to the IGA grocery store near my grandmother's house when it would have fit into just a couple of aisles of today's huge, well-stocked stores. Immigrant labor has not only fed us for years, but it has contributed to the wider range of foods and products we enjoy.

Immigrant labor has also helped to house us. According to the National Association of Home Builders, analysis of the latest U.S. Census data shows that immigrants make up about 20 percent of construction workers in the United States, compared to 15 percent of the general workforce.[15] Housing, of course, represents a major driver of economic growth in the United States. It plays a key role in the U.S. economy, because it "affects related industries, such as banking, the mortgage sector, raw materials, employment, construction, manufacturing, and real estate."[16] Just like home construction has a ripple effect on the whole economy, so do other sectors involving immigrant labor. The system would not work if any major sector of it disappeared. Without immigrant labor, America's economy would have suffered grave harm in the last fifty years.

ARE IMMIGRANTS INDISPENSABLE TO AMERICA'S ECONOMY?

In 2004, the film *A Day Without a Mexican* depicted the effects on the California economy that would occur if Mexicans disappeared for a day.[17] According to the *New York Times*,

> The mockumentary postulates that the lack of Latino gardeners, nannies, cooks, policeman, maids, teachers, farm workers, construction crews, entertainers, athletes, and the world's largest growing consumer market would create a social, political, and economic disaster, leaving the concept of the "California Dream" in shambles.[18]

The film made a strong argument to anyone who would listen to it, but many people still refuse to consider the question seriously. Let no one doubt that a single factor explains the entire failure of the U.S. government to keep immigrants from crossing the Mexican border. The same factor explains why the Department of Homeland Security does not deport all undocumented immigrants. The simple truth? Stopping immigration would inflict grave harm on the American economy.

ENTREPRENEURSHIP

Immigrants play a major role in the most important source of economic renewal—entrepreneurship. (Ironically, no authentic English word exists to name the agents of new business formation, so we have to employ a French word, *entrepreneur*, to refer to them.) "From Google's Sergey Brin to Ebay's Pierre Omidyar to thousands of local and neighborhood businesses, there's no denying the impact of immigrant entrepreneurs," says *Forbes* magazine contributor Cheryl Conner.[19] "According to the U.S. Chamber of Commerce, immigrant-owned companies created nearly half a million jobs and more than $50 billion in revenue in 2012."[20] As the stories of Brin, Omigyar, and Celis illustrate, immigrants in high-tech industries and corporate America have played major roles in the revitalization of the American economy over the past twenty years.

In fact, immigrants have founded more than 25 percent of the scientific and technology firms in the United States.[21] Thomas Donahue, CEO of the U.S. Chamber of Commerce, stated an obvious truth at a conference on the State of American Business in 2012:

> We should allow the world's most creative entrepreneurs
> to stay in our country. They are going to contribute and
> succeed somewhere—why shouldn't it be in the United

States? America's prosperity has always depended on the hard work, sacrifice, drive, and dreams of immigrants. Our future will depend on them even more.[22]

The complaint sometimes arises among opponents of immigration that foreign-born computer scientists take high-tech jobs that Americans should have. No one has proven yet whether they actually decrease the number of such jobs available to Americans. But one can hardly argue that entrepreneurs steal jobs from Americans. By definition, they create jobs for Americans.

Those who would assume that the only impact made on business formation comes from world-class geniuses fail to see the true picture. In fact, immigrants make a large contribution to the formation of small- and medium-sized businesses as well. I always note the irony when I eat in a Mexican or other immigrant-founded restaurant and notice native-born American employees of another ethnic origin. As Conner notes, "U.S. Census data also report that immigrants are more likely than native citizens to choose self-employment—5.1 percent are self employed in their own incorporated businesses as compared to only 3.7 percent of native-born U.S. entrepreneurs."[23] In other words, immigrants are 38 percent more likely to start businesses than native-born Americans.

Andrés Panasiuk, an Argentine immigrant to the United States, has achieved fame through his nonprofit financial literacy organization, *Cultura Financiera*. Following in the footsteps of the late Dr. Larry Burkett, Panasiuk provides financial education through books and mass media programs to Spanish-speaking immigrants in the United States, reaching a worldwide audience as well.

He explains from his personal experience and observation what academic theory on immigration has long held—immigrants are self-selected for economic success.[24]

> I believe that when you are willing to leave your house, leave your community, leave the safety net of your friends and family, leave your culture, language, and country; and then, you are willing to risk your time, your money, and sometimes even your life to come to America, then you are made up of something very special. You are an entrepreneur all the way to the level of your own DNA! You will not behave in any other way: risk and entrepreneurship is in your personality profile.[25]

Panasiuk's personal life nicely illustrates the entrepreneurial drive of immigrants. His Ukrainian parents had migrated to Argentina, where they attended a Russian-speaking church in an Italian neighborhood. In 1985, his family sold a property in order to send him to the United States to pursue a university degree. Since he had an uncle in Chicago who pastored one of the city's largest Spanish-speaking churches, he followed the historic, family-based, migrational pattern that immigrants have always preferred, and enrolled at the famous Moody Bible Institute in Chicago.

Through a combination of thrift, hard work, and the support of his family, Panasiuk managed to graduate from Moody and finish a bachelor's degree in communication at Trinity International University with only minimal student loans. Although he had intended to return to Argentina, he grew to love the Chicago neighborhoods where he had ministered alongside his uncle, and he wound up accepting the pastorate of a Puerto Rican church in Humboldt Park. The church could not afford to pay him a salary, so he accepted a position as administrator of a radio station in order to support his wife and newborn daughter. Like most Americans, he and his wife fell into a pattern of debt, and after three years, they had sunk into $65,000 of debt. He explains, "Our lack of understanding of the American economy, of sound financial decision-making, and of the dangers associated with indebtedness led us to fall into financial bondage."

As Panasiuk and his wife learned to manage their own finances and get out of crippling debt, they found that many immigrant families in America shared their situation. Their lifestyle of ministering to others led them in 1996 to begin teaching other immigrants the principles of financial management that had helped them achieve financial freedom. He explains,

> Teaching and serving our community in the most extreme sectors of our society helped my wife and me identify with the poorest of the poor and gave us a unique understanding of the challenges and dynamics of the immigrant's financial life.[26]

Today their ministry has taught biblical stewardship to more than twenty-one million Spanish-speaking people around the world through their writing, conference speaking, programs for pastors and leadership development, and appearances on radio and television. Undoubtedly, their nonprofit entrepreneurship has contributed to the financial freedom and upward mobility of untold numbers of immigrants who adopt their principles of financial responsibility.

IMMIGRANT ENTREPRENEURS AND RECESSION

In hard economic times, such as the recent recession, immigrants are even more likely to start new businesses. According to CNNMoney, in 2011 "Immigrants created 28% of all new firms" and were "twice as likely to start a new business when compared to those born in the United States."[27] Hispanic immigrants especially stand out among immigrant entrepreneurs who took the lead in replacing jobs the recession eliminated, as they "are creating new businesses at a faster clip than any other ethnic group. Hispanics make up more than half of the nation's 40 million foreign-born, and they are starting businesses at a rate that exceeds even their population growth."[28] According to DeVere Kutscher of the United States Hispanic Chamber of Commerce, "Hispanic entrepreneurs are driving economic development, and their enterprises are creating jobs and helping lead the country out of recession."[29]

The entrepreneurial drive of immigrants shines in the fact that while they make up only 16 percent of American workers, they own 28 percent of Main Street businesses, a phenomenon that stands out even more in urban areas.[30] Across the country, according to 2013 data,

> The entrepreneurial drive of immigrants shines in the fact that while they make up only 16 percent of American workers, they own 28 percent of Main Street businesses.

immigrants make up 61 percent of all gas station owners, 58 percent of dry cleaners owners, 53 percent of grocery store owners, 45 percent of nail salon owners, . . . 38 percent of restaurant owners, and 32 percent of both jewelry and clothing store owners.[31]

A casual visit to small, independent hotels will also give consumers a likely opportunity to meet immigrant business owners, often renewing the life of businesses that had previously suffered decline.

When I lived in New York and New Jersey, home to Ellis Island and launching pad for American immigrants for many years, I often noticed the way immigrants move into blighted slum areas and immediately go to work to create employment and to revitalize the communities they live in. According to Borges-Mendez, Liu, and Watanabe,

> Immigrants often move into low-rent neighborhoods that have little economic activity and deteriorating physical conditions. Many establish businesses as an alternative to working at low-wage jobs, usually within 3 to 10 years after they arrive in the United States. These businesses are typically small to moderate in size and include real estate firms, restaurants, food stores, nail salons, and gift shops. Many of these businesses offer retail or personal services needed by neighborhood ethnic groups.[32]

It would be a mistake to assume that immigrant businesses do not enjoy financial success. According to Robert Fairlie of the Small

Business Administration, "Immigrant-owned firms have $435,000 in average annual sales and receipts, which is roughly 70 percent of the level of non-immigrant owned firms at $609,000."[33] Given the obstacles immigrants face in adjusting to a new culture, language, legal system, and business practice, 70 percent seems like admirably strong performance.

HOW DO IMMIGRANTS FINANCE NEW BUSINESSES?

Among native-born Americans, two of the most important sources of start-up capital for new businesses have traditionally been small business loans and home equity loans from banks and other traditional financial institutions.[34] Those sources dried up considerably during the recent recession, even as immigrants increased their entrepreneurial drive and performance. How did they do it? Most immigrant start-up capital, as with all entrepreneurs, comes from personal savings.

During a total of nine years living in Costa Rica, El Salvador, and Ecuador, years of traveling to all of the countries of Latin America except Venezuela, and forty years of close contact with Latinos, I have often marveled over how apparently poor people manage to save money. Often, when I have asked them where they got money for something they needed or wanted, they have smiled proudly and said, "*Siempre tengo mis ahorritos*" (Always have my little savings). The use of the diminutive form of the word *ahorros* (with the *ito* ending) not only suggests the relatively small amounts of the savings but also a certain endearment the saver feels toward them. Many Latinos proudly save up their money so they can travel, help a family member, or *save the day* when things go wrong.

Obviously, not everyone in Latin America (or anywhere else) has developed the habit of saving money. All cultures include people of different personality types, and often people in any culture spend everything they earn on their immediate needs. According to Andrés Panasiuk, that is the reality for most immigrants.

My experience is that immigrants are thrifty, but don't know how to save, especially for the long-term. They may send their savings back home to support family members or they may save by investing in businesses or real estate. Saving for the future is a topic I always have to take time to teach in my conferences.[35]

Nevertheless, those immigrants who do know how to save money also tend to reinvest those savings in new businesses, rental properties, or other profitable strategies.

The culture of credit card debt that rules the finances of many Americans has become quite widespread in Latin America, and I have found no data to suggest that Latinos save more than Americans do.[36] But reasons do exist that support the casual observation and general nostrum that many immigrants show special diligence in saving.

First of all, today's immigrants, as always, represent the thriftiest of all Americans. Many of them come from poor countries where they have survived almost on pure frugality, and when they come to the United States, they live incredibly frugal lives. Often such immigrants have grown accustomed to surviving on rice and beans—a very nutritious but equally cheap diet—and do not eat "feast food" every day the way many Americans do. On feast days, they feast. But on most days, they eat simple, inexpensive food. They often live in the cheapest housing available, and they pack a lot of people into their apartments. They wear the same clothes more often, mending them when necessary to squeeze every bit of utility out of them before handing them down to another immigrant less fortunate than they are.

Not only do they practice frugality, they also work constantly. Immigrants will often work as many jobs as they can find, putting in eighty-hour weeks if they can get enough work to do so. They like to work, because work brings them a sense of pride and allows them to take a proactive approach to solving their problems. They came to America for opportunity, risking everything. Now that they have arrived, they know it is time to make the most of it.

A very simple but passionate motivation often drives their frugality and industry. They send high percentages of their earnings home to their families in Latin America, where the rise in immigration to the United States in the 1990s and afterward has created a whole new economic model based on remittances from America. According to the World Bank, "Remittances exceed the foreign exchange reserves in at least 15 developing countries, and are equivalent to at least half of the level of reserves in over 50 developing countries."[37] Without such remittances, the economies of many developing countries would collapse overnight, along with the families of immigrants who depend on them.

In many cases, the families have chosen which member will immigrate and send back money to support them. Such members feel enormous pride in being the breadwinner of the family. Yet they have a responsibility beyond mere remittances. They also have to save money that will later allow them to bring family members to the United States to join them. This pattern holds true for immigrants from all over the world, as well as for Latinos.

Not all immigrants achieve impressive savings, but those who do become entrepreneurs or stakeholders in entrepreneurial efforts on the part of other immigrants. In Pedro Celis' case, his financial success in the computer industry led him to start Plaza Bank along with other immigrants. Such banks have a long tradition in America, best exemplified perhaps by the eponymous Emigrant Savings Bank, the oldest and ninth-largest bank in New York City, which Irish immigrants founded in 1850. But formal banks only represent one of the ways immigrants create pools of funds to fuel start-ups. Informal lending circles, "called *tandas* in Latin America, *susu* in West Africa, and *hui* in China . . . offer pooled-risk loans from informal groups with family honor as collateral."[38]

> In many cases, the families have chosen which member will immigrate and send back money to support them. Such members feel enormous pride in being the breadwinner of the family.

Such sources of capital, especially crucial to undocumented entrepreneurs, underscore the community values of immigrants as well as the traditional moral virtues that made America great throughout its history.

The renewal of America's faith includes the formation of social capital (i.e. trust) among immigrants, who hold strongly to communitarian values. Not trusted by people and institutions outside their communities, they turn to each other for mutual aid and support. As social capital increases, money flows into new ventures, and financial capital growth follows as a direct consequence. Nothing holds greater importance for the renewal of inner-city communities.

MOVING TO THE HEARTLAND

I have often noted how such immigrant families move out of urban neighborhoods in the generations born in America, assimilating into the heartland of America. Such assimilation represents one of America's greatest glories, and the entry of second- and third-generation Americans into the heartland brings fresh blood, fresh perspectives, and often, new businesses to aging towns and cities.

Thirty years ago I used to visit the Chambersburg neighborhood of Trenton, which enjoyed widespread fame for its spectacular Italian restaurants. I have never eaten in finer restaurants, some of which commanded one hundred dollars per diner because of the high quality of the food and the elegance of the setting. Today those restaurants have all closed. The prosperous Italian immigrants have moved out into the suburbs and across the country. In their place, Mexican immigrants have taken up the baton to rebuild and renew the inner city. From the most impoverished neighborhoods of our oldest East Coast cities to the shining new towers of Silicon Valley, California, and Bellevue, Washington, up and down the nation, from sea to shining sea and across the amber waves of grain, the New Pilgrims are renewing America's economy and beaming out to the world the message that, in this shining city, anyone can succeed. Liberty, prosperity, dignity, and faith still radiate around the world from the hill of America.

11

RENEWING HIGHER EDUCATION

D r. Jesse Miranda, at the age of seventy-eight, figures as the apostle of higher education in the minds of many Christian Hispanic immigrants to the United States. Jesse began life as a Hispanic-American in New Mexico, where members of his mother's family prided themselves as having come to America from Spain before the American conquest of the Southwest during the Mexican-American War (1846–47). "I didn't cross the border; the border crossed me," his mother would always say.[1] Americans in the Southwest might consider that the concept of "illegal immigration" did not seem to bother the American soldiers who took Arizona, New Mexico, Colorado, Nevada, California, and Utah away from Mexico by force just a few generations ago.

Dr. Miranda's maternal ancestors fit into John Ogbu's category of involuntary minority rather than voluntary immigrant, so their perspective on American identity made success in America a more complicated concept.[2] Spanish-Americans—the preferred ethnic description before the 1960s—who lived in the American

Southwest at the time of the American conquest have historically struggled to prosper in American higher education and in society in general. A friend of mine recently told me of a case where an American angrily confronted a woman after she finished her conversation on the phone in a language he assumed was Spanish. "You should learn to speak English!" he told her. "The language of the United States of America is English, and you should adapt to speak the native language of the nation where you live."

"Sir," she replied, "I was speaking in Navajo." My friend did not know whether the irony was lost on the man. People with a conquest mentality do not often consider the reasons why others do not yield to their forceful efforts to stamp out difference. Consequently, involuntary minorities that resist pressure to assimilate tend to face obstacles and hostility in the pursuit of success, including in the field of higher education.

Dr. Miranda's own desire to pursue an education in spite of his family's poverty and estrangement from the American mainstream began at his Pentecostal church when he was nine or ten years old. In what Pentecostals call "the Afterglow" of the church service, when members stand, kneel, and lie in prone or supine positions praying around the front of the church after the sermon, his mother came over and sat next to him. She said, *"Hijo, cuándo tú seas hombre* (Son, when you grow up), *quiero que tú seas un hombre educado* (I want you to be an educated man)."

"Sí, Mamá," he replied.

"Allí está un hombre educado (There's an educated man)," she explained, pointing to a man who lay sprawled on the floor—the youth director for the church and the soloist for the church's radio program, who also served as a deacon. Dr. Joe Martínez was young

and brilliant—a professor at the University of New Mexico who held a PhD in engineering. But he lay semiconscious in ecstatic prayer before the altar area of the church.

"What I got in my mind was that an educated man was a man with a heart on fire and a mind ablaze—because he had both. He was sprawled on the floor, and yet he had an academic position. So that was the image I got. He was my mentor. That was the image I took from there," recalled Dr. Miranda.

No one in Jesse's family had ever been to college. His father, an immigrant from Mexico, had spent six weeks in school as a child but always pointed out that the teacher was sick and absent for three of those weeks. In contrast, Jesse always planned to go to college as Dr. Martínez had done. Like many ethnic minority students, he faced cultural, social, and even religious obstacles to his plan.

Jesse's friends at church gave him his most important advantage in overcoming adolescent obstacles:

I lived in the *barrio*, with tough kids, and I could have gone that way too, but Joe Martínez helped to get a good group of young people together in the church and mentored us well. Iron sharpens iron. We used to pray together, do things unlike other young people who do strange things. No, we would have prayer sessions ourselves and so, I was sixteen years old in the eleventh grade, and my friends were older than I was. Clovis and Richard, two young men in the church, and there were others, went to Bible school. So there I was—five of my friends in church left for Bible school—and I missed them. They came back saying Bible school is this, that . . . so I went to Brother Girón, the superintendent [of the Assemblies of God Hispanic District] at that time, and I said, "Brother, you know, the Lord is calling me to go to Bible school." "Did you finish school?" he asked me. "No. I have one more year." He said, "Son, if that's what you feel, you should do that. Go. But I want you to promise one thing. That you're going to finish high school somehow, later.[3]

Sure enough, Jesse went to Latin American Bible Institute (LABI) in El Paso (now in San Antonio). After graduating from LABI with a three-year diploma, he went up to pastor a church in Chama, New Mexico, at the ripe old age of twenty years.

After he began his work as a pastor, Miranda approached the principal of the local high school and told him, "I need to finish my diploma." He said, "Reverend, I cannot see you sitting in a classroom with your church members. Here . . ." and the principal gave him an address in Santa Fe, the state capital of New Mexico. "See this person, and he's going to give you a test, and you're gonna get your GED diploma," and so Miranda continued his education.[4]

After two years in the pastorate, Miranda received an invitation from Latin American Bible Institute in La Puente, California, to join their faculty. Although he had no college degree, he had built a reputation as a leader at his Bible school and as a smart pastor. Bible schools in those days, as well as now, tended to care more about a teacher's practical abilities and spiritual maturity than about his or her formal qualifications. So Miranda moved to La Puente and presented himself as a student at Mount San Antonio College, a nearby community college.

Miranda recalled that he ran into obstacles immediately. After standing in line to enroll, they informed him that he could not be admitted with a GED diploma.

> So I took off, but one fellow that was standing in line came after me and said, "Listen, listen, I overheard what they told you, and don't give up"—because I was going to leave and say I couldn't enroll. But he said, "This is what you do. I did the same thing. You go and take classes at night, not the regular program, but at night, and get good grades and then come and tell them, "Look, I can do the work." So I went and did that, and I got through junior college.[5]

After finishing his associate's degree, Miranda continued at Vanguard University and graduated with his BA in Bible. From there, he went on to a master's degree in religious education at Talbot Theological Seminary (Biola University). He soon became the principal of a Christian day school and the co-pastor of an Assemblies of God church in the Southern California District— not the Hispanic District. During his two years in those roles, he saw the need to get a master's degree in educational administration from California State University, Fullerton.

Two master's degrees later, Miranda enrolled at the University of Southern California in a PhD program in social ethics. Hardly a professional student, he had worked through his first four degrees and entered his fifth degree program while raising a family and working two full-time jobs. Immigrants in general—like other adult students—tend to take a very pragmatic approach to learning.[6] As Miranda finished his second year in the PhD program, he realized that the things the school focused on lacked relevance for his people. "They were talking about in vitro fertilization, and I said, 'That will not preach in our community; that's the least thing our people need.'"[7] So he transferred to the first doctor of ministry program at Fuller Theological Seminary and finished his doctorate there.

Dr. Miranda's education, combined with his administrative experience, superior people skills, and outstanding ministry talents helped him rise through the ecclesiastical ranks quickly, and he served as executive secretary, assistant superintendent, and then finally as superintendent (for eight years) of the Pacific Latin District of the Assemblies of God. As a key leader of Hispanic churches around the United States, and especially in California, Miranda constantly pushed young leaders to go to college and seminary.

> My method of encouraging is to model. Jesus said, "Come and see," and I've used that model. Our people like to see models rather than hear ideas. I "show and tell" my story to encourage people. Later, the general superintendent of the Assemblies of God did research and discovered that the Pacific Latin District had the most highly educated ministers in the whole AG. One graduates, then others; then others follow and model.[8]

To anyone familiar with immigration and with Pentecostal churches, such a model stands apart as truly distinctive. Over the years, Miranda has inspired countless numbers of ministers to press on to higher learning, with many of his students and disciples going on to earn master's degrees and doctorates at schools such as Harvard, Yale, Princeton, and other top schools.

As Miranda's career in church leadership continued, race riots broke out in Los Angeles, and he felt he needed to get more involved in addressing the needs of society. So he left his executive position to train pastors and leaders as a faculty member and Associate Provost of the School of Theology at Azusa Pacific University (APU). In response to the social upheaval, APU had committed itself to working with minority communities to raise up leaders, and Miranda had long proven his leadership skills.

In his new position, Miranda opened up extension sites of APU for training leaders in the African-American, Asian, and Latino communities. He said,

> As I worked in those communities, I saw the need to organize the Hispanic community. During the Reagan amnesty, a lot of Latinos came to America and they became the topic of discussion in every institution—schools, government, the church. So the Pew Foundation got interested in how to assist Hispanics.[9]

The Pew Charitable Trusts had hired Luis Lugo from Calvin College to lead research projects and, together with Danny Cortés, a minister in Philadelphia, they gathered selected Latino leaders to discuss the needs of the Latino population. The group came to the conclusion that organization and unity constituted the greatest needs, so Pew offered funding to help in forming a new association to bring Hispanic leaders together. At an organizational meeting in Long Beach, California, in 1992, a new national group emerged with Miranda as its president, the *Asociación de Ministerios Evangélicos Nacionales* or AMEN.

As an organizational acronym, AMEN had special relevance for Latino leaders. As in English, the word *amen* means "yes" or "I agree" in Spanish, reminiscent of César Chávez's famous cry, "*Sí, se puede*" (Yes, it can be done). Latino Christians say "amen" to everything they like. The organization rallied Hispanic leaders from across the nation—young and old, from all Evangelical denominations and lonely corners, among Hispanics from all Latin American nations—and gave them a focal point.

For ten years, Miranda led the organization, sponsoring four national conventions and many seminars and regional meetings. They sponsored the first Hispanic Presidential Prayer Breakfast, a meeting that continues to this day. Miranda met with Presidents Reagan (before AMEN came together), Bush, and Clinton, and when George W. Bush became president, he featured AMEN in a national press conference related to his Faith-Based Initiative. After ten years, in a search for a younger leader, Miranda led AMEN to merge with the National Hispanic Christian Leadership Conference (NHCLC), with Reverend Samuel Rodríguez as president of the combined effort. Today NHCLC is the largest Hispanic organization in the nation.

NEW GENERATION OF HISPANICS IN AMERICA

Jesse Miranda modeled the way for the New Pilgrims of today, who believe strongly in the value of higher education. Highly educated Christian leaders like Isaac Canales, Wilfredo de Jesús, Samuel

Rodríguez, and Gaston Espinoza stand in the penumbra of his leadership. But they are not unique in seeking to take advantage of the opportunities for higher education our system provides. Jessica Domínguez, a prominent immigration lawyer in the Los Angeles area, provides a great example that parallels that of Jesse Miranda. Born in Iquitos, Peru, Domínguez came to the United States at the age of fourteen to join her mother, an undocumented immigrant. Like many immigrants, Jessica came to the United States on a legal tourist visa but stayed on in the country after its expiration.[10]

Like many immigrant teenagers of her generation, she had to drop out of high school to work in support of her family. She could barely speak a word of English, but she got a job at a cookie factory in New Jersey and started taking English as a Second Language (ESL) classes, determined to learn the language as quickly as possible.

> Jessica Domínguez, a prominent immigration lawyer in the Los Angeles area, came to the United States on a legal tourist visa but stayed on in the country after its expiration.

After a short while, she got laid off from her job at the cookie factory, but she quickly found other jobs, working at Burger King and at a cosmetics factory. Her natural intelligence and leadership abilities shone through, and within two weeks of beginning her work at the cosmetics factory, she earned a promotion to a supervisory job—at age fifteen! Later that year, she and her mother moved to Los Angeles, where she tried to attend high school, but found it necessary to drop out and work full-time. Rising at 3:00 a.m. each day to open the drive-thru window at a local McDonald's, she served customers with such charm and efficiency that she couldn't escape notice. Before much time had passed, a senior citizen who drove through every day for early morning coffee said to her, "You should work in an office. Come and work for me at my insurance agency and I'll teach you all you need to know about insurance."[11]

Like the typical immigrant family discussed in Chapter 9, Jessica's family worried that the old man might try to take advantage of the seventeen-year-old, so eight members of the family accompanied her to her job interview! Jessica quickly learned about the insurance business and gained office skills, then took a second job working for another insurance agent. After eight months, a third agency offered her more money to come and work for them.

Despite her blooming success in the insurance business, Jessica had dreams to pursue. When she was a child in Peru, her middle-class family had always expected her to become a doctor or a lawyer, but she seriously began to dream of being a lawyer when she experienced the divorce case of her parents. "On the last day of court," she said, "I was told the judge would ask me questions, but it didn't happen. I should have had an opportunity to speak!" Disappointed at the injustice suffered by children in divorce cases, she determined to fight for justice for children in domestic law. Coming to the United States actually made that dream harder to fulfill, since poverty made it very difficult for her to remain in school.

"When I came to this country, I had nothing but a backpack full of dreams," she said, but despite the challenges of survival as an undocumented immigrant, she never let go of her dreams. "I have a lot of hope in my life. I thought that someday, somehow, it was going to happen. I had no [plan with steps] A, B, C. You do what you have to do. But I always believed there would be something greater."[12]

Jessica's office work resulted in meeting and marrying her husband, Javier Domínguez, at age eighteen. When he went to her mother to ask for Jessica's hand—an absolute requirement in Latino families—her mother asked him to make sure Jessica would succeed in going to law school. But things got more difficult before they got easier. She soon had her first baby, and when a second child entered the world with special needs, she had to quit work to stay home and take care of him. Ironically, this hardship also provided her with enough time to go back to school, and she set to work on earning a GED diploma as soon as possible.

Community colleges play an enormous role in making a way for immigrants into higher education, and Domínguez enrolled at Pierce College as soon as she finished her GED program. "I don't know what gave me the guts to enroll in honors classes at Pierce College," she said, "but I did, and that wound up getting me a scholarship to finish my degree at Pepperdine."[13] After finishing a BA in sociology from a highly prestigious school, she went on to earn a law degree studying part-time at University of Laverne Law School.

As a student at Laverne, Domínguez impressed the dean, Robert Ackrich, who hired her as a law clerk after her graduation in 2000. "I was going to be a family law attorney, but every time we went to court, I'd come back crying. The parent with the most money always got the best decision, not the children. My family was very aware that I felt like a failure. I wasn't getting justice for children. So my mother told me I should be in immigration law. I didn't know anything about it, so I asked Mr. Ackrich, 'Could you refer me to an immigration attorney, because I'd like to learn about that?'"[14]

Her mentor immediately called a friend, and two days later she went to court on an immigration case. She loved it—the fact that she could get justice for her clients. The new firm hired her as a law clerk, and that decision set her calling into motion. She is now "one of the most sought-after immigration attorneys in Los Angeles."[15]

Domínguez quickly began to gain notoriety as a lawyer who was telegenic and articulate in explaining American immigration law in Spanish. Her big break came in 2013 when she found out about María Suárez, a Mexican sex slave who was being deported from the United States. When a neighbor of the man who had bought María and abused her killed her tormentor by beating him to death with a table leg, she was arrested for conspiracy to commit murder.[16] The innocent woman had spent twenty-two years in prison, and now she faced deportation.

Horrified by the injustice the woman had suffered, Domínguez took up the woman's cause and "helped organize rallies, started a letter-writing campaign, and besieged elected representatives."[17] As her campaign garnered international attention, Marta Sahagún de Fox—first lady of Mexico at the time—got involved, as well as U.S. Congresswoman Hilda Solís. Eventually, María's lawyers succeeded in getting her a visa as a victim of human trafficking, and as she celebrated her release along with her family, she said of

> More than ever before, today's Christian immigrants believe in the value of higher education. Immigrants are represented in the college student population at the same rates as whites.

Domínguez, "She is my angel."[18] From that moment Domínguez became known as "the angel of justice." Her sharp intelligence and attractive personality has opened up opportunities as a frequent contributor on media outlets like Fox News, the *Huffington Post*, and Univisión, where she presents a weekly feature called "Angel de Justicia" on the program *¡Despierta, America!* (Wake up, America!).[19]

Dr. Miranda noted that, more than ever before, today's Christian immigrants believe in the value of higher education. The facts bear him out. For the first time in history, immigrants are represented in the college student population at the same rates as whites. In other words, whites go to college at a rate about equal to their percentage of the population. Similarly, 23 percent of college students are immigrants or first-generation Americans, equal to the percentage of youths in that group.[20] The percentages of undergraduates coming from immigrant families are even higher in America's most populous states of California (45 percent) and New York (35 percent).[21]

When I was in graduate school in 1996, I remember a report that came out that said 50 percent of Hispanic high school graduates attended college within four years of graduating, compared to 67 percent of white graduates. Less than fifteen years later, Hispanic college attendance has soared, along with the high school graduate rate. According to Pew Research in 2013:

> A record seven-in-ten (69 percent) Hispanic high school graduates in the class of 2012 enrolled in college that fall, two percentage points higher than the rate (67 percent) among their white counterparts.[22]

You read that right. A higher percentage of Latino high school graduates enroll in college than do white graduates. Furthermore, the percentage of high school graduates among Latinos has soared. Pew noted that "in 2011 only 14% of Hispanic 16- to 24-year-olds were high school dropouts, half the level in 2000 (28%)."[23] Most of this improvement has occurred over the past six years as attitudes have changed dramatically since the recession of 2008.

For years, scholars wrote about how Latino culture placed a low value on higher education. Earlier generations of Hispanics in America often descended from the earlier populations who became minorities through conquest rather than immigration, and their societal status directly affected their confidence and desire to pursue a college education. Ogbu and Simons wrote that, despite their recognition that success in America requires education and hard work, involuntary minorities develop, over the course of several generations, a point of view that their status exposes them to unfair discrimination as well as other barriers to success. Accordingly,

> They have come to believe that (1) job and wage discrimination is more or less institutionalized and permanent, and (2) individual effort, education, and hard work are important but not enough to overcome racism and discrimination.[24]

Their belief that society has stacked the deck against them may not even be conscious, but it affects their lives powerfully.

Even as they encourage their children to stay in school, promising them that it will enable them to succeed in later life, from their personal and group experiences with employment discrimination they know only too well that school success often does not lead to a good job. Moreover, they often engage in various forms of "collective struggle" with whites for more job opportunities. Involuntary minority children are affected by this actual texture of their parents' lives: they observe and hear about their parents' experiences. Eventually they share their parents' ambivalence. Thus, involuntary minorities are less sure that education leads to success or helps to overcome barriers to upward mobility.[25]

Ogbu and Simons contrasted the involuntary minorities with voluntary immigrants, who

> see school success as a major route to making it in the United States. The community, family, and students believe strongly that the same strategies that middle-class white Americans employ for success, namely, hard work, following the rules, and getting good grades, will also work for them in school and in the future job market.[26]

It would appear that today's Latinos in the United States have increasingly adopted the immigrant mindset.

Everything has changed now, as it has for other ethnic minorities. The *Chronicle of Higher Education* has reported, "Over the last generation, students of all racial and ethnic groups increased their college-going rates by double-digit percentage points."[27] But recently, the growth of minority groups has outpaced that of white

Americans in college attendance. "Black and Asian enrollment rates also grew from 2009 to 2010, with 88,000 and 43,000 more young black and Asian students enrolling, respectively. White students were the only ethnic group for which the Pew Hispanic Center reported negative growth . . . a 4-percent drop."[28]

The *Chronicle* specially notes the "importance that Latino families place on a college education":

> According to a 2009 Pew Hispanic Center survey, 88 percent of Latinos ages 16 and older agreed that a college degree is necessary to get ahead in life today. By contrast, a separate 2009 survey of all Americans ages 16 and older found that fewer (74 percent) said the same. *The Huffington Post* notes the change from past values, as 94 percent of Hispanic parents "say they expect their children to actually go to college—more than double the number who say their own parents expected them to do so."[29]

Christian immigrants have especially grown wise to the value of higher education. According to Dr. Miranda,

> They've seen the results of education and what it has done for others. Here's a kid from the *barrio*, who dropped out of high school, got a GED. Students see the results of it in my life, and they see others graduating and becoming an asset in our movement. Today's immigrants have a greater desire for education than earlier ones did. They come here, yes, to survive, but they also see the benefits of an education, that it can take them farther, that their investment

of time and money in [education] takes them farther in the long run. Because students today are more informed through the media, the Internet, and computers, the news about higher education can reach more people. They are no longer in a mental *barrio*, but they're hearing the success stories of others and that's encouraging.[30]

According to the Associated Press, the fall semester of 2014 marks the first time in history that a majority of students in America's primary and secondary schools did not come from white families.[31] The growth of the Latino population, with a spike in both immigration and birthrates, has played a large role in this new reality. As today's K–12 students progress through the system and head to college, non-white students will make an increasing impression on collegiate student bodies. Among them, the children of Christian immigrants will make an impact as they bring with them a more intense religious commitment and stronger family values. Dr. Miranda says, "I think they'll come with a lot of fire, a lot of hope, and I think that if we, as a nation, if we as a church, open the doors and give them an opportunity, there's no limit to what they can do."

One way the children of the New Pilgrims will affect colleges, as seen in the example of Ilona Trofimovich, involves their greater commitment to their families and to the community around them. While many traditional American students have tended to

> The children of Christian immigrants will make an impact as they bring with them a more intense religious commitment and stronger family values.

evaluate colleges in terms of which schools partied the hardest, many immigrants and first-generation Americans go to college with a much deeper sense of the seriousness of the matter, of how much their parents have sacrificed to get them there, and of what they owe their families. Dr. Miranda suggested,

I think their experience, the need of their families perhaps, will cause them to look not just for advancement of themselves but also to carry their family with them. They grow up with that mentality of family, so it's not just the individualism that we see in America. They want their families' lives to be improved, not just their own individual lives. Many also come to school as parents, not just as children, and that will make a big difference.[32]

RECRUITING STRATEGY FOR COLLEGES

As colleges seek to attract the New Pilgrims to their campuses, they would do well to take families very seriously. Miranda commented:

The American family says you're your own person, you're an individual, whereas a Hispanic family says, no, you're part of the family, and the family makes the decision. So you don't go to college because of the nice catalog or where they ranked in American higher education, in the top 10 or top 100. I don't think they look at that. They ask, "What is the benefit and what's going to happen after the education?" I always say to convince a child to get them to school, you talk to the parents and you talk to the pastor. Those are the two guidelines.[33]

Miranda recalled the story of one student whose father was an area presbyter and pastor in Fresno. The father came to him and said, "I don't know why she wants to go east to school when she can go right here to Fresno State. She wants to go east and that's far away from our family, and second, I don't know what kind of church there is, and she's grown up in the church. She's a pastor's daughter, and she'll step away from the church if we're not careful. Could you tell her to stay here and go to Fresno State, because I know you know education?"

Miranda said, "Okay I'll talk to her." So he asked her, "Why do you want to go east? Your father wants you to stay here in Fresno; he wants you to continue going to church."

The young woman replied, "Brother, I have a full four-year scholarship to Harvard, and I cannot turn it away."

Miranda laughed knowingly and said, "Okay, let me talk to your dad." Returning to the father, he said, "Brother, you don't know what she's been offered. Not only is it thousands of dollars, but it's the best education in the country. No, if she goes and you allow me, I'll keep in touch. I'll write to her every month and I'll find out where there is a church over there, and I'll hold her accountable to that, and I'll report back to you."[34]

Four years later, she graduated from Harvard and eventually became a state department official in Costa Rica. Today she works as a vice president in a bank in Los Angeles. Her story illustrates, however, that parents and pastors play an important role in the college decisions of Latino and other Christian immigrant youths. "She took me as a bishop, as a superintendent and said, 'Okay, let's make this work,'" Miranda summed up.[35] The same thing holds true among Asians and other immigrant groups. The parents and the pastors can play crucial roles in the educational choices of youth. Getting Hispanics on the faculty and in the student body only adds a small part of a successful program. A successful multicultural environment requires a combination of recruitment, retention, climate issues, pedagogy and the curriculum, organizational values, culture, structure, and staff development.

LIFE IN THE MIDDLE

As Pew Charitable Trusts has described in a research report entitled "Between Two Worlds: How Young Latinos Come of Age in America," Latino immigrants and their children, like all other immigrant groups, live in the tension of two different worlds.[36] They speak multiple languages and live between two or more different cultural milieus. Often, the children of working-class immigrants bridge different social classes as they become college-educated professionals. They juggle different communities and loyalties. In telling his life story, Miranda drew over and over from the concept of *nepantla*.[37]

As Miranda noted, the Aztec Indians, during the Spanish Conquest of Mexico, used the word *nepantla* to describe the dynamics they were experiencing. The word refers to "in-betweenness" or "both/and." He explained,

> The Spanish would ask, "Are you going to be loyal to us or to them?" and they would say "*Nepantla*"—both/ and. What happened is you get a reconfiguration of your being, because you see the negative and the positive. And so you're able to take away the myths of your own culture or the fears of another conquering society, so you're able to

see yourself in a different reality, and there's going to be a change, and you want to be part of that change. So this is pretty wise of them to opt for "in-betweenness" and say, "I'll go with your side and come with my side as things go." And I think that is a key in relation to education. Education opens your eyes to a reality and you see those things in your life that are myths and fictions.[38]

Pew recognized the tension in today's Hispanic community by noting the contradictions in the community:

Young Latinos are satisfied with their lives, optimistic about their futures, and [they] place a high value on education, hard work, and career success. Yet they are much more likely than other American youths to drop out of school and to become teenage parents. They are more likely than white and Asian youths to live in poverty. And they have high levels of exposure to gangs. These are attitudes and behaviors that, through history, have often been associated with the immigrant experience.[39]

As the Hispanic community deals with the same *anomie* that all immigrant groups have faced in American history, churches and universities have their work cut out for them.

OVERCOMING PREJUDICE BASED ON RELIGION

As much as *anomie* contributes to student attrition among immigrants, factors beyond dissolute behavior also lead to dropping out. Although research has long demonstrated that Evangelical

Christians face special challenges in higher education and stand at-risk in terms of dropping out of school,[40] the professional journals that publish research on the efforts of student affairs specialists to retain other categories of at-risk students show virtually no interest in the question of how to help Evangelical students succeed in college. The problem derives from unrecognized prejudice against students who take their religion seriously.

If higher education researchers will address this issue, they will find that Evangelicals often face hostility toward their faith from professors, administrators, and fellow students. Those who care about Latino and Latina students should consider how to defend them from religious persecution and create safer environments for them to prepare for professional careers and engaged citizenship. They should especially open space for campus ministries to operate freely. The New Pilgrims and their children deserve assistance from collegiate communities that will recognize the many dimensions of their "in-betweenness" and give them space to be themselves in every way, not just in terms of their color and culture.

> Those who care about Latino and Latina students should consider how to defend them from religious persecution and create safer environments for them to prepare for professional careers and engaged citizenship.

When he was a young man, Miranda's mother often invited Demetrio Bazán to their home for dinner. As Bazán served as superintendent of their Hispanic district of the Assemblies of God, Miranda asked him, "Why is it that we are with Springfield [the Missouri-based headquarters of the Assemblies of God]? We are Assemblies, they're Assemblies, but we speak Spanish and they speak English. They're in Springfield and we're in New Mexico." Bazán answered, *"Hijito, estamos con Springfield—cerca de ellos para aprender de ellos, pero lejos para ser lo nuestro"* (Son, we are with Springfield—close to them to learn from them, but far enough away to be ourselves).[41] As a result, Miranda has always worked to keep the Hispanic churches in fellowship with the national organization of his church, and Hispanics now make up fully 20 percent of all AG members in the United States.[42]

Neither churches nor universities enjoy immunity from the racial and ethnic divisions that society experiences as a whole. Successful religious organizations in the future—as well as successful universities—will have to become comfortable with the reality of *nepantla*. When immigrants are marginalized and pushed into ghettos and balkanized communities, *anomie* rules. Wise intercultural leadership takes *nepantla* seriously, giving people room to be themselves while also making space inside organizations (not only making them feel like guests but making them cohosts of the institution). The best way to learn how the mainstream culture flows requires plunging into it.

12

RENEWING AMERICAN POLITICS

Chapter 5 discussed the issue of immigration and the Rule of Law. In an interview with Dr. Varun Laohaprasit, I asked him why some Christian immigrants feel justified in breaking American laws to enter the country. His response left me stunned. He said,

> I have travelled all over the world—to many countries. The American system is very organized and safe for your family. There's no perfection here, but overall, the environment is safer, the law is more—how can I say it in English—people respect the law in America. The society really respects the law. It backs you up with the law. In the Third World country, there is no law. You have the law, but people don't care.[1]

I responded, "So you're telling me that people break the law in order to come under the security of the law?"

"Yes, that's right," he acknowledged. "Because they know they will be more secure here, to live here, for their kids and for themselves."

"People break the law to gain the Rule of Law?" I verified, stunned at the irony.

"That's right. Because in their country, people can shoot you and you die, and no one cares, because the law is not protected. There's so much corruption. So if you have money you can pay somebody to do anything."[2] As he spoke, I remembered a time in Quito, Ecuador, when a friend told me that the going rate to hire a *sicario*—a hit man—was a mere fifty U.S. dollars. As the vile Nazi Captain Strasser famously said in *Casablanca*, "Perhaps you have already observed that in Casablanca human life is cheap."[3] In underdeveloped nations around the world, similar conditions hold.

The moral dilemma faced by immigrants today puts them in a no-win situation. No realistic legal way for them to enter the country exists, so they live exposed to lawlessness in their countries of origin. To gain equal justice under law, they must break the law once and then live in its shadows. As a consequence, immigrants then become the most law-abiding people in society. Undocumented immigrants come to America to work, and knowing that committing even a minor infraction of the law will lead to possible deportation, they do everything possible to avoid breaking the law after arriving. Sociologist Rubén G. Rumbaut of the University of California, Irvine, found in 2007 that incarceration rates among immigrants were lower than those of any ethnic group in America, including Whites and other native-born groups.[4] For example, in 2000 the incarceration rate of the native-born was five times higher than that of foreign-born among men between the ages of eighteen and thirty-nine.

As a missionary who has lived in three different countries of Latin America and has visited every country in Latin America except Venezuela, I have often heard Latinos marvel over the fact that Americans generally obey the law, including such minor laws as coming to a full stop at stop signs or laws against littering. In contrast, Argentine evangelist Albert Mottesi, in a book observing the five hundredth anniversary of Columbus' discovery of America, called attention to a phrase that Spanish conquistadors made famous in colonial days, "*Acato la ley, pero no la cumplo*" (I abide by the law, but I do not fulfill it). He noted how that attitude had contributed to a culture of ingovernability and lawlessness in today's Latin American culture.[5] Indeed, the theme of *ingobernabilidad* represents one of the most vexing problems in the economic and social development of the region.[6]

Peruvian politician Ricardo Palma described the origin of the phrase *Acato la ley pero no la cumplo* as follows:

> In Colonial times, the Viceroy had his way of not fulfilling the norms and it was this: After recognizing the seal on the Royal Accord, he would stand up on the tip of his toes, take the paper or the folder that contained it, kiss it if the urge moved him, and afterward, elevating it to the level of his head, would say with a robust voice, "I abide by it and I do not fulfill it."[7]

In American idiom, we would say that the viceroy paid lip service to the king's law.

As the twentieth-century Peruvian politician Carlos Torres y Torres-Lara explained, such behavior illustrated that (1) there were laws, without the institutionality to enforce them, and (2) there was no institutionality because the laws were not enforceable. He concluded that under such conditions, "it would be preferable that there were no law, rather than having law that no one enforced, since that foments another 'institutionality'—the non-fulfillment of all legal norms."[8]

> If we do not either enforce or change the law to legalize their situation, we will erode and potentially destroy the very framework of justice that drew them to America in the first place.

The ironic situation of today's undocumented immigrants—having to violate the law in order to come under its protection—speaks analogously to the governmental dilemma faced by American citizens in trying to deal with the twelve to thirteen million unauthorized foreigners in the country. If we do not either enforce or change the law to legalize their situation, we will erode and potentially destroy the very framework of justice that drew them to America in the first place. If the Rule of Law does not survive in America, where can it stand? As Ronald Reagan said in 1964,

If we lose freedom here, there's no place to escape to. This is the last stand on earth. And this idea that government is beholden to the people, that it has no other source of power except the sovereign people, is still the newest and the most unique idea in all the long history of man's relation to man.[9]

The ultimate injustice America could possibly visit upon immigrants would be to extinguish the beacon of the Rule of Law.

EXECUTIVE ORDERS AND
CONGRESSIONAL REFORM OF THE LAW

In 2011, President Obama eloquently described his duties to enforce the laws passed by Congress in a town hall meeting on the Spanish-language television network, *Univisión*. Following up on a question from an undocumented college student, anchorman Jorge Ramos asked President Obama if he could sign an executive order preventing deportations. The president aptly responded,

> With respect to the notion that I can just suspend deportations through executive order, that's just not the case, because there are laws on the books that Congress has passed . . . We've got three branches of government. Congress passes the law. The executive branch's job is to enforce and implement those laws. And then the judiciary has to interpret the laws. There are enough laws on the books by Congress that are very clear in terms of how we have to enforce our immigration system that for me to simply through executive order ignore those congressional mandates would not conform with my appropriate role as President.[10]

Obama promised, however, that his administration would continue to propose "legislation that would change the law in order to make it more fair, more just."

President Obama's commitment to the Rule of Law in that

speech represents a crucial factor in preserving the America that immigrants come to participate in, and since that time, both parties and both houses of Congress have made efforts to pass an immigration reform bill. No one sees the current immigration laws as adequate, and everyone understands the political challenge of reforming the law at a time when the country stands divided on the issues. Partisan wrestling over the issue has, however, stymied progress in both gaining control of the entry of new immigrants at our borders and airports as well as in reforming the law to make it both beneficial and enforceable.

As a result, President Obama threatened to address the issue through executive orders, a prospect that greatly agitated his political enemies. But as attorney Jessica Domínguez notes,

> President Obama is not the first president to use executive actions to try to deal with a broken immigration system— a system that Congress refuses to change because they are too busy playing political football.[11]

Domínguez explains that the history of presidential executive orders on immigration

> makes it clear that presidents have ample legal authority—and abundant historical precedent—supporting their discretion to take action in immigration matters. Since at least 1956, every U.S. president has granted temporary immigration relief to one or more groups in need of assistance.[12]

At the same time, presidential executive orders do not address problems as systematically and permanently as laws passed by Congress and an orderly process of bipartisan adjustments to laws that do not work out as planned. For example, the inaptly named Deferred Action for Childhood Arrivals Order (DACA)[13] achieved its intended purpose of contributing to the short-term security of longstanding undocumented immigrants who accompanied their parents as children and know no other home but America, but it may have also provoked the unintended result of suggesting to children that they will be welcomed into America and that "Obama will take care of them."[14]

In all fairness to President Obama, DACA did not create the phenomenon of unaccompanied children crossing the U.S. border. They have been coming by the thousands for many years, but the recent surge of child migrants emerged through a distorted interpretation of DACA promoted by unscrupulous *coyotes* (human traffickers) and unintended consequences of a 2008 law passed by Congress during George W. Bush's administration. Under the Trafficking Victims Protection Reauthorization Act, Central American children "must be given a court hearing before they are deported (or allowed to stay)."[15] The fact that we have not provided sufficient funding to appoint enough judges to deal with their cases in a timely way means that the Obama administration is required by law to give them a "*permiso*," a paper permitting them to stay until they get the legally required hearing. Obama has no legal choice but to "take care of them," and that is the right thing to do as well.

Under the structure of the United States Constitution, the

president carries the responsibility of ensuring that the executive branch of government enforces the bills passed by Congress and signed into law by the president. The president does not, however, control the budgeting process. If Congress passes laws without approving sufficient funds to enforce them—as the case now stands with regard to immigration laws—the president cannot guarantee the full enforcement of the laws. In such cases, the president has no choice except to exercise discretion in terms of what violations constitute the greatest danger to American society and direct the efforts of law enforcement on those types of cases through lawful executive orders.

I am personally a Republican and have very little praise to offer the Obama administration in general. I do not admire President Obama's reticence in the past to offer real leadership on immigration reform legislation. His unwillingness to invest political capital in the issue until it could no longer affect him politically resulted in a record number of deportations and tragic disruption of immigrant families. He has lacked moral courage for six years in letting the situation get to where it has gone. But in the matter of Deferred Action for Childhood Arrivals, President Obama made a justifiable decision that immigrant children raised in America and educated in our school system posed a truly minimal threat to the nation's well-being.

In formally defining a particular group as deserving deferred action, Obama did nothing that immigration officials have not done for a long time. As Jessica Domínguez points out,

Deferred action has been on the books for years. It allows ICE and CIS officers to use their discretion to do just that: "defer action"—the action of deporting individuals that are in the country without legal immigration status. Government officials for years have granted deferred action to families who show that they deserve the opportunity to stay in the country.[16]

The relief provided by such actions does not give immigrants any legal status or amnesty but rather it only provides them temporary relief from deportation. Executive orders authorizing massive deferred actions that provide only temporary relief offer imperfect substitutes for a permanent solution. To fix our laws, we will need the best minds in our government all working together, compromising, and demonstrating political courage to bring the nation together.

As President Obama acknowledged under questioning at the *Univisión* town meeting, a presidential executive order granting what his audience requested—an end to all deportations—would result in the nullification of current immigration laws and a de facto amnesty for the millions of immigrant workers who have become an integral part of the American economy and would unquestionably bring relief and freedom from fear to them. Obama understands that adopting a presidential policy of "*Acato la ley, no la cumplo*" would set into motion a retreat from the very tradition of legality and equal protection under law that brings immigrants to America in the first place. No American president can ever surrender the dignity

> Executive orders authorizing massive deferred actions that provide only temporary relief offer imperfect substitutes for a permanent solution.

of serving under the United States Constitution by adopting the governing philosophy of the colonial viceroys who set themselves above the Rule of Law and contributed to a political culture that created much of the Third World as we know it today. We could too easily become the Third World of the future.

Short of a cooperative governmental climate in which all three branches of government work together to reform our immigration laws, the president has to set priorities for using scarce funds to address overwhelming needs. On November 20, 2014, President Obama announced a new executive order that provided minimal relief and precarious quasi-legal status to millions of people by identifying new categories of immigrants he would not seek to deport. As expected, this brought comfort to many immigrants and enraged his political opponents. Only time will tell the unintended consequences that his unilateral and very temporary action will bring. The best answer, as President Obama has pointed out repeatedly, requires the Congress to get busy and reform our immigration laws in a way that ensures the best possible outcomes for our country and ensures the establishment of justice for the long term.

In the meantime, the issue of the legality of President Obama's executive action will ultimately wind up in the hands of the Supreme Court. Executive orders should never nullify the law, but rather provide for the wisest and most effective administration of them. For that reason, it is troubling that President Obama responded to a group of pro-immigration hecklers a couple of days after announcing his order, saying:

Now, you're absolutely right that there have been significant numbers of deportations. That's true. But what you are not paying attention to is the fact that *I just took an action to change the law.*[17]

Speaking off the cuff, President Obama probably did not mean to say that he had literally "changed the law." But in making such a statement, he at least superficially contradicted his own earlier explanation of his legal position during the *Univisión* interview. In fact, executive orders do not change the law. Only Congress and the Supreme Court can truly do that. But in all fairness, the current situation has the president in an impossible position, in which a great gulf lies between what current law allows and what he believes to be right. It lacks dignity for Congress to stand by and criticize him in his dilemma or scrutinize his technique as he walks a political tightrope.

Part of the role of the president involves representing the American people. President Obama's discomfiture accurately represents our national reality in terms of immigration policy. Like Obama, we have become, as a country, a walking contradiction, insisting on the rule of laws we cannot enforce, declaring justice for all as we deny it to many. Until Congress steps up and reforms our immigration laws, the light from the City of America shines dimly indeed.

THE CITY ON A HILL

As discussed earlier, John Winthrop's vision for America foresaw a nation that would stand as a shining city on a hill, reflecting to the world an example of the Kingdom of God at work and proving that "the God of Israel is among us."[18] Over the course of the centuries, as nonsectarian American Civil Religion and a secular state properly took hold under the disestablishment clause of the United States Constitution, Winthrop's vision became a quest for American leadership as a beacon of freedom and democracy to the rest of the world. If America meant to establish true religious freedom, it could take no other avenue.

A Latin American friend once mentioned to me that American comic book characters such as Mickey Mouse and Superman acted as world missionaries for "truth, justice, and the American Way." Enemies of American virtues around the world revile our role as the world's policeman, even as many of our own citizens have grown weary of the role after more than a decade of war in the Middle East. But friends and admirers of America around the world marvel at the willingness of our soldiers to obey orders, sometimes marching into certain death in battle in order to secure the blessings of freedom and democracy for foreign nations. A walk through the cemeteries of Normandy never fails to provoke wonder among lovers of freedom. Year after year, members of the American military offer their lives as missionaries of freedom wherever our nation may send them.

> A Latin American friend once mentioned to me that American comic book characters such as Mickey Mouse and Superman acted as world missionaries for "truth, justice, and the American Way."

President Woodrow Wilson declared America's God-given, manifest destiny to defend democracy in his eighth "Annual Message to the Congress" in 1920, two years after the end of World War I. He averred:

It is surely the manifest destiny of the United States to lead in the attempt to make this spirit prevail. There are two ways in which the United States can assist to accomplish this great object. *First, by offering the example within her own borders of the will and power of Democracy to make and enforce laws which are unquestionably just and which are equal in their administration*—laws which secure its full right to labor and yet at the same time safeguard the integrity of property, and particularly of that property which is devoted to the development of industry and the increase of the necessary wealth of the world. *Second, by standing for right and justice as toward individual nations.* The law of Democracy is for the protection of the weak, and the influence of every democracy in the world should be for the protection of the weak nation, the nation which is struggling toward its right and toward its proper recognition and privilege in the family of nations.[19]

America would shine the light of democracy around the world by its own domestic example and by the force of its military and its diplomatic influence, as Theodore Roosevelt had earlier said, "speaking softly and carrying a big stick."

Our current domestic political realities and foreign policies have put that historic mission at significant risk of failure. This book has not sought to treat American foreign policy and must forgo the temptation to further discussion of it here, because the greatest threat to our national mission at present involves our internal politics. The current gridlock between the executive branch of government and the legislative branch gives aid and comfort to the enemies of America's doctrine of freedom and democracy around the world. If the light of the American Way does not shine brightly here, no military force—nor any diplomatic corps—can project it to the world.

THE LAMB'S AGENDA

John Winthrop warned, in his famous sermon about the City on a Hill, "The only way to avoid this shipwreck, and to provide for our posterity, is to follow the counsel of Micah, to do justly, to love mercy, to walk humbly with our God." The "shipwreck" he referred to involved the judgment of God on the people of Massachusetts if they were to fail to live up to the laws they had agreed upon:

> Now if the Lord shall please to hear us, and bring us in peace to the place we desire, then hath He ratified this covenant and sealed our commission, and *will expect a strict performance of the articles contained in it.*[20]

America's national covenant requires the Rule of Law and justice, guided by the exercise of mercy. No issue in domestic politics puts the issues of law and justice and mercy into starker contrast than our current debate over immigration law.

One of the questions that concerns Americans today in terms of the near-term legalization of residency and eventual citizenship of today's immigrants—and the topic of this chapter—asks about the future impact of Christian immigrants on our nation's political life. Remember that about 80 percent of immigrants either come to America as Christians or convert to Christianity after arriving (overwhelmingly in Evangelical churches). A clear answer emerges from analysis of public speaking by Christian immigration advocates, from interviews with Christian immigrants, and from analysis of the issues that drove them from their own countries to America. Christian immigrants take conservative positions on social/moral issues such as family values, abortion, and sexual morality. They hold liberal views on the issue of the responsibility of government to provide a safety net for the poor. As immigrants establish themselves and join the lower middle class, they often tend to adopt more conservative views on government. No genetic component influences their political views.

Obviously, immigrants think for themselves, just like all other human beings, and they will not all vote the same way. Cubans and immigrants from Eastern Europe who lived under communist oppression may often vote for Republicans, while immigrants from Latin America may continue to vote for Democrats as long as they think Republicans hold a prejudice against Latinos. Immigrants, like native-born Americans, will "vote their pocketbooks" when it comes down to the moment of truth. They came here for their families to prosper economically and spiritually, and they will vote for the party that offers them the best opportunity to do so. No one should ever forget that opportunity brought immigrants to this country, and they will consistently seek to maximize it.

The immigrant vote can be won by either Democrats or Republicans, depending on who campaigns the hardest to get it and offers immigrants the best chance for success. Immigration means struggle, and immigrants tend to get bruised in the process of adjustment to American life. Figuratively, politicians should neither see them as "Red" nor as "Blue" but rather as "Purple."

Saturnino González, pastor of the five-thousand-member *Iglesia El Calvario* in Orlando, Florida, challenges Republicans in particular to take another look at Hispanic voters:

> Republicans need to read us well. I think they are reading us wrong . . . They automatically assume that Hispanics are automatic Democrats, and they don't know that there is a new breed coming up, which is Latino Evangelicals. They don't know who we are. And we're not even on their radar. They just put a brand on us: "Okay, Latino. Automatically Democrat. So let's just change the page." They're reading us wrong. I don't know how long it's gonna take for them to notice there is a group that is coming up, that has a completely different mentality than the regular Democrat (Latino) . . . That's why they don't invest in us . . . We have a radio station in Orlando, an Evangelical Christian station, and we've been telling the political people, "Hey, you know what? You can put an announcement here. Invest in our community. Invest in our radio station." Republicans don't do that. They don't want to do that because they automatically assume, "We can't win them." I've been sitting with them, and they're reading us wrong.[21]

Republicans have, nevertheless, taken notice of Samuel Rodríguez and his wife, Eva, each of whom has offered prayers at the Democratic and Republican presidential election conventions.[22]

Neither party can afford to ignore the rising electoral power of immigrants, especially Latinos. The National Hispanic Prayer Breakfast annually convenes over seven hundred Latino faith and community leaders in Washington, D.C. The event, sponsored by Reverend Luis Cortés and Esperanza, consists of one of the largest and most active networks of Latino ministries in the United States and "features prominent speakers from both the Republican and the Democratic parties and has been keynoted by President George W. Bush on six occasions, President Barack Obama twice, and Vice President Joe Biden."[23] Esperanza's work focuses on issues that lift Latinos out of poverty, including everything from education ventures to real estate and other economic development issues. The organization values real solutions to the problems that debilitate people, not party affiliations.

Rodríguez sums up the politics of today's Christian immigrants as "not the Donkey, not the Elephant, but the Lamb."[24] He explains, "There are many good, Christ-loving, Bible-believing Christians who identify themselves as Democrats . . . It is not hard to find a large number of pro-life, pro-family African-Americans and Hispanics who vote Democrat."[25] Such ethnic-minority Democrats, however, chafe severely at the liberal moral agenda of the Democratic Party. Rodríguez warns, "Unless the Donkey reconciles with the Lamb, the Donkey may finish this Century in the pony show of the politically obscure."[26]

> Neither party can afford to ignore the rising electoral power of immigrants, especially Latinos.

On the other hand, Republicans have a significant opportunity to gain the support of Christian immigrants. He counsels:

The Elephant must determine whether Conservatism stands defined as the preservation of life, liberty, family, religious freedom, limited government, and free markets or the preservation of a monolithic voting constituency. In other words, the Elephant will make significant advances if it intentionally moves forward with the justice mission of Lincoln and the moral optimism of Ronald Reagan.[27]

Rodríguez emphasizes the fact that Christian immigrants do not want to be torn between biblical righteousness (defined as moral rightness) and biblical justice (defined as mercy toward the poor). As Gabriel Salguero has written, "We think that poverty, economic inequality, and the environment are just as important moral issues as abortion, stem cell research, and same-sex marriage."[28]

CHANGE IN POLITICS

Rodríguez likes to frame political issues as both vertical and horizontal—involving a vertical, spiritual dimension as well as a horizontal, social dimension. He sees the crosslike intersection of the vertical and the horizontal as the natural home of Christian immigrants. He has a strong point, but reality has more than just vertical and horizontal dimensions. In fact, reality resembles a sphere more than any sort of linear chart. Reality defies linearity. As Rodríguez understands, reducing politics to a fight between the right and the left leaves most of the important questions unanswered.

For example, the issue of compassion for the poor does not belong to the left or the right. The question does not revolve around whether to help the needy but rather how to help them. Democrats currently try to help them with big, government-controlled programs, whereas Republicans usually try to help with programs that incentivize the poor to show initiative on their own. Immigrants tend to show a remarkable work ethic and self-sufficiency, especially those who have come without legal authorization. Their political loyalties will owe much more to what they perceive as helping them rather than to any predetermined ideology.

The history of American politics demonstrates an incontrovertible fact: Political parties change. In recent memory, Republicans strongly opposed the use of the American military to engage in nation building during the Clinton administration and then became the champions of that practice during the Bush administration. My grandmother used to say, "Never vote for the Democrats because they will get us into a war," offering the presidencies of Roosevelt (World War II), Truman (Korean War), and Kennedy (Vietnam) as evidence. Today, the Republicans have earned a reputation as hawks, with Reagan invading Grenada, George H. W. Bush leading us into the liberations of Panama and Kuwait, and George W. Bush leading the nation to war in Iraq and Afghanistan.

> For most of their history, the Republicans stood as the champions of African-Americans—Lincoln having freed the slaves—with Democrats from the "Solid South" standing against civil rights legislation.

For most of their history, the Republicans stood as the champions of African-Americans—Lincoln having freed the slaves—with Democrats from the "Solid South" standing against civil rights legislation. Democrats in Teddy Roosevelt's time stood on the side of billionaires and industrialists, while the Republican Roosevelt led "the Progressives" in standing up for consumer protection from corporate trusts and manufacturers. Which way is right? Which way is left?

No one could even feign surprise when the United States Conference of Catholic Bishops called for comprehensive immigration reform in a gospel-saturated position paper in 2013.[29] Roman Catholics have always defied characterization as liberal or conservative in their politics, and the six Roman Catholics who serve on the United States Supreme Court represent opposite sides of the left-right divide. Political questions for authentic Roman Catholic thinkers do not revolve so much around labels such as "conservative" or "liberal" but rather around truth, righteousness, and justice.

Many people assume that Evangelical Christians support a right-wing political agenda, but history does not support such pigeonholing. As Donald Dayton argued in a powerful book in 1976, *Discovering an Evangelical Heritage,* Evangelicals led the crusade against slavery and poverty and for women's rights in the nineteenth century.[30] In the current climate, Evangelical churches stand strongly in support of immigrants, seeing their responsibility as ministry to them, not border control. The National Association of Evangelicals (NAE), the most important political voice of the Evangelical movement and a stalwart supporter of pro-life politics and other issues seen as belonging to the right wing, issued a strong statement calling for immigration reform in 2009.[31]

Leading Evangelical denominations in the country have also made strong statements in favor of immigrants and reform of immigration laws.[32] The Southern Baptists, representing sixteen million members in fifty thousand churches, approved a carefully nuanced but pro-immigrant resolution:

That we ask our governing authorities to implement, with the borders secured, a just and compassionate path to legal status, with appropriate restitutionary measures, for those undocumented immigrants already living in our country; and be it further resolved, that this resolution is not to be construed as support for amnesty for any undocumented immigrant.[33]

Similarly, the Assemblies of God denomination called for "comprehensive immigration reform"—one of the most loaded terms in today's American politics—stating:

It is appropriate for the borders of the United States to be secure in order for immigration to conform to the laws of the United States. As people of faith we support comprehensive immigration reform that reflects human dignity, compassion, and justice integral to a "nation under God." Apart from issues related to governmental jurisdiction, we believe that the gospel of Jesus Christ compels us to minister to all who live or work within our country.[34]

The majority of Assemblies of God members have traditionally supported Republican candidates dating back to the beginning of the Reagan Revolution, and AG member and former Senator and Attorney General John Ashcroft has cut a heroic figure in American conservatism. Yet he has offered stalwart support to immigrants, supporting President George W. Bush's efforts to achieve comprehensive immigration reform a decade ago.[35]

Republicans cannot question the conservative bona fides of

Evangelicals, but the question remains: what makes hostility to immigration "conservative"? The more religious the conservative, the more likely he or she will support the merciful treatment of immigrants. Immigration is as American as apple pie and always has been.

In 2012, the NAE and many Evangelical denominations, along with an impressive list of individual luminaries from Evangelical institutions, joined the Evangelical Immigration Table, "a broad coalition of evangelical organizations and leaders advocating for immigration reform consistent with biblical values."[36] Defying characterization as representing the right or the left, the Table promotes a set of biblical principles to guide the U.S. Congress in legislation for comprehensive immigration reform. Their statement reads:

> As Evangelical Christian leaders, we call for a bipartisan solution on immigration that:
>
> - Respects the God-given dignity of every person
> - Protects the unity of the immediate family
> - Respects the Rule of Law
> - Guarantees secure national borders
> - Ensures fairness to taxpayers
> - Establishes a path toward legal status and/or citizenship for those who qualify and who wish to become permanent residents.[37]

Their position does not represent the Elephant or the Donkey, but rather a sober and judicious consideration of what their faith requires of them, what serves the nation best, what solves the problems we face together, and what brings an end to an unnecessarily divisive issue in a nation of immigrants.

In the future, the ever-swirling tides of American life will change the issues our political parties debate. Politics may not spring up like the mercies of God, "new every morning," but the issues on the front burner tend to change continually. Today's immigrants will play a major role in the future renewal of American politics, but their party affiliation—whether Democrat, Republican, or a third party to be named later—will depend on the issues that emerge and the way the current parties adjust to them.

Religiously identified immigrants—86 percent of all immigrants—will vote for the political party that offers the best solutions to America's problems.[38] Since no one can predict how the parties themselves will change in the near future, no valid reason exists to assume that they will automatically prefer one party or the other. When they have legal documents, safety, security, opportunity to work, a loving family around them, and a church or other religious community that offers them the right hand of fellowship—when they have a real stake in the national well-being—America can depend on them to vote for policies that support opportunity and the national interest.

13

THE BIBLE AND OUR IMMIGRATION CRISIS

A friend of mine in the Washington, D.C., area recently sent me a link to a website that purports to explain "What the Bible Says About Our Illegal Immigration Problem."[1] The study, prepared for a "Members Bible Study" offered to the United States Congress, intends to give biblical guidance to legislators. The title itself implies that the Bible has something to say *directly* about our "illegal immigration problem." In fact, the Bible does not speak directly to our situation—which differs tremendously from that of ancient Israel—but rather offers principles that can guide our thinking about the problem.

Nonreligious citizens may object to the very idea that the Bible should have any influence on legislative and other governmental functions in the United States, believing that our public affairs should be purely secular. I remember a particular mini-scandal of the 1980s that involved accusations that Ronald Reagan made foreign and military policy decisions based on biblical expectations for the apocalypse.[2] Objections also arose when the news emerged that Nancy Reagan had consulted astrologers in planning the president's schedule after a would-be assassin had wounded her husband.[3] As much as Evangelicals complained about the idea of Reagan's possible reliance on astrology, and as much as secularists may object to Evangelical use of the Bible for guidance, people have religious beliefs and the First Amendment's "Free Exercise Clause" guarantees their right to participate in society as religious beings. If voters do not like the particular religiosity of a politician, they have every right to vote that person out of office.

Once Christians have determined what the Bible's teaching has to say about the issues of human life, they take it very seriously. For that reason, Christian theology obligates Christians not only to read the Bible but also to consider its meaning for our context carefully. In all Christian theological traditions, believers are expected not only to identify scriptural references and precedents but also to engage in a process of prayerful, moral reasoning to let the Holy Spirit guide them in understanding God's will for particular situations. Our own prejudices and predetermined conclusions can very easily lead us to interpret the Bible in ways that unfairly favor us while disfavoring other people. Unfortunately, the Members Bible Study document on immigration lacks the rigor that Christian theological consideration of complex problems deserves, and it draws unfounded conclusions about what the Bible actually says about immigrants.

THE *GER* AND THE *NEKHAR*

The study points out that the Hebrew Bible recognizes two kinds of non-Israelite in Ancient Israel, the *ger* and the *nekhar*. Without a doubt, the word *ger* in Hebrew refers to aliens, sojourners, or immigrants while the word *nekhar* refers to foreigners or literally, "strangers." The question at stake involves the exact difference between the two words. With regard to the two words, the study states:

> An Israelite citizen is referred to as a "countryman" *ach* in Scripture, whereas a legal immigrant is referred to as a "sojourner" *ger* . . . , and a foreigner is called an illegal *nekhar*. Important to this study, and evident from the OT, is that an illegal did not possess the same benefits or privileges as a sojourner or countryman.[4]

In effect, the study draws an unfounded, direct equivalence between the *nekhar* in ancient Israel and the illegal immigrant in the United States today.

The study goes on to illustrate the use of the word *nekhar* in the case of Ruth, the grandmother of King David:

> Notice for instance the words of Ruth the Moabite, and her response to Boaz the Israelite in Ruth 2:10: "Then she fell on her face, bowing to the ground and said to him, 'Why have I found favor in your sight that you should take notice of me, since I am a foreigner?'" Not only was Ruth a *foreigner* (nekhar), an illegal immigrant, she was a Moabite illegal, who according to Deuteronomy 23:3 was forbidden to migrate into Israel altogether! For *Citizen* Boaz to entertain Ruth at all was remarkably generous and gracious, and possibly even illegal. (Perhaps Boaz already had in mind legitimizing her status by marriage). The point is that Ruth's self-declaration serves to underscore the classification of people in and by ancient Israel.[5]

Such an interpretation of Ruth shocks any biblically literate reader, as it accuses the grandmother of Israel's greatest king, the iconic King David, of immigrating illegally to Israel!

Consider the details of Ruth's migration to Israel. Her deceased husband, apparently named Kilion, had migrated from Israel to Moab during a famine, and she had returned to Israel as the only source of sustenance for her mother-in-law, Naomi. She went to Israel, where she took up the rights accorded to a *ger* and gleaned harvest fields without anyone objecting to her presence or challenging her rights. Boaz clearly saw her as part of his extended family and offered to marry her in the role of a kinsman-redeemer, as *per* the opportunities provided in the law (Leviticus 25:25). Yet because she refers to herself as a *nekhar* or foreigner, and since the authors of the study "know" that *nekhar* refers to an *illegal immigrant*, they jump to the conclusion that Ruth lacked legal authorization to live and work in Israel.

Pretending to know things one does not really know can lead to gross errors! Sticks and stones and word studies apparently can hurt real people, especially those who are the most vulnerable.

Such an interpretation of Ruth's situation tacitly projects an odd but very interesting semblance between the situation in Israel during Ruth's time and that of American immigrants today, namely, that apparently no one paid any attention to the laws regarding immigration. The Members Study thinks Ruth disobeyed the law as she supported her Israelite mother-in-law economically though backbreaking labor. It also holds little regard for Boaz as a law-abiding citizen, since it accuses him of breaking the law (Deuteronomy 7:3–4) by marrying a *nekhar*. Further, it tacitly recognizes that the whole nation ignored the law when it accepted

David as king two generations later, since Deuteronomy 23:3—the putative primary legal code for Ancient Israel—states that "no Ammonite or Moabite or any of their descendants may enter the assembly of the LORD, not even in the tenth generation." David's rule over Israel apparently constitutes a flagrant violation of that law.

IGNORANCE OF THE LAW

Such violations of the law may not constitute so much a refusal to obey the Mosaic Law as ignorance of it. While elements of the Mosaic Law (or perhaps Ancient Near Eastern cultural traditions) such as the kinsman-redeemer provision occur in the biblical record of Israel's early history, the Bible offers no clear evidence that Israel ever enforced the Mosaic laws strictly before the reign of Josiah, centuries after the time of Ruth, and near the end of Israel and Judah's sovereign possession of the Holy Land.[6] Regardless of whatever degree of force the Mosaic Law may have held at different times in Israel's history, the book of Judges makes it imminently clear that the rule of Mosaic Law did not hold sway in Israel during Ruth's time, repeating the refrain, "In those days Israel had no king; everyone did as they saw fit" (Judges 17:6; 21:25).

Instead of obeying the laws (as the Members Study would posit them), everyone in the story of Ruth did what they considered fair and just. These facts notwithstanding, the study treats Ruth's self-description as a *nekhar* differently than does the source text it drew its definitions from. The main source for the study, James K. Hoffmeier, states: "It is curious that she calls herself a 'foreigner' (*nokhariah*, literally 'a foreign woman') when she seems to fit the classic definition of an alien (*ger*)." He goes on to add,

"She may have used the term in a self-deprecating manner in order to accentuate the generosity of Boaz."[7] So was Ruth or was she not an illegal immigrant?

Christian theology demands the utmost care in handling the scriptures. The lives of precious people literally hang in the balance. The study that was prepared for the purpose of orienting members of Congress based its arguments on Hoffmeier's more learned research, but even Hoffmeier—an otherwise well-trained Old Testament scholar with a PhD from the prestigious University of Toronto—commits two anachronistic errors: the first by assuming the force of Mosaic Law during the pre-monarchic period of Israel's history, and the second by importing modern American categories, i.e., "legal" and "illegal" immigrants, into the meaning of Hebrew words *ger* and *nekhar.*

> Christian theology demands the utmost care in handling the scriptures. The lives of precious people literally hang in the balance.

Hoffmeier does well in recognizing that the difference between a *ger* and a *nekhar* does not involve an essential element but rather a situational element. Not everyone has made that distinction, and at least one interpreter adds ugly racial overtones to the question by suggesting that *nekhar* always referred to people of other races.[8] Hoffmeier recognizes the difference as follows: the alien (*ger*) came to Israel to become a permanent resident. The foreigner (*nekhar*) allegedly did not. He notes:

In several passages the terms are used in a parallel manner (Exodus 30:33; Isaiah 28:21; Lamentations 5:2), showing that they carried *a nearly identical meaning.* The difference hinged on permanence. The *nokharim* passed "through the land with no intention of taking residence, or perhaps they would be temporarily or seasonally employed."[9]

In contrast, Hoffmeier alleges that the alien (*ger*) "entered Israel and followed legal procedures to obtain recognized standing as a resident alien."[10] Unfortunately for Hoffmeier, he cannot have it both ways. Either the words do or do not carry the technical distinction he wishes to load them with. In fact, Old Testament contextual usage of the words *ger* and *nekhar* carry virtually synonymous meanings. Hoffmeier would have done better to have limited himself to the correct observation that the two words are treated as synonyms in many poetic passages of the Old Testament, such as Job 19:15: "My guests and my female servants count me a [*ger*]; they look on me as on a [*nekhar*]."

In using modern American categories of immigration control to explain ancient Israelite practice, Hoffmeier pretends to possess more knowledge of the legal customs of ancient Israel than any extant evidence can offer. He undermines his own argument later in his book when he writes that a *ger* is "one who leaves home to establish a new permanent residence *with the approval of a citizen-host.*"[11] While Hoffmeier states on the same page that to become a *ger*, a *nekhar* had to "receive the formal agreement of the leader or official representative of that nation," he does so on the flimsy evidence that Abraham and Isaac—wealthy nomadic ranchers with large flocks and many employees and slaves—sought out permission from several kings in Genesis to live in their territory. He does not consider whether individual immigrants or small families would need to get such high-level permission, and he has no evidence for his pretensions of knowledge about official immigration procedures in Old Testament times. Neither does he consider whether customs in effect during the time of the patriarchs would remain in effect hundreds of years later. Furthermore, he ignores all evidence that contradicts his opinion.

Ruth presents the perfect case in point: she did indeed come to Israel as a *nekhar*. Despite Hoffmeier's casual dismissal of Ruth's self-acknowledgment, no people fit the description of *nekhar* better than highly despised Moabites did. Nevertheless, Ruth only needed a "citizen-sponsor" (as Hoffmeier himself notes) in order to gain recognition as a *ger*. Such a sponsor would allow her to glean in his fields or—on the happy occasion of finding a beautiful and marriageable young *nekhar* like Ruth—take her as his wife. When all the biblical evidence comes into account, we see that kings could offer permission for a *nekhar* to reside in their territory, as well as employers, or even householders. The Mosaic Law, as well as the more determinant cultural background of the ancient Near East, required Israelites to offer at least temporary hospitality to travelers, whether they intended to stay or merely pass through the land. As long as the hospitality offer remained in force, the *nekhar* had the privileges of a *ger*.

ANCIENT ISRAEL AND MODERN AMERICA

The immigration cultures and laws of ancient Israel and modern America could hardly offer a more striking contrast. To compare the ancient *nekhar* with modern undocumented immigrants fails the test of the most elemental fairness. The question in Ruth's case, indeed, hinged on fairness—what justice demanded. The current situation in America hinges on unenforceable and unfair laws that our people have the power to change—and should.

If we make biblical categories like *ger* and *nekhar* applicable to American immigrants, then perhaps we should adopt the whole biblical framework. A half-biblical indictment of weak and defenseless farm workers and other low-wage, manual laborers surely cannot reflect any reasonable standard of justice. If, on the other hand, America were to adopt the biblical practice of allowing not only kings but also employers and host families to request and promptly receive temporary or permanent residency visas for foreigners (and take responsibility for their behavior), then the categories of *ger* and *nekhar* would fit perfectly. Something along those lines might actually work, although the current political realities do not suggest a high probability of passing such laws.

In view of the very fluid difference in the categories of *ger* and *nekhar, a* Christian ethic of immigration demands more than just an ideologically biased linguistic study to guide contemporary Christians in their attitudes and actions toward undocumented immigrants. In today's context, a foreigner whose presence in the United States includes nefarious intentions and violations of criminal law deserves harsh treatment, including deportation or incarceration. Immigrants—whether legally sanctioned or not—who have come to the United States to settle, work, and contribute to the society deserve the considerations afforded the *ger*.

BEYOND MERE WORD STUDIES

The Old Testament speaks univocally about the duties of Israelites toward the *ger* or immigrant. The book of Genesis, as mentioned earlier, follows the migration of humanity from Eden through the call of Abraham to migrate from Ur through the wanderings of the families of Isaac and Jacob and the trafficking of Joseph as a slave to his reunion with his extended refugee family in Egypt. The sufferings of the Israelites under Egyptian oppression marked the way God would expect them to treat immigrants in the Promised Land.

In Exodus 22:21–22, God commands Israel as follows: "Do not mistreat or oppress a foreigner, for you were foreigners in Egypt. Do not take advantage of the widow or the fatherless." In that command, the love of God for the weak and vulnerable stands as the basis of this provision for immigrants, widows, and orphans. Exodus 23:9 repeats the command, appealing directly to the empathy that the Israelites had earned during their own suffering: "Do not oppress a foreigner; you yourselves know how it feels to be foreigners, because you were foreigners in Egypt."

> The Old Testament repeats over and over again the moral equivalence before God of widows, orphans, and immigrants.

The Bible repeats this same command over and over. Indeed, it stands as one of the most often repeated ethical norms for Israel.[12] Deuteronomy 10:19 says, "You are to love those who are foreigners, for you yourselves were foreigners in Egypt." Leviticus 19:33–34 takes the command a step further: "When a foreigner resides among you in your land, do not mistreat them. The foreigner residing among you must be treated as your native-born. Love them as yourself, for you were foreigners in Egypt. I am the LORD your God." The reader should not gloss over this latter commandment without recognizing the progression of its gravity and the complexity of its implications:

1. Good treatment only begins to fulfill the obligation of the Israelites toward immigrants in their land.

2. The Israelites must not lose the empathy they gained during their own experience as foreigners in a distant land.

3. The full human rights and dignity of immigrants must remain intact, with the same privileges as the native born.

4. Immigrants deserve not only justice, but love from the Israelites.

5. The love immigrants receive must equal the love of one's self.

6. This commandment flows out of God's own identity. The command stands under the invocation of the divine name over it: "I am the LORD your God."

Israel rightly took pride in her election as the people of God, but Psalm 94:5–6 mentions other kinds of people as God's own. In describing oppressors of God's people, the psalm says, "They crush your people, O LORD; they oppress your inheritance. They slay the widow and the foreigner; they murder the fatherless." In promising God's vengeance against such enemies, the text includes Israelites, widows, orphans, immigrants, and other vulnerable people as God's people.

The Old Testament repeats over and over again the moral equivalence before God of widows, orphans, and immigrants. Deuteronomy 24:17–18 says: "Do not deprive the foreigner or the fatherless of justice, or take the cloak of a widow as a pledge. Remember that you were slaves in Egypt and the LORD your God redeemed you from there. That is why I command you to do this." The same text goes on to promise God's blessings on those who show kindness to the weak: "When you are harvesting in your field and you overlook a sheaf, do not go back to get it. Leave it for the foreigner, the fatherless, and the widow, so that the LORD your God may bless you in all the work of your hands" (verses 19–20). Not only do these verses suggest that God will bless such generosity, they also imply that failure to show kindness prevents God from blessing "the work of your hands."

It serves little purpose to go on citing all the other verses that drive these points home over and over in the Old Testament. The Israelites' history as oppressed immigrants left them with a moral obligation to offer outstanding hospitality to immigrants of good intent in their land. Their duties went beyond those of other nations. They owed their freedom to the God whose very nature promised liberation to the captive and a new home for the homeless and displaced. No other kind of God would deserve their worship, and Heaven stands as the Bible's ultimate symbol and final fulfillment of God's freedom-loving, place-making, home-giving nature.

Whether an American confesses Christian faith, any other faith, or none at all, the principle behind Israel's duty to immigrants can serve to inform our own personal practices and national laws. The principle at stake here is moral reciprocity. Israelites owed a debt to their immigrant ancestors to remember their struggles and to treat contemporary immigrants with kindness, justice, and hospitality. In the same way, Americans today owe a debt to their immigrant ancestors that they can only pay through kindness to today's immigrants. Other than the Native Americans whose ancestors crossed the Pacific to populate a virgin continent many millennia ago, all the rest of us either discovered America through immigration or as descendants of immigrants. As a nation, we have always struggled with the challenge of welcoming new immigrants, but the best moral agents and heroes of our past have championed the rights of immigrants. America's heritage demands that we do no less in our time.

IMMIGRATION AND THE NEW TESTAMENT

Some Christians may feel a temptation to say, "That's the Old Testament." In fact, Christians have considered the rejection of the Old Testament both false and heretical since the days of Jesus and the apostles. While the apostles recognized that Christians do not share the ritual obligations of Jews under the Sinai Covenant, the stories of the Old Testament "happened to [the Israelites] as examples and were written down as warnings for us, on whom the culmination of the ages has come."[13] The confession of historic Christian faith cannot include a rejection of the Old Testament, and believers of any faith or even none at all can derive instruction from its moral precepts, as America's leaders from Washington to Obama have always acknowledged publicly.

In any case, the New Testament follows in the tradition of the Hebrew Bible in urging an ethic of hospitality. In the very first chapter of the New Testament, Matthew showed that Jesus' family tree illustrated a love for foreigners. In fact, all of the women mentioned by name in the genealogy of Jesus were either foreigners themselves or were married to foreigners—and not just foreigners, but foreigners with a checkered reputation.[14] Tamar, the mother of Perez, was a Canaanite who had to prostitute herself to Judah in order to get what he owed her. Rahab, also a Canaanite, left a life of prostitution to marry an Israelite. Ruth, the Moabitess and self-described *nekhar*, engaged in some very suspicious late-night activities in her romance with Boaz. Bathsheba, whose adultery with a lecherous King David colors her memory forever, first married Uriah the Hittite, an immigrant in Israel. The second chapter of the New Testament goes on to tell the immigration story of Jesus' nuclear family, in which Mary became a foreigner in Egypt, a political refugee who fled from the murderous designs of King Herod.[15]

Like the Israelites, Jesus Himself spent time as a foreigner in Egypt, and He obeyed the Old Testament injunction to treat foreigners with love. Just as the Old Testament enjoined the Israelites to love foreigners as they loved themselves, Jesus taught His disciples that the two greatest commandments require us to love God with all of our hearts . . . and our neighbors *as ourselves*.[16] In response to this command, a man asked Jesus, "And who is my neighbor?"[17] Jesus responded scandalously with the parable of the Good Samaritan, which ends with the question "Which of these three do you think was a neighbor to the man who fell into the hands of robbers?"[18] The answer? The hated foreigner—the Samaritan— acted as a neighbor. Clearly, Jesus put a twist on the story. Instead of a Jew loving the Samaritan neighbor, the Samaritan *nekhar*/foreigner in Israel loved the Jewish man as his neighbor. If a despised Samaritan had the capacity to love his Jewish neighbor as himself, followers of Christ could hardly claim lesser obligation.

Jesus followed up on the issue of loving one's neighbors when

He told His disciples that, at the reception of the righteous into Heaven, the King will say:

> I was hungry and you gave me something to eat, I was thirsty and you gave me something to drink, I was a stranger and you invited me in, I needed clothes and you clothed me, I was sick and you looked after me, I was in prison and you came to visit me.[19]

The word *stranger* in this verse translates the word *xenos* in the original Greek version, a word that means "foreigner" or stranger. In modern English, the word *xenophobia* means "the fear or hatred of foreigners." Just like the Mosaic Law included foreigners along with widows and orphans as recipients of God's love and protection, Jesus includes foreigners along with the hungry, the naked, and the captive, and He calls upon Christians to champion their cause.

The parable goes on to state that the righteous will reply to the King, asking when they had ever seen him hungry, thirsty, a foreigner, naked, or in prison. Jesus said, "Truly, I tell you, whatever you did for one of the least of these brothers and sisters of mine, you did for me" (verse 40). Jesus considered the weak and vulnerable His own "brothers and sisters"—children of God who deserve our love and compassion just as Jesus Himself did. Some might protest, "But when He says 'the least of these my brothers and sisters,' He refers to the Christian poor." That interpretation will not hold water, but let's give them the benefit of the doubt for a moment. If Jesus meant that Christians should pay special attention to the Christian immigrant, today's immigrants to America qualify remarkably.

But non-Christian immigrants may indeed deserve even great-er consideration on the part of American Christians than Christian immigrants do. A friend of mine once said of America's immi-grants, "They either came here to evangelize or to be evangelized." Sharing the good news of God's love in Jesus Christ constitutes the essential Evangelical ethical duty, and it can have no other start-ing place than treating every vulnerable person with the same love and care that Jesus Himself would offer them if He stood in our midst. And every Christian believes that He does indeed stand in our midst. But that misses the point Jesus makes in the parable: the presence of Jesus remains with the immigrant, the poor, the vulnerable, and what we do for them, we do for Him.

BIBLICAL HOSPITALITY

The New Testament calls upon Christians to show hospitality in many passages, but Hebrews 13:2–3 especially applied the Old Testament moral standard to Christians: "Do not forget to show hospitality to strangers [foreigners], for by doing so some people have shown hospitality to angels without knowing it. Continue to remember those . . . who are mistreated as if you yourselves were suffering." Not only does this verse allude to Old Testament teach-ings about God's love for the weak and vulnerable and Jesus' call to love our neighbor, it also recalls a specific event in the life of Abraham, who entertained angelic visitors in Genesis 18.

Many people, even devoted Christians, may doubt that angels exist or that they visit people in our time. The New Pilgrims do not doubt it, as they frequently give testimony to miraculous interven-tions that brought them safely through "many dangers, toils, and snares" to America. I have never seen an angel, but when I was a young man working in Mexico, my American traveling companions and I got lost on the way to Tampico. A seemingly interminable line of traffic formed and we didn't know where we were; nor did we know where the traffic was going. As we moved further along, we realized that everyone had to board a ferry that would transport them to the other side of a large lake. We could not turn around, nor did we understand how to get our car onto the ferry in the midst of what seemed like total chaos, every driver jockeying forward to get aboard.

All of the sudden, a man appeared who took charge of us. Although I could barely speak Spanish at the time, he kindly helped me understand that we were going the right way and that we had no choice except to cross the lake. He helped us get on the ferry, protecting us from the terrible disorder and the many people that competed with us to board the ferry. He showed us on a map where to go to arrive at our destination. When we reached the other side, he left in his automobile, and I never saw him again. The only thing that convinced me that he was not an angel was the business card he gave me that indicated his occupation as an auto parts salesman.

Like the Mexican who helped me cross the water, the immigrant who crosses your path may be the very angel God has sent you, your very own Good Samaritan. But once again, the field has flipped. I started out talking about helping immigrants and all of the sudden I find myself talking about a foreigner who helped me in his own country. As the ancient Greek fable of the Lion and the Mouse teaches, sometimes the weak person can step up to help the strong. In Mexico I played the role of the weak person. In America, I hope to offer as much help to people in crisis as I once received on that Mexican ferry. The roles tend to toggle as to who helps whom.

The biblical ethic of offering help to the weak and the vulnerable—especially to widows and orphans as "pure and faultless religion" requires—also applies to assisting our immigrant peers.[20] The Bible does not tell us exactly how to shape American immigration policy to achieve optimal justice. The principles of the Evangelical Immigration Table offer a good starting place for legal reform, but the nation as a whole will have to come together to craft the best possible strategy for restoring the Rule of Law to our country by drafting a realistic, just, and enforceable immigration code that does not crush the "tired, poor, huddled masses."

The Bible clearly teaches that we have an ethical responsibility to offer assistance to those who have given up everything they once knew and often have risked their very lives to come to America. But this book presents the inverse argument. The New Pilgrims have come to America *to help us*—to renew our faith, strengthen our families, transform our churches, and fill our schools and universities with hope in the form of ambitious learners who dream of a better future. As more and more American Christians are feeling like foreigners in our own land in the face of opposition to the Church and the attack on biblical morality, isn't it ironic that these Evangelical immigrants may very well tip the scale back to a conservative America at some point?

14

THE CITY ON A HILL

Ronald Reagan, one of America's greatest presidents, often referred to Winthrop's vision of America as "a shining city on a hill." Many people today assume that when Reagan signed the Immigration Reform and Control Act in 1986 to create a path to citizenship for millions of undocumented immigrants, he acted out of mere political necessity. But in fact, his decision to sign that legislation stood in perfect integrity with his lifelong political philosophy and vision. In his presidential farewell address in January, 1989, he said:

I've spoken of the shining city all my political life, but I don't know if I ever quite communicated what I saw when I said it. But in my mind it was a tall proud city built on rocks stronger than oceans, wind-swept, God-blessed, and teeming with people of all kinds living in harmony and peace, a city with free ports that hummed with commerce and creativity, *and if there had to be city walls, the walls had doors and the doors were open to anyone with the will and the heart to get here.* That's how I saw it and see it still.[1]

Open to anyone with the will and the heart to get here: that was Reagan's view of America's ideal stance toward immigrants.

Reagan's vision of America stood in the Pilgrim tradition, depending on the blessing of God to crown the efforts of a virtuous citizenry and a steady flow of industrious immigrants in an unending reign of freedom. Today's immigrants offer our best hope to restore the values that once established it and without which, it cannot stand.

About the same time as Reagan spoke those words as president, Ben Sterciuc suffered persecution for his faith in Communist Romania. "I grew up in a small village in Romania in a Pentecostal family," he recalls. "As a boy, I would read about America—how everyone had an equal chance to go to school and practice their faith. I yearned for that kind of freedom, but it didn't seem possible."[2] Because of his faith in Christ, Ben refused to join the Communist Party, thus giving up the opportunity to go to college, to get a well-paying job, and to start a business. After he married his wife, Lia, their son, Flavius, was born in 1987. As Ben's dreams of being a father came true, though, the responsibilities he faced to provide a future for his son weighed heavily on him. How could he subject his son to a life of oppression? In a moment, he knew what he had to do.

> "As a boy, I would read about America—how everyone had an equal chance to go to school and practice their faith. I yearned for that kind of freedom, but it didn't seem possible."

Ben knew who Ronald Reagan was. He would listen to Americans talk about freedom on Radio Free Europe, lying in bed with the pillows wrapped around the transistor radio to keep the neighbors from hearing, and dreaming of an escape to freedom.

> We viewed Reagan as the savior of the world—the person or the president who had all the answers, who had the greatest power in the world in his hands. Decisions that he would make affected the entire globe, the whole world. I loved that grandfatherly voice, even though I couldn't understand his English.[3]

In August 1988, Ben tried to leave. Along with a friend they tried to cross the border into Yugoslavia, but they were captured and thrown into prison for three months.

His windowless cell permitted no light to enter the pitch-black darkness. The heartless guards crammed twelve people into a cell designed for four people and cruelly denied them water for three days and food for seven. Leaving the cell meant interrogations and beatings. "It was a low point for any human being," Ben remembers, "to be put in prison and beaten into obedience for simply wanting to be free, for wanting a better life for your family. It was very hard to take."[4]

Prison only deepened Ben's commitment to Christ. He found time there to reflect, pray, and fast, but "the fasting was not always by choice," he chuckled. "That was the time when I really deepened my relationship with Christ. It was there that I knew, whatever happens—whether I live or die—I'm going to follow Jesus Christ."[5] His eventual release from prison did not mean freedom, as he found his life just as restricted as before, but now he faced additional surveillance, harassment, and detentions from the authorities. "They wanted to make a case out of me, to show that a Pentecostal Christian would become an atheist."[6] But stern oppression only hardened Ben's determination to escape to a new life.

As Reagan addressed America for a final time on the other side of the world, Ben made his plans. In June of 1989 he fled with a group of two others, leaving his wife and child behind until he could make arrangements for them to leave as well. While one of his friends got caught, two escaped, running across a field of sunflowers through a hail of bullets, their lives at grave risk, dogs chasing them as they crossed into Hungary. "That was the closest moment of my life to death," Ben reflects.[7] Their entry into Hungary violated the laws of both Romania and Hungary, and within hours the Hungarian authorities arrested them. After three days and nights of interrogating, the Hungarians believed their stories of being political and religious refugees and allowed them to stay. Ben lived on the streets, under bridges, and in parks for five weeks, looking for leftover change in phone booths to buy food.

After deciding that Hungary had nothing to offer him, he used his knowledge as a railroad mechanic to stow away on a train (in a secret compartment above the water tank and the toilet in a passenger car) and escape, again illegally, into Austria at the end of July.

Through an amazing series of events, God created a moment when I was able to connect with someone. I was sitting in a corner, praying to God and asking God for direction about what to do, and an elderly gentleman approached me, out of the blue. I had on the same blue jeans I had when I escaped from Romania—that was all I had—so I probably looked pretty miserable and pretty different from the nice clean Austrians in the train station. So he came to me and kept saying something, and one word just popped, kind of, out of the sentences he was saying, and that was *hilfe*. Later I learned that means help.

Not understanding, Ben resisted the man's attempts to help, but eventually, the man was able to connect Ben with a Romanian friend who helped Ben communicate with the United Nations Refugee services in Austria.

Was Ben an illegal immigrant? He certainly left Romania as an illegal *émigré*, and he entered Hungary as an illegal immigrant, doubly illegal in his escape to freedom, as illegal in his actions as those Central Americans who leave their nation without legal sanction, pass illegally through Mexico, and swim the dark waters of the Rio Grande to enter America. Ben entered Austria just as illegally, if not more so, than the thousands who fly to the United States on a tourist or student visa and stay on past the expiration date, considering no price too high to pay in order to purchase life in America. In Ben's case, the laws of Romania and Hungary were unjust, and his illegality there remains a badge of honor, a shame now swallowed up in the glory of American citizenship.

Some would ask, "Why don't they wait in line like everyone else?" There is no line. They cannot wait. Their situation hangs too precariously; the dangers they face are too real. Their passion for freedom and justice drives them through the darkness toward America, the Land of the Free and the Home of the Brave. No one can argue that they don't count as brave.

By the spring of 1990, the Romanian Communist regime had fallen, and Ben Sterciuc would stand in a train station in Vienna, flowers in hand to welcome his wife and son from Romania. "I cannot express in words what that moment meant to us," Ben reminisced. "It was like we were given a chance to live again. It was a rebirth."[8] As refugees protected by the United Nations, Ben and Lia applied for visas to settle in Canada, South Africa, or the United States. Canada offered them visas first, but their heart's desire was to go to America, and they waited until they received word that America would receive them.

Joining distant relatives in Olympia, Washington, they worked hard to create a new life in America. They studied English ten to twelve hours a day and worked at night cleaning buildings. After gaining command of English, Ben went to college to study nursing, and while working as a nurse assistant, he conceived an idea to start a business providing referrals of patients to nursing homes and other care facilities. As soon as he finished school and got a nursing license, he bought a home and started an "adult family home" to provide care for seniors. He later bought another home to establish a second facility. After finishing a master of science in nursing degree at the University of Washington in Bothell, he became an adjunct faculty member and began to teach nursing at Northwest University. He then enrolled at the university to complete a second bachelor's degree in music ministry, and then, with his wife, Lia, he recently finished a master's degree in theology and culture.

In 2012, Ben planted Elevation Church, a growing ministry in Kirkland, Washington, that reaches out to people from a wide variety of ethnic groups, both immigrants and native-born Americans.[9] Through hard work, he not only mastered English and became a citizen but he also finished the education he had dreamed of as a child and earned success as an American businessman and employer. He has made a place for himself in America—a place of leadership and a place of gratitude:

> The life that God gave us here is so much more than I even knew how to dream. All we wanted was to live in a country where we could be free, where we could worship and not worry about being put in prison. But God has been so gracious in the way He molded us through this process. He gave us favor when we needed it. He gave us life. He has been so faithful to us. There are no words to describe our gratitude.[10]

Ben stands proud among the New Pilgrims. The old Pilgrims—indeed pilgrims from every American generation—would embrace him as an equal.

"The Land of the Free and the Home of the Brave" can never survive on what men and women did in the long shadows of our past. Its permanence depends on the constant striving of those who refuse to live without freedom and will bravely run any risk and pay any price to achieve it. Without them, we cannot continue to be America, nor can we even see it. Those of us born here, who have enjoyed freedom all of our lives, find ourselves too often blinded by the light, unable to perceive the dim and simple glories detectable only by eyes that have known the jet blackness of oppression.

If people like Ilona Trofimovich, Ben Sterciuc, Varun Laohaprasit, and Roberto Tejada do not continually lend us their eyes by describing the subtle majesties of the land we take for granted, we will find ourselves trampling them.

Ronald Reagan was thinking of people like them when he wound up his service as president, going on to conclude his farewell address with these words:

> And how stands the city on this winter night? . . . After 200 years, two centuries, she still stands strong and true on the granite ridge, and her glow has held steady no matter what storm. And she's still a beacon, still a magnet for all who must have freedom, for all the pilgrims from all the lost places *who are hurtling through the darkness toward home* . . .[11]

As I write this sentence, twenty-five years have passed—a full tithe of America's history. May we never abandon Reagan's vision, nor Winthrop's, nor that of Rodríguez, so that America's light will shine forever.

NOTES

Introduction

1. G. K. (Gilbert Keith) Chesterton, *What I Saw in America* (London: Hodder and Stoughton, Ltd., 1922), 7.

2. Ibid, 5.

3. Ibid.

4. Ibid.

5. Ibid.

6. The same researchers who report a 70 percent loss of youth also report that 65 percent of those who abandon church in their teens and twenties return to church by age thirty, thus preserving a minimum of 75 percent of Evangelical youth. See Scott McConnell, "LifeWay Research Finds Reasons 18- to 22-Year-Olds Drop Out of Church," *LifeWay*, August 7, 2007, http://www.lifeway.com/ArticleView?storeId=10054&catalogId=10001& langId=-1&article=LifeWay-Research-finds-reasons-18-to-22-year-olds-drop-out -of-church. For a thorough summary of literature on the topic of youth abandonment of faith, see J. Warner Wallace, "Are Young People Really Leaving Christianity?" *Cold Case Christianity*, September 27, 2013, http://coldcasechristianity.com/2015/are-young-people -really-leaving-christianity/ (both accessed May 19, 2015).

7. Pew Research Center, "Christians Decline Sharply as Share of Population," The Pew Forum on Religion & Public Life, May 12, 2015, http://www.pewforum.org/2015/05/12/ americas-changing-religious-landscape/ (accessed June 23, 2015).

8. Pew Research Center, "The Religious Affiliation of U.S. Immigrants: Majority Christian, Rising Share of Other Faiths," The Pew Forum on Religion and Public Life, May 17, 2013, http://www.pewforum.org/2013/05/17/the-religious-affiliation-of-us-immigrants/ (accessed May 19, 2015).

9. Pew Research Center, "'Nones' on the Rise."

10. Pew Research Center, "The Religious Affiliation of U.S. Immigrants."

11. Readers interested primarily in the growth of non-Christian religions in America will find that story in *A New Religious America* by Diana L. Eck (New York: HarperCollins Publishers, 2009) or in *Parade of Faiths: Immigration and American Religion* by Jenna Weissman Josselitt (New York: Oxford University Press, 2011).

12. Robert Neely Bellah, "Civil Religion in America," *Journal of the American Academy of Arts and Sciences,* Winter 1967, http://www.robertbellah.com/articles_5.htm (accessed May 19, 2015). For more on Washington's faith, see Ron Chernow, *Washington: A Life* (New York: Penguin, 2010).

13. Emma Lazarus, "The New Colossus," http://en.wikipedia.org/wiki/The_New_Colossus (accessed May 19, 2015).

14. Gillian Flaccus, "Atheist 'Megachurches' Crop Up Around the World," *Huffington Post*, November 10, 2013, http://www.huffingtonpost.com/2013/11/10/atheist-mega -church_n_4252360.html (accessed May 19, 2015).

Chapter 1

1. George Soule (Mayflower Passenger), Wikipedia, accessed July 6, 2014, http:// en.wikipedia.org/wiki/George_Soule_(Mayflower_passenger) (accessed May 19, 2015).
2. Roger Finke and Rodney Stark, *The Churching of America, 1776–2005: Winners and Losers in Our Religious Economy* (New Brunswick, NJ: Rutgers University Press, 2005), 10.
3. By no means can one maintain that Jews or Muslims, or for that matter, new Christian sects (such as the Latter-day Saints) thrived in a persecution-free environment throughout American history, but they did enjoy an unprecedented measure of toleration.
4. Pew Research Center, "'Nones' on the Rise: One-in-Five Adults Have No Religious Affiliation," The Pew Forum on Religion and Public Life, October 9, 2012, http:// www.pewforum.org/files/2012/10/NonesOnTheRise-full.pdf (accessed May 19, 2015); James Emery White, *The Rise of the Nones: Understanding and Reaching the Religiously Unaffiliated* (Grand Rapids, MI: Baker Books, 2014).
5. Scott McConnell, "LifeWay Research Finds Reasons 18- to 22-Year-Olds Drop Out of Church," *LifeWay*, August 7, 2007, http://www.lifeway.com/ArticleView?storeId=10054& catalogId=10001&langId=-1&article=LifeWay-Research-finds-reasons-18-to-22-year-olds -drop-out-of-church (accessed May 19, 2015); Todd Hillard, Britt Beemer, and Ken Ham Green, *Already Gone: Why Your Kids Will Quit Church and What You Can Do to Stop It* (Green Forest, AR: Master Books, 2009). For discussion of reasons for attrition among Christian youth, see David Kinnaman, *You Lost Me: Why Young Christians Are Leaving Church . . . and Rethinking Faith* (Grand Rapids, MI: Baker, 2011).
6. Robert Wuthnow, *After the Baby Boomers: How Twenty- and Thirty-Somethings Are Shaping the Future of American Religion* (Princeton, NJ: Princeton University Press, 2007).
7. 2 Peter 3:9 KJV.
8. Pew Research Center, "'Nones' on the Rise."
9. T. J. Espenshade, J. C. Guzman, and C. F. Westoff, "The surprising global variation in replacement fertility," *Population Research and Policy Review*, No. 22 (5/6),(2003): 575.
10. In 2002, the birthrate of undocumented immigrant women was about 3.1 while the birthrate for legal immigrants stood at 2.6. Steven A. Camarota, "Birth Rates Among Immigrants in America: Comparing Fertility in the U.S. and Home Countries," Center for Immigration Studies, October 2005, http://www.cis.org/ImmigrantBirthRates -FertilityUS; Associated Press, "Utah fertility rate tops the U.S. charts," *Deseret News*, Nov. 7, 2010, http://www.deseretnews.com/article/700079435/Utah-fertility-rate-tops-the-US -charts.html; L. P. Greksa, "Population Growth and Fertility Patterns in an Old Order Amish Settlement," *Annals of Human Biology*, Mar-Apr, 2002, 29(2), 192–201; as for birth rates among Orthodox Jews, Jack Wertheimer has written, "An informed estimate gives figures ranging upward from 3.3 children in 'modern Orthodox' families to 6.6 in Haredi or 'ultra-Orthodox' families to a whopping 7.9 in families of Hasidim." Jack Wertheimer, "Jews and the Jewish Birthrate," Aish.com, October 2005, http://www.aish

.com/jw/s/48899452.html (all accessed May 19, 2015).

11. Erick Kaufmann, *Shall the Religious Inherit the Earth?* (London: Profile Books, 2010), xi.

12. Assemblies of God, "AG U.S. Adherents 1975–2013," http://agchurches.org/Sitefiles/Default/RSS/AG.org%20TOP/AG%20Statistical%20Reports/2014/Adhs%20Ann%20 2013.pdf (accessed May 19, 2015).

13. Ibid.

14. U.S. Census Bureau, "The White Population: 2000," *Census 2000 Brief*, August 2001, http://www.census.gov/prod/2001pubs/c2kbr01-4.pdf (accessed May 19, 2015).

15. Assemblies of God, "AG U.S. Adherents by Race 2001–2012." Obtained from Sherri Doty, Statistician, Assemblies of God National Resource Office, Springfield, Missouri, on June 25, 2014.

16. Interview with Scott Temple, Springfield, Missouri, June 25, 2014.

17. Luis Carlos Lopez, "Minorities Will Become the Majority in the U.S. By 2043," *Huffington Post*, March 25, 2013, http://www.huffingtonpost.com/2013/03/25/ minorities-will-become-th_n_2948188.html (accessed May 19, 2015).

18. Assemblies of God, "AG Worldwide Churches And Adherents 1987–2013," agchurches .org, http://agchurches.org/Sitefiles/Default/RSS/AG.org%20TOP/AG%20Statistical%20 Reports/2014/AdhWW%202013.pdf (accessed May 19, 2015).

19. Assemblies of God, "AGWM Vital Stats," Assemblies of God World Missions, December 31, 2013, http://agwm.com/assets/agwmvitalstats.pdf (accessed May 19, 2015).

20. William Molenaar, "Intercultural Ministries," *Celebrating 75 Years of Ministry: U.S. Missions . . . that none perish* (Springfield, MO: Gospel Publishing House, 2012), 64.

21. Ibid.

22. James Kessler, "New Dimensions in Mission America," *Pentecostal Evangel*, August 4, 1985, 26.

23. Interview with Scott Temple, Springfield, Missouri, June 25, 2014.

24. Roland Allen, *Missionary Methods: St. Paul's or Ours?* (Grand Rapids: Wm. B. Eerdmans Publishing Company, 1962). For the classic AG articulation of these principles at work in Latin America, see Melvin L. Hodges, *The Indigenous Church* (Springfield, MO: Gospel Publishing House, 1976).

25. Interview with Scott Temple, Springfield, Missouri, June 25, 2014.

26. Interview with Saturnino González, Tampa, Florida, November 2, 2014.

27. Ibid.

28. Ibid.

29. Ibid.

30. Archbishop Jose H. Gomez, *Immigration and the Next America: Renewing the Soul of Our Nation* (Huntington, IN: Our Sunday Visitor, June 28, 2013).

31. Pew Research Center, "America's Changing Religious Landscape," The Pew Forum on Religion and Public Life, May 12, 2015, http://religions.pewforum.org/reports (accessed May 19, 2015).

32. Archdiocese of Milwaukee, "Hispanic Ministry in the United States," accessed July 10, 2014, http://www.archmil.org/Resources/HispanicMinistryintheUnitedStates.htm (accessed May 19, 2015). Obviously, not all American Hispanics are immigrants or the

children of such, but immigrants account for the lion's share of the growth, as American-born Hispanics have traditionally claimed Roman Catholic identity and, since American-born Hispanics have birthrates similar to other native-born Americans, would not account for much of the growth.

33. Pew Research Center, "America's Changing Religious Landscape."

34. Pew Research Center, "The Global Catholic Population," The Pew Forum on Religion and Public Life, February 13, 2013, http://www.pewforum.org/2013/02/13/the-global -catholic-population/ (accessed June 15, 2015).

35. Gretchen Livingston and D'vera Cohn, "U.S. Birth Rate Falls to a Record Low; Decline Is Greatest Among Immigrants," *Pew Research Social and Demographic Trends*, November 29, 2012, http://www.pewsocialtrends.org/2012/11/29/u-s-birth-rate-falls-to-a-record-low -decline-is-greatest-among-immigrants/ (accessed May 19, 2015).

36. Ibid.

37. Elizabeth Dias, "¡Evangélicos!," *Time*, April 2013, 20–29. See also Pew Research Center, "The Shifting Religious Identity of Latinos in the United States," The Pew Forum on Religion and Public Life, May 7, 2014, http://www.pewtrusts.org/our_work_report_ detail.aspx?id=85899545262 (accessed May 19, 2015).

38. Roger Finke and Rodney Stark, *The Churching of America, 1776–2005: Winners and Losers in Our Religious Economy* (New Brunswick, NJ: Rutgers University Press, 2005), 241.

39. Ibid.

40. Philip Jenkins, *The Next Christendom: The Coming of Global Christianity* (New York: Oxford University Press, 2011).

41. Pew Research Center, "Global Christianity – A Report on the Size and Distribution of the World's Christian Population," The Pew Forum on Religion and Public Life, December 29, 2011, http://www.pewforum.org/2011/12/19/global-christianity-exec/ (accessed May 19, 2015).

42. Pew Research Center, "The Future of the Global Muslim Population," The Pew Forum on Religion and Public Life, January 27, 2011, http://www.pewforum.org/2011/01/27/the -future-of-the-global-muslim-population/ (accessed May 19, 2015).

43. Pew Research Center, "The Global Religious Landscape: Hindus," The Pew Forum on Religion and Public Life, December 18, 2012, http://www.pewforum.org/2012/12/18/ global-religious-landscape-hindu/ (accessed May 19, 2015).

44. Peter Berger, "Counting Christians in China," The American Interest, August 17, 2010, http://www.the-american-interest.com/berger/2010/08/17/counting-christians-in-china/ (accessed May 19, 2015).

45. Peter Berger, "Counting Christians in China." See also World Christian Database, http:// www.worldchristiandatabase.org/wcd/about/country.asp (accessed May 19, 2015).

46. Peter Berger, "Counting Christians in China."

47. Berkley Center on Religion, Peace, and World Affairs, George Washington University, "South Korea," *Resources on Faith, Ethics, and Public Life*, http://berkleycenter.georgetown .edu/resources/countries/print?id=south-korea (accessed May 19, 2015).

48. U.S. Department of State, "Vietnam: International Religious Freedom Report 2006" *Diplomacy in Action*, accessed August 6, 2014, http://www.state.gov/j/drl/rls/ irf/2006/71363.htm (accessed May 19, 2015).

49. Staff, "The Explosion of Christianity in Africa," Christianity.com, http://www.christianity
.com/church/church-history/timeline/2001-now/the-explosion-of-christianity-in-africa
-11630859.html (accessed May 19, 2015).

50. Robbie Corey-Boulet, "With 176 million Catholics, Africa gains prominence," *USA Today*, March 12, 2013, http://www.usatoday.com/story/news/world/2013/03/12/
catholic-church-africa/1963171/ (accessed May 19, 2015).

51. Lillian Kwon, "Pew Part Two: Pentecostalism in Africa," *Christian Post*, November 18, 2006, http://www.christianpost.com/news/pew-part-two-pentecostalism-in-africa-23528/
(accessed May 19, 2015).

52. Pew Research Center, "Overview: Pentecostalism in Latin America," The Pew Forum on Religion and Public Life, October 5, 2006, http://www.pewforum.org/2006/10/05/
overview-pentecostalism-in-latin-america/ (accessed May 19, 2015).

53. Pew Research Center, "Spirit and Power – A 10-Country Survey of Pentecostals," The Pew Forum on Religion and Public Life, October 5, 2006, http://www.pewforum.
org/2006/10/05/spirit-and-power/ (accessed May 19, 2015).

54. Pew Research Center, "Global Survey of Evangelical Protestant Leaders," The Pew Forum on Religion and Public Life, June 22, 2011, http://www.pewforum.org/2011/06/22/
global-survey-of-evangelical-protestant-leaders/ (accessed May 19, 2015).

55. Alex Murashko, "Samuel Rodriguez on Mega Merger of over 500,000 Latino Churches: We're Not Drinking the Kool-Aid, Christianity Is Not in Decline," *Christian Post,* June 27, 2014, http://www.christianpost.com/news/samuel-rodriguez-on-mega-merger-of-over
-500000-churches-were-not-drinking-the-kool-aid-christianity-is-not-in-decline-122252/
(accessed May 19, 2015).

Chapter 2

1. "Pilgrim," *Dictionary.com*, http://dictionary.reference.com/browse/pilgrim?s=t (accessed June 15, 2015).

2. David Aikman reports on the widespread belief in China that the West has prospered as a result of its Christian worldview in his classic report, *Jesus in Beijing: How Christianity Is Transforming China and Changing the Global Balance of Power* (Washington, D.C.: Regnery, 2003).

3. Interview with Edgardo Montano, Sarasota, Florida, August 1, 2014.

4. Ibid.

5. Ibid.

6. According to Sir William Ramsey, the Greek writer Dion Chrysostom refers to Heracles as the "*archegos*" of Paul's home city of Tarsus, noting that the term refers to a "leader in a migration." For a thorough discussion of this concept, see Irad Malkin, *Religion and Colonization in Ancient Greece,* Studies in Greek and Roman Religion, number 3 (New York: Brill, 1987), 241–60; and William Ramsey, *The Cities of St. Paul: Their Influence on His Life and Thought: The Cities of Eastern Asia Minor* (Grand Rapids, MI: Baker, 1960), 136. For a further discussion of the usage of *archegos* in Hebrews, see David E. Aune, "Heracles and Christ: Heracles Imagery in the Christology of Early Christianity," *Greeks, Romans, and Christians: Essays in Honor of Abraham J. Malherbe* (Minneapolis: Fortress, 1990), 3–19.

7. Hebrews 11:8–10.
8. Hebrews 11:13–16, emphasis added.
9. Hebrews 11:39–40.
10. Traditional folk song, "The Wayfaring Stranger," no date.
11. See Don Piper and Cecil Murphey, *90 Minutes in Heaven: A True Story of Death & Life* (Grand Rapids, MI: Revell, 2004); Todd Burpo, *Heaven Is for Real: A Little Boy's Astounding Story of His Trip to Heaven and Back* (Nashville, TN: Thomas Nelson, 2011).
12. Genesis 1:26.
13. Genesis 1:27.
14. Tom Rath and Jim Harter, *Wellbeing: The Five Essential Elements* (New York: Gallup Press, 2010).
15. Genesis 1:28.
16. Revelation 7:9–10.
17. Genesis 3:23–25.
18. Genesis 4:13–14.
19. Genesis 9:1.
20. For more detail, see Joseph L. Castleberry, *Inmigrantes de Dios: A Bilingual Blog for Immigrants and People Who Love Them,* http://www.inmigrantesdedios.org.
21. Genesis 11:4.
22. Genesis 12:1–3.
23 Genesis 12:10–20.
24. Genesis 14:1–24.
25. Genesis 16:1–16. The Bible does not protect the reputation of its heroes from their worst deeds. Abraham enjoyed God's election through grace, not through his own personal righteousness, and like us, he was a sinner saved by grace.
26. Genesis 20:1–18.
27. Genesis 24:1–66.
28. For more on these episodes, see Joseph Castleberry, *Immigrants in the Heart of God*, www.inmigrantesdedios.org.
29. See Peter Harrison, "Fill the Earth and Subdue It: Biblical Warrants for Colonization in Seventeenth Century England," *Journal of Religious History*, 2005, 3–24. See also John White, *A Commentary upon the First Three Chapters of the First Book of Moses called Genesis,* Book 1 (London: 1656), 113. For a late Colonial Era commentary, see H. C. Leupold, *Exposition of Genesis,* vol. 1 (Grand Rapids, MI: Baker Book House, 1942), 96.
30. Isaiah 49:6.
31. Deuteronomy 26:5; Matthew 1:1–21.
32. Matthew 28:19.
33. "Crop Facts," *Washington Apples*, accessed August 25, 2014, http://bestapples.com/facts/facts_crop.aspx (accessed May 19, 2015).
34. "Washington Apple History," *Washington Apples*, accessed August 25, 2014, http://www.bestapples.com/facts/facts_washington.aspx (accessed May 19, 2015).
35. Telephone interview with Jesús De Paz, August 25, 2014.
36. Ibid.
37. Ibid.

38. Ibid.
39. Ibid.

Chapter 3

1. Bob Young, "Retail pot to get rolling Tuesday," *Seattle Times*, July 6, 2014, A1.
2. Tamar Lewin, "Coming to U.S. for baby—and womb to carry it," *Seattle Times*, July 6, 2014, A11.
3. Maureen Dowd, "Who Do We Think We Are?" *New York Times*, July 6, 2014, SR1.
4. Kevin Drum, "Liberals Started the Culture War, and We Should Be Proud of Continuing It," *Mother Jones*, March 19, 2012, http://www.motherjones.com/kevin-drum/2012/03/liberals-started-culture-war-we-should-proud-continuing-it (accessed May 19, 2015).
5. Maureen Dowd, "Who Do We Think We Are?" *New York Times*, July 6, 2014, SR1.
6. Ibid.
7. "Mexican Standoff," Wikipedia, http://en.wikipedia.org/wiki/Mexican_standoff (accessed July 6, 2014).
8. Samuel Rodríguez, *The Lamb's Agenda: Why Jesus Is Calling You to a Life of Righteousness and Justice* (Nashville: Thomas Nelson, 2013).
9. "The Mayflower Compact," U.S. Constitution, accessed July 6, 2014, http://www.usconstitution.net/mayflower.html.
10. John Winthrop, "A Model of Christian Charity (1630)," The Gilder Lehrman Institute of American History, http://www.gilderlehrman.org/sites/default/files/inline-pdfs/A%20Model%20of%20Christian%20Charity.pdf (accessed August 1, 2014).
11. Matt Hansen and Mark Boster, "Protesters in Murrieta block detainees' buses in tense standoff," *Los Angeles Times*, July 1, 2014, http://www.latimes.com/local/lanow/la-me-ln-immigrants-murrieta-20140701-story.html (accessed June 15, 2015).
12. Contrary to popular belief, Alexis de Tocqueville was not the author of the quote. See John J. Pitney Jr., "The Tocqueville Fraud," *The Weekly Standard*, November 13, 1995, http://www.weeklystandard.com/Content/Protected/Articles/000/000/006/951lhlhc.asp (accessed June 15, 2015).
13. Samuel Rodríguez, *The Lamb's Agenda: Why Jesus is calling you to a life of righteousness and justice* (Nashville: Thomas Nelson, 2013), xvii–xix.
14. Katharine Lee Bates, "America the Beautiful," 1913, USA Flag Site, http://www.usa-flag-site.org/song-lyrics/america.shtml (accessed July 6, 2014).
15. Bono, "U2's Bono: Budget Cuts Can Impact Social Enterprise, Global Change," Georgetown University, November 12, 2012, http://www.georgetown.edu/news/bono-speaks-at-gu.html (accessed June 15, 2015).
16. Bradley R. E. Wright, *Upside: Surprising Good News about the State of Our World* (Minneapolis: Bethany House, 2011); Andrea Palpant Dilley, "The Surprising Discovery about Those Colonialist, Proselytizing Missionaries," *Christianity Today*, January 18, 2014, http://www.christianitytoday.com/ct/2014/january-february/world-missionaries-made.html?paging=off (accessed June 15, 2015).
17. William Butler Yeats, "The Second Coming," *Michael Robartes and the Dancer* (Kuala Press, 1921).
18. Zechariah 4:6 (NKJV).

19. Philippians 4:13.

20. Randy Hurst, "How Can the Lost Billions Be Reached?" *Today's Pentecostal Evangel, World Missions Edition*, June 2008, http://world.ag.org/article/how-1 (accessed June 15, 2015).

21. *Time* Staff, "The 2013 Time 100 Poll: Sammy Rodríguez," *Time*, March 22, 2013, http://time100.time.com/2013/03/28/time-100-poll/slide/samuel-Rodríguez/ (accessed July 6, 2014).

22. Rick Warren, "The 2013 Time 100: Wilfredo de Jesús," *Time*, April 18, 2013, http://time100.time.com/2013/04/18/time-100/slide/wilfredo-de-jesus/ (accessed July 6, 2014).

23. "Rev. Samuel Rodríguez," NHCLC, http://nhclc.org/rev-samuel-Rodríguez/ (accessed July 6, 2014).

24. William Shakespeare, *Romeo and Juliet*, act 2, scene 2.

25. Frederick Clarkson, "Rev. Samuel Rodríguez: Not So Moderate," *The Public Eye*, Fall, 2012, http://www.politicalresearch.org/wp-content/uploads/downloads/2012/12/Fall.2012.Public-Eye.pdf (accessed July 6, 2014).

26. Gabriel Salguero, "God's Politics: My Living Paradox,"*Beliefnet*, April, 2007, http://www.beliefnet.com/columnists/godspolitics/2007/04/rev-gabriel-salguero-my-living-paradox.html (accessed May 4, 2015).

27. Frederick Clarkson, "Rev. Samuel Rodriguez: Not So Moderate," Political Research Associates, October 2, 2012, accessed June 11, 2015, http://www.politicalresearch.org/2012/10/02/rev-samuel-rodriguez-not-so-moderate/#sthash.ACfiAOSo.KXjeWiY8.dpbs ((accessed July 6, 2014).

Chapter 4

1. Revelation 6:2 (NKJV). This appropriation of biblical language does not imply any prophetic claim, but rather a simple analogy.

2. Charles C. Mann, *1491: New Revelations of the Americas Before Columbus* (New York: Knopf, 2006).

3. José Casanova, "Religion, European Secular Identities, and European Integration," *Religion in the New Europe*, vol. 2 (Budapest, Hungary: Central European University Press, 2006), 30.

4. Richard F. Kuisel, "Coca-Cola and the Cold War: The French Face Americanization, 1948–1953," *French Historical Studies*, 1991, 96–116.

5. Barry R. Chiswick, "Immigration Policy and Immigrant Quality: Are Immigrants Favorably Self-Selected?" *AEA Papers and Proceedings,* May 1999, 181.

6. Interview with Hilario Garza, Kirkland, Washington, July 8, 2014.

7. Joseph L. Castleberry, "The Immigrant and the Four Freedoms," *TuDecides/You Decide: A Bilingual Newspaper*, http://tudecidesmedia.com/our-faith-the-immigrant-and-the-four-freedoms-p4890-128.htm (accessed July 25, 2014).

8. Gabriel García Márquez, *El Coronel No Tiene Quien le Escriba* (New York, NY: Vintage Español, 2010), 64.

9. *Which Way Home.* Directed by Rebecca Cammisa. United States: HBO, 2009, https://www.netflix.com/WiMovie/70117031?trkid=2361637 (accessed July 25, 2014).

10. Ross Douthat, "The Parent Trap," *New York Times*, July 20, 2014, http://www.nytimes

.com/2014/07/20/opinion/sunday/ross-douthat-the-parent-trap.html?_r=0 (accessed July 25, 2014).

11. Joseph L. Castleberry, *Your Deepest Dream: Discovering God's True Vision for Your Life* (Colorado Springs: NavPress, 2012), 121.

Chapter 5

1. Matthew Soerens, "Are There Aliens in the Bible?" *G92*, September 26, 2011, http://g92.org/are-there-aliens-in-the-bible/ (accessed October 2, 2014)

2. Elizabeth Burnes and Marisa Louie, "THE A-FILES: Finding Your Immigrant Ancestors," *Genealogy Notes*, Spring 2013, 54, http://www.archives.gov/publications/prologue/2013/spring/a-files.pdf (accessed October 2, 2014).

3. Acts 4:19; 5:29; Daniel 3:18.

4. Subcommittee on Africa, *Global Health, and Human Rights of the Committee on Foreign Affairs, U.S. House of Representatives, China's One Child Policy: The Government's Massive Crime Against Women and Unborn Babies* (Washington, D.C.: U.S. Government Printing Office, 2011).

5. Emma Goldman, "People & Events: Immigration and Deportation at Ellis Island," *American Experience*, Public Broadcasting System, http://www.pbs.org/wgbh/amex/goldman/peopleevents/e_ellis.html (accessed October 2, 2014).

6. Genesis 26:22 (NLT).

7. Jeremiah 29:7.

8. Samuel Rutherford, *Lex Rex, or The Law and the Prince* (London: 1644).

9. Dan Berger and Angélica Cházaro, "What's behind the hunger strike at Northwest Detention Center," *Seattle Times*, March 19, 2014, http://seattletimes.com/html/opinion/2023173231_danbergerangelicachazaroopedprisonhungerstrike20xml.html (accessed June 11, 2015).

10. Alex Altman, "Prison Hunger Strike Puts Spotlight on Immigration Detention," *Time*, March 17, 2014, http://time.com/27663/prison-hunger-strike-spotlights-on-immigration-detention/ (accessed June 11, 2015).

11. Peter Ferrara, "Reaganomics vs. Obamanomics: Facts and Figures," *Forbes*, May 5, 2011, http://www.forbes.com/sites/peterferrara/2011/05/05/reaganomics-vs-obamanomics-facts-and-figures/ (accessed June 11, 2015).

12. Mark Hugo Lopez and Ana Gonzalez-Barrera, "High rate of deportations continue under Obama despite Latino disapproval," Pew Research Center, Fact Tank, September 19, 2013, http://www.pewresearch.org/fact-tank/2013/09/19/high-rate-of-deportations-continue-under-obama-despite-latino-disapproval/; Nora Kaplan-Bricker, "Who's the Real Deporter-in-Chief: Bush or Obama?," *New Republic*, April 17, 2014, http://www.newrepublic.com/article/117412/deportations-under-obama-vs-bush-who-deported-more-immigrants (both accessed June 11, 2015).

13. "Silly Laws," kubik.org, accessed July 30, 2014, http://www.kubik.org/lighter/silly.htm.

14. G. E. Miller, "The U.S. Is the Most Overworked Developed Nation in the World—When Do We Draw the Line?" *20 Something Finance,* July 20, 2014, http://20somethingfinance.com/american-hours-worked-productivity-vacation/ (accessed June 11, 2015).

15. John Lantigua, "Illegal Immigrants Pay Social Security Tax, Won't Benefit," *Seattle Times*, December 28, 2011, http://seattletimes.com/html/nationworld/2017113852_immigtaxes29.html (accessed June 11, 2015).

Chapter 6

1. Emile Durkheim, *The Division of Labour in Society* (New York: The Free Press, 1993), ix.

2. Roger Finke and Rodney Stark, *The Churching of America, 1776–2005: Winners and Losers in Our Religious Economy* (New Brunswick, NJ: Rutgers University Press, 2005), 35.

3. For more on this topic, see Oscar Handlin, *The Uprooted: The Epic Story of the Great Migrations that Made the American People* (Boston: Little, Brown and Company, 1952).

4. William G. McLoughlin, *Revivals, Awakenings, and Reform*, Chicago History of American Religion (Chicago: University of Chicago Press, 1978), 2.

5. William Fogel, *The Fourth Great Awakening and the Future of Egalitarianism* (Chicago and London: University of Chicago Press, 2000).

6. Thomas Picketty, trans. Arthur Goldhammer, *Capital in the Twenty-First Century* (Cambridge, MA: Harvard University Press, 2013).

7. David Goldman, *How Civilizations Die (and Why Islam Is Dying Too)* (Washington, D.C.: Regnery Publishing, 2011).

8. Most churches being planted in Europe today depend on immigrant/missionary leadership, but the bigger story in Europe is the founding of mosques by the burgeoning Muslim immigrant population that will almost certainly come to dominate European demographics over the next century. See André Droogers, Cornelis van der Laan, Wout van Laar, eds., *Fruitful in This Land: Pluralism, Dialogue and Healing in Migrant Pentecostalism* (Zoetermeer, Netherlands: Boekencentrum, 2006); Bruce Bawer, *While Europe Slept: How Radical Islam Is Destroying the West from Within* (New York: Broadway Books, 2006); Bat Ye'or, *Eurabia: The Euro-Arab Axis* (Madison and Teaneck, NJ: Farleigh Dickinson University Press, 2005); Bruce S. Thornton, *Decline & Fall: Europe's Slow Motion Suicide* (New York: Encounter Books, 2007). For an opposing view on the eventual Muslim domination of Europe, see Pew Research Center, "The Future of the Global Muslim Population," The Pew Forum on Religion and Public Life, January 27, 2011, http://www.Pewforum.Org/2011/01/27/The-Future-Of-The-Global-Muslim-Population/ (accessed August 15, 2014).

9. Roger Finke and Rodney Stark, *The Churching of America, 1776–2005: Winners and Losers in Our Religious Economy* (New Brunswick, NJ: Rutgers University Press, 2005), 88.

10. "History of immigration to the United States," *Wikipedia*, http://en.wikipedia.org/wiki/History_of_immigration_to_the_United_States (accessed August 15, 2014).

11. Roger Finke and Rodney Stark, *The Churching of America, 1776–2005: Winners and Losers in Our Religious Economy* (New Brunswick, NJ: Rutgers University Press, 2005), 32.

12. Roger Finke, "The Illusion of Shifting Demand: Supply-Side Interpretations of American Religious History," *Retelling U.S. Religious History* (Berkeley: University of California Press, 1997), 108–26.

13. Mark Noll, *A History of Christianity in the United States and Canada* (Grand Rapids, MI: Eerdmans, 1992), 90.

14. Ibid., 105; Edward Davis, "Early Advancement Among the Five Civilized Tribes," *Chronicles of Oklahoma*, June, 1936, 163.

15. Christine Leigh Heyrman, "The First Great Awakening," *Divining America: Religion in American History*, http://nationalhumanitiescenter.org/tserve/eighteen/ekeyinfo/grawaken .htm (accessed July 10, 2014).

16. Jesse Wendell Castleberry and Rosalie Nieft Castleberry, *Castleberry and Allied Families*, vol. 1 (Windermere, FL: Jesse Wendell Castleberry, 1966).

17. Roger Finke and Rodney Stark, *The Churching of America, 1776–2005: Winners and Losers in Our Religious Economy* (New Brunswick, NJ: Rutgers University Press, 2005), 23.

18. J. Edwin Orr, *Campus Aflame: Dynamic of Student Religious Revolution* (Glendale, CA: Regal Books, 1971), 19.

19. Ibid., 17.

20. J. Edwin Orr, "The Role of Prayer in Spiritual Awakening," *Anglican Revivalist*, http:// anglicanrevivalist.blogspot.com/2008/01/j-edwin-orr-role-of-prayer-in-spiritual.html (accessed 6/3/2014).

21. Mark Noll, *A History of Christianity in the United States and Canada* (Grand Rapids, MI: Eerdmans, 1992), 166.

22. Noll, Ibid.

23. Albert Raboteau, *Slave Religion: The "Invisible Institution" in the Antebellum South* (New York: Oxford University Press), 132.

24. Noll, *A History of Christianity in the United States and Canada* (Grand Rapids, MI: Eerdmans, 1992), 167. For uninitiated readers, the "barking exercise" involved ecstatic worshippers who would literally bark like dogs as an act of praise. The phenomenon has recurred all over the world and still characterizes some of the most frenzied revival meetings in America and Canada.

25. Raboteau, *Slave Religion: The "Invisible Institution" in the Antebellum South* (New York: Oxford University Press), 132.

26. Noll, *A History of Christianity in the United States and Canada* (Grand Rapids, MI: Eerdmans, 1992), 167.

27. Ibid.

28. Ibid.

29. Ibid.

30. "History of immigration to the United States," *Wikipdedia*, http://en.wikipedia.org/wiki/ History_of_immigration_to_the_United_States (accessed 6/3/2014).

31. Jenna Weissman Josselitt, *Parade of Faiths: Immigration and American Religion* (New York: Oxford University Press, 2011), 27.

32. Mark Noll, *A History of Christianity in the United States and Canada* (Grand Rapids, MI: Eerdmans, 1992), 205. For another more nuanced view of the statistics, see Roger Finke and Rodney Stark, *The Churching of America, 1776–2005: Winners and Losers in Our Religious Economy* (New Brunswick, NJ: Rutgers University Press, 2005), 118–20.

33. Ibid., 207.

34. Ibid., 210.

35. Ibid., 212; Jenna Weissman Josselitt, *Parade of Faiths: Immigration and American Religion*

(New York: Oxford University Press, 2011), 29.

36. Jenna Weissman Josselitt, *Parade of Faiths: Immigration and American Religion* (New York: Oxford University Press, 2011), 30.

37. Ibid., 36.

38. Ibid., 22.

39. Mark Noll, *A History of Christianity in the United States and Canada* (Grand Rapids, MI: Eerdmans, 1992), 220.

40. William G. McLoughlin, *Revivals, Awakenings, and Reform: Chicago History of American Religion* (Chicago: University of Chicago Press, 1980), chapter 4.

41. Pew Research Center, "Global Christianity: A Report on the Size and Distribution of the World's Christian Population," December 2011, http://www.pewforum.org/files/2011/12/Christianity-fullreport-web.pdf (accessed June 11, 2015).

42. Noll, *A History of Christianity in the United States and Canada* (Grand Rapids, MI: Eerdmans, 1992), 179–80.

43. "A. T. Pierson," *Wikipedia*, http://en.wikipedia.org/wiki/Arthur_Tappan_Pierson (accessed August 1, 2014).

44. Michael Parker, "Mobilizing a Generation for Missions," *Christianity History*, August 6, 2009, http://www.christianitytoday.com/ch/bytopic/missionsworldchristianity/mobilizinggenerations.html (accessed August 1, 2014).

45. Ibid.

46. Ibid.

47. Vinson Synan, *The Holiness-Pentecostal Movement in the United States of America* (Grand Rapids, MI: Eerdmans, 1971).

48. Frank Bartleman, *Another Wave Rolls In!: What Really Happened at Azusa Street* (Monroeville, PA: Whitaker Books, 1970), 55.

49. Harvey Gallagher Cox, *Fire from Heaven: The Rise of Pentecostal Spirituality and the Reshaping of Religion in the Twenty-First Century* (Cambridge, MA: Da Capo Press, 2001).

50. Douglas Peterson, Murray Dempster, and Byron Klaus, eds., *The Globalization of Pentecostalism: A Religion Made to Travel* (Oxford: Regnum Books, 1999).

51. Andrew Chesnut, "Pope Francis Joins the 'Samba School' of Charismatic Catholicism," *Huffington Post*, June 5, 2014, http://www.huffingtonpost.com/r-andrew-chesnut/charismatic-pope-francis_b_5444340.html (accessed August 1, 2014).

52. Robert Crosby, "A New Kind of Pentecostal," *Christianity Today*, August 3, 2011, http://www.christianitytoday.com/ct/2011/august/newkindpentecostal.html?paging=off (accessed August 1, 2014).

53. Assemblies of God, "AG Worldwide Churches And Adherents 1987–2013," agchurch.org, http://agchurches.org/Sitefiles/Default/RSS/AG.org%20TOP/AG%20Statistical%20Reports/2014/AdhWW%202013.pdf (accessed August 1, 2014).

Chapter 7

1. Associated Press, "Papal First: Francis Visits Pentecostal Church, *New York Times*, July 28, 2014, http://www.nytimes.com/aponline/2014/07/28/world/europe/ap-eu-rel-vatican-pentecostals.html?_r=0 (accessed August 2, 2014).

2. Sarah Eekhoff Zylstra, "Pope Francis Apologizes for Pentecostal Persecution, But Italy's Evangelicals Remain Wary," *Christianity Today*, July 30, 2014, http://www .christianitytoday.com/gleanings/2014/july/pope-francis-apologizes-for-pentecostal -persecution-italy.html (accessed August 2, 2014).

3. Cindy Wooden, "Meeting 200 Pentecostals, Pope Renews Friendship, Talks Unity," *Catholic News Service,* August 1, 2014, http://www.cdom.org/CatholicDiocese.php?op =Article_Meeting+200+Pentecostals%2C+pope+renews+friendship%2C+talks+unity (accessed August 2, 2014).

4. John L. Allen Jr., "The Top Five 'Missing Mega-trends' Shaping Catholicism,"*National Catholic Reporter,* December 28, 2006, http://ncronline.org/blogs/all-things-catholic/ top-five-%C3%ABmissing-mega-trends-shaping-catholicism (accessed August 2, 2014).

5. Ibid.

6. Pew Research Center, "The Shifting Religious Identity of Latinos in the United States," The Pew Forum on Religion and Public Life, May 7, 2014, http://www.pewforum.org/ 2014/05/07/the-shifting-religious-identity-of-latinos-in-the-united-states/ (accessed August 2, 2014).

7. Virginia Garrard-Burnett, "Catholicism Can Win Back Evangelicals in Latin America," *New York Times*, March 15, 2013, http://www.nytimes.com/roomfordebate/2013/03/14/ does-pope-franciss-election-signal-a-catholic-comeback-for-latin-america/catholicism-can -win-back-evangelicals-in-latin-america (accessed August 2, 2014).

8. Ibid.

9. Elizabeth Dias, "¡Evangélicos!," *Time*, April 2013, 20–29. See also Pew Research Center, "The Shifting Religious Identity of Latinos in the United States," The Pew Forum on Religion and Public Life, May 7, 2014, http://www.pewtrusts.org/our_work_report_ detail.aspx?id=85899545262 (accessed August 2, 2014).

10. Pew Research Center, "The Shifting Religious Identity of Latinos in the United States," The Pew Forum on Religion and Public Life, May 7, 2014, http://www.pewforum.org/ 2014/05/07/the-shifting-religious-identity-of-latinos-in-the-united-states/ (accessed August 2, 2014).

11. "Erwin McManus," *Wikipedia*, http://en.wikipedia.org/wiki/Erwin_McManus (accessed August 2, 2014).

12. Thomas Bergler, *The Juvenilization of American Christianity* (Grand Rapids: Eerdmans, 2012).

13. Elizabeth Dias, "¡Evangélicos!"

14. Roger Finke and Rodney Stark, *The Churching of America, 1776–2005: Winners and Losers in Our Religious Economy* (New Brunswick, NJ: Rutgers University Press, 2005), 1.

15. Ibid.

16. Elizabeth Dias, "¡Evangélicos!"

17. For more on Pentecostalism as a global culture, see Karla Poewe, ed., *Charismatic Christianity as a Global Culture* (Columbia, SC: University of South Carolina Press, 1994).

18. Galatians 5:1.

19. For further discussion of these terms, see Darrell Guder, ed., *Missional Church: A Vision for the Sending of the Church in North America* (Grand Rapids, MI: Wm. B. Eerdmans

Publishing Company, 1998); Billy Hornsby, *The Attractional Church: Growth Through a Refreshing, Relational, and Relevant Church Experience* [Kindle Edition] (New York: FaithWords, 2011).

20. Elizabeth Dias, "¡Evangélicos!"
21. David Briggs, "Fire in the Pews: Pentecostal-Catholic Competition Reviving Religion in Latin America," *Huffington Post*, November 4, 2013, http://www.huffingtonpost.com/david-briggs/fire-in-the-pews-pentecos_b_4212677.html (accessed June 15, 2015).
22. Pew Research Center, "The Shifting Religious Identity of Latinos in the United States," The Pew Forum on Religion and Public Life, May 7, 2014, http://www.pewforum.org/2014/05/07/the-shifting-religious-identity-of-latinos-in-the-united-states/ (accessed August 2, 2014).

Chapter 8
1. Roger Finke and Rodney Stark, *The Churching of America, 1776–2005: Winners and Losers in Our Religious Economy* (New Brunswick, NJ: Rutgers University Press, 2005), 241.
2. Garrison Keillor, *A Prairie Home Companion*, accessed January 2, 2015, http://prairiehome.org/listen/podcast/ (accessed July 25, 2014).
3. Jenna Weissman Josselitt, *Parade of Faiths: Immigration and American Religion* (New York: Oxford University Press, 2011), 30.
4. Ibid., 31.
5. Finke and Stark, *The Churching of America, 1776–2005: Winners and Losers in Our Religious Economy* (New Brunswick, NJ: Rutgers University Press, 2005), 241.
6. For more on this phenomenon, see Jaweed Kaleem, "Hispanic Churches, Historically Spanish-Speaking, Adopt More English to Appeal to U.S.-Born Latinos," *Huffington Post*, December 26, 2012, http://www.huffingtonpost.com/2012/12/26/hispanic-churches-latinos-spanish-english-language_n_2333178.html (accessed July 25, 2014).
7. Interview with Samuel Rodríguez, Sacramento, California, July 10, 2014.
8. William A. Henry III, "Beyond the Melting Pot," *Time*, April 9, 1990, http://content.time.com/time/magazine/article/0,9171,969770,00.html (accessed July 25, 2014).
9. Interview with Varun Laohaprasit, Bellevue, Washington, July 24, 2014.
10. Ibid.
11. Ibid.
12. Ibid.
13. Ibid.
14. Ibid.
15. Ibid.
16. Ibid.
17. Ibid.
18. Martin Luther King Jr., "Communism's Challenge to Christianity" speech, Atlanta, Georgia, August 9, 1953, The Martin Luther King, Jr. Papers Project, http://mlk-kpp01.stanford.edu/primarydocuments/Vol6/9Aug1953Communism%27sChallengetoChristianity.pdf (accessed July 25, 2014).
19. For a listing of a few large multi-ethnic churches, see "Multi-ethnic Churches listed in

Outreach's 2009 Top 100 & Fastest Growing and Largest Churches," *Unity in Christ*, http://unityinchristmagazine.com/misc/side-bars/multi-ethnic-churches-listed-in-outreach's-2009-top-100-fastest-growing-and-largest-churches/ (accessed August 2, 2014).

20. For a representative sample, see United Church of Christ, "Immigration," United Church of Christ, http://www.ucc.org/justice/immigration/ (accessed August 15, 2014).

21. Fed Ranches, Marjorie Royle, and Richard Taylor, "Now Is the Time for New Church Development: A Report on 50 Years of Church Development in the United Church of Christ," United Church of Christ, January 5, 2008, http://www.ucc.org/newchurch/pdfs/50-yr-nc-report1.pdf (accessed August 15, 2014).

22. Presbyterian Mission Agency, "The Top 10 Most Frequently Asked Questions about the PC(USA)," Presbyterian Mission Agency, https://www.presbyterianmission.org/ministries/research/10faq/#7 (accessed August 10, 2014).

23. Korean Congregational Support Office, "2013 Directory Korean Congregations," Korean Congregational Support Office, accessed August 10, 2014, https://www.pcusa.org/site_media/media/uploads/korean/pdf/directory.pdf.

24. Presbyterian Mission Agency, "The Top 10 Most Frequently Asked Questions about the PC(USA)," Presbyterian Mission Agency, accessed August 10, 2014, https://www.presbyterianmission.org/ministries/research/10faq/#7.

25. "What Are the Origins of Hispanic Mennonites in North America?," *Thirdway: Simply Following Jesus*, http://thirdway.com/faq/what-are-the-origins-of-hispanic-mennonites-in-north-america/ (accessed June 15, 2015).

26. Rafael Falcón, "Hispanic Mennonites," *Global Anabaptist Mennonite Encyclopedia Online*, 1989, http://gameo.org/index.php?title=Hispanic_Mennonites (accessed August 10, 2014).

27. Lancaster Mennonite Historical Society, "Statistics," *LMHS.com*, November 27, 2010, http://www.lmhs.org/Home/About/Anabaptist_Statistics (accessed August 10, 2014).

28. Rafael Falcón, "Hispanic Mennonites," *Global Anabaptist Mennonite Encyclopedia Online*, 1989, http://gameo.org/index.php?title=Hispanic_Mennonites (accessed August 10, 2014).

29. "The Mennonites," *Thirdway: Simply Following Jesus*, http://thirdway.com/mennonites/ (accessed June 15, 2015).

30. Thom S. Rainer, "The 15 Largest Protestant Denominations in the United States," *Christian Post*, March 27, 2013, http://www.christianpost.com/news/the-15-largest-protestant-denominations-in-the-united-states-92731/ (accessed June 15, 2015).

31. "Ethnic Specific and Multicultural Ministries," *Evangelical Lutheran Church in America*, http://www.elca.org/Our-Work/Congregations-and-Synods/Ethnic-Specific-and-Multicultural-Ministries (accessed June 15, 2015).

32. "U.S. Religious Landscape Survey: Religious Beliefs and Practices, Diverse and Politically Relevant: Detailed Data Tables Washington D.C.," Pew Forum on Religion and Public Life, June 2008.

33. "Churches of Christ," *Wikipedia*, http://en.wikipedia.org/wiki/Churches_of_Christ (accessed August 10, 2014).

34. Martin Marty, "Southern Baptists Waning," *Huffington Post*, June 17, 2014, http://www

.huffingtonpost.com/martin-marty/southern-baptists-waning_b_5505166.html (accessed August 10, 2014).

35. Tobin Perry, "Ethnic Congregations up 66% for Southern Baptists Since '98," *Baptist Press*, January 23, 2013, http://www.bpnews.net/39568/ethnic-congregations-up-66-for -southern-baptists-since-98 (accessed August 10, 2014).

36. Ibid.

37. Ibid.

38. Melissa Steffan, "African Americans (Not Latinos) Lead Surge in 'Non-Anglo' Southern Baptist Congregations," *Christianity Today*, January 30, 2013, http://www .christianitytoday.com/gleanings/2013/january/african-americans-not-latinos-lead-surge -in-non-anglo.html?paging=off (accessed August 10, 2014).

39. Beth Byrd, "Filipinos gather for fellowship & partnership," *Baptist Press*, June 18, 2013, http://www.bpnews.net/40554/filipinos-gather-for-fellowship—partnership (accessed August 10, 2014).

40. Beth Boyd, "Chinese Baptists set church planting goal," *Baptist Press*, June 18, 2013, http://www.bpnews.net/40555/chinese-baptists-set-church-planting-goal (accessed August 10, 2014).

41. Karen L. Willoughby, "Koreans to Grow Churches, Increase Giving," *Baptist Press*, June 18, 2013, http://www.bpnews.net/40557/koreans-to-grow-churches-increase-giving (accessed August 10, 2014).

42. Wayne Clark and Helen Rountree, "The Powhatans and the Maryland Mainland," *Powhatan Foreign Relations, 1500–1722* (University of Virginia Press, 1993), 114.

43. Cathy Taylor, *Historic Falls Church: Images of America* (Charleston, SC: Arcadia, 2012); Bradley E. Gernand and Nan Netherton, *Falls Church: A Virginia Village Revisited* (Merceline, MO: Wallsworth, 2000), 7, 19.

44. The Falls Church Anglican, "History," *Tfcanglican.org*, 2012, http://www.tfcanglican.org/ pages/page.asp?page_id=185903 (accessed May 21, 2014).

45. Melvin Lee Steadman Jr., *Falls Church by Fence and Fireside* (Falls Church, VA: Falls Church Public Library,1964), 13–17, 37.

46. "Act for Establishing Religious Freedom, January 16, 1786," *Shaping the Constitution*, Virginia Memory, Library of Virginia, http://www.virginiamemory.com/online_ classroom/shaping_the_constitution/doc/religious_freedom; Joan R. Gundersen, "How 'Historic' Are Truro Church and The Falls Church?," Rutgers, December 22, 2006, http:// www.rci.rutgers.edu/~lcrew/dojustice/j392.html (both accessed August 14, 2014).

47. Leith Anderson, *A Church for the 21st Century* (Grand Rapids: Baker Books, 1992).

48. Mary Frances Schjonberg, "Falls Church Episcopal celebrates past, looks to future: Episcopal congregation may still face at least one more legal hurdle," Episcopal News Service, May 15, 2013, http://episcopaldigitalnetwork.com/ens/2013/05/15/falls-church -episcopal-celebrates-past-looks-to-future/ (accessed August 14, 2014).

49. John Yates, "Congregation of The Falls Church Must Begin Again," *Washington Post*, May 11, 2012, http://www.washingtonpost.com/local/congregation-of-the-falls-church-must -begin-again/2012/05/11/gIQA7zZMJU_story.html (accessed August 14, 2014).

50. For more on these developments, see Miranda K. Hassett, *Anglican Communion in Crisis:*

How Episcopal Dissidents and Their African Allies Are Reshaping Anglicanism (Princeton, NJ: Princeton University Press, 2007).

51. Anglican Church in North America, "About the Anglican Church in North America," Anglican Church in North America, http://anglicanchurch.net/?/main/page/abacna (accessed April 27, 2015).

52. "Religious Bodies of the World with at Least 1 Million Adherents," Adherents.com, accessed August 13, 2014, http://www.adherents.com/adh_rb.html (accessed August 14, 2014).

53. Robert E. Weber and Lester Ruth, *Evangelicals on the Canterbury Trail: Why Evangelicals Are Attracted to the Liturgical Church* (New York: Morehouse Publishing, 2013).

54. Robert Duncan, "Anglican Immigrant Initiative," Anglican Church in North America, http://www.anglicanchurch.net/?/main/page/732 (accessed August 13, 2014).

55. Ibid.

Chapter 9

1. Ilona Trofimovich, Northwest University Commencement, Redmond, Washington, May 10, 2014.

2. Ibid.

3. Josiah Bushnell Grinnell, *Men and Events of Forty Years* (Boston, MA: D. Lothrop Company), 87.

4. Herbert Hoover, "Rugged Individualism," speech delivered on October 22, 1928, *Teaching American History*, accessed July 10, 2014, http://teachingamericanhistory.org/library/document/rugged-individualism/.

5. Susan Brown, *The Politics of Individualism: Liberalism, Liberal Feminism, and Anarchism* (Black Rose Books, 1993).

6. George Peter Murdock, *Social Structure* (New York: Macmillan, 1949), 1–22.

7. Jonathan Vespa, Jamie M. Lewis, and Rose M. Kreider, "America's Families and Living Arrangements: 2012," United States Census Bureau, August, 2012, http://www.census.gov/prod/2013pubs/p20-570.pdf (accessed July 10, 2014).

8. Geert Hofstede, Gert Jan Hofstede, and Michael Minkov, *Cultures and Organizations: Software of the Mind, Intercultural Cooperation and Its Importance for Survival* (New York, NY: McGraw-Hill, 2010).

9. Alan Roland, *In Search of Self in India and Japan: Toward a Cross-Cultural Psychology* (Princeton, NJ: Princeton University Press, 1991).

10. *Star Trek: The Next Generation,* "I Borg," Season 5, Episode 23. Directed by Robert Lederman. Written by Gene Roddenberry and René Echevarria. Los Angeles, CA: Paramount Studios, May 9, 1992.

11. *Star Trek, First Contact.* Directed by Jonathon Frakes. Hollywood, CA: Paramount Pictures, 1996.

12. Bruce Bretts and Matt Roush, "Baddies to the Bone: The 60 Nastiest Villains of All Time," *TV Guide*, March 25, 2013, 14–15.

13. R. Stephen Parker, Diana L. Hayko, and Charles M. Hermans, "Individualism and Collectivism: Reconsidering Old Assumptions," *Journal of International Business Research,*

January 2009, http://www.freepatentsonline.com/article/Journal-International-Business
-Research/208956140.html (accessed July 10, 2014).

14. Interview with Hilario Garza, Kirkland, Washington, July 8, 2014.

15. Ibid.

16. Steven A. Camarota, "Illegitimate Nation: An Examination of Out-of-Wedlock Births
Among Immigrants and Natives," Center for Immigration Studies, June 2007, http://
www.cis.org/illegitimate_nation.html (accessed July 10, 2014).

17. Adam Davidson, "It's Official: The Boomerang Kids Won't Leave," *New York Times*, June
20, 2014, http://www.nytimes.com/2014/06/22/magazine/its-official-the-boomerang
-kids-wont-leave.html (accessed July 10, 2014).

18. *Born in East L.A.* Directed by Cheech Marin. United States: Universal Studios, 1987.

19. "Senior Pastor," The Mission, Ebenezer Family Church, http://missionebenezer.com/
seniorpastor.html (accessed August 1, 2014).

20. Telephone interview with Isaac Canales, August 1, 2014.

21. Ibid.

22. Ibid.

23. Ibid.

24. Ibid.

25. Mary Eberstadt. *How the West Really Lost God: A New Theory of Secularization* (West
Conshohocken, PA: Templeton Press, 2013), 5.

26. For historical evidence, see David Goldman, *How Civilizations Die (and Why Islam Is
Dying Too)* (Washington, D.C.: Regnery Publishing, 2011).

27. John Adams, "Quotes of the Founding Fathers: The Importance of a Moral Society," Free
to Pray, http://www.free2pray.info/5founderquotes.html (accessed July 30, 2014).

28. Warren D. TenHouten, *Time and Society* (Albany, NY: SUNY Press, 2006), 58.

Chapter 10

1. Ninoska Marcano, "Mexican-American Pedro Celis vies to unseat Democratic
Congresswoman in Washington state," Fox News Latino, October 21, 2014, http://latino
.foxnews.com/latino/politics/2014/10/21/mexican-american-pedro-celis-hopes-to-unseat
-republican-representative-for/(accessed January 4, 2015).

2. "Board of Directors," Plaza Bank, http://www.plazabankwa.com/about-plaza-bank/board
-of-directors/ (accessed January 4, 2015).

3. Ibid.

4. Ibid.

5. "Meet Pedro Celis," Pedro Celis for Congress, https://pedroforcongress.com/meet-pedro
-celis/ (accessed January 4, 2015).

6. Jens Manuel Krogstad, "Visa cap cuts off immigrants with advanced degrees," *USA
Today*, January 9, 2013, http://www.usatoday.com/story/money/business/2013/01/09/
immigration-science-technology-engineering-math-jobs/1566164/ (accessed January 4,
2015).

7. Mark Gongloff, "The One Chart That Explains Our Grim Economic Future," *Huffington
Post*, April 23, 2014, http://www.huffingtonpost.com/2014/04/23/population-growth

-chart_n_5198251.html (accessed January 4, 2015).

8. Mark Mather, "Fact Sheet: The Decline in U.S. Fertility," *Population Reference Bureau,* July 2012, http://www.prb.org/publications/datasheets/2012/world-population-data-sheet/fact-sheet-us-population.aspx (accessed January 4, 2015).

9. Ibid.

10. Justin Fox, "Piketty's 'Capital,' in a Lot Less than 696 Pages," *Harvard Business Review,* April 24, 2014, https://hbr.org/2014/04/pikettys-capital-in-a-lot-less-than-696-pages/ (accessed January 4, 2015).

11. The U.S. population grew by 105 million people between 1970 and 2010, from 203,302,031 to 308,745,538. See "History," U.S. Census Bureau, August 7, 2014, https://www.census.gov/history/www/through_the_decades/fast_facts/ (accessed January 4, 2015).

12. CAP Immigration Team, "The Facts on Immigration Today," Center for American Progress, October 23, 2014, https://www.americanprogress.org/issues/immigration/report/2014/10/23/59040/the-facts-on-immigration-today-3/ (accessed January 4, 2015).

13. Ian Urbina, "Short on Drivers, Truckers Offer Perks," *New York Times,* February 28, 2006, http://www.nytimes.com/2006/02/28/national/28truckers.html?pagewanted=print (accessed January 4, 2015).

14. Neil Irwin, "The Trucking Industry Needs More Drivers. Maybe It Needs to Pay More," *New York Times,* August 9, 2014, http://www.nytimes.com/2014/08/10/upshot/the-trucking-industry-needs-more-drivers-it-should-try-paying-more.html?abt=0002&abg=1 (accessed January 4, 2015).

15. Natalia Siniavskaia, "Immigrant Workers in Construction," National Association of Home Builders, accessed December 7, 2014, http://www.nahb.org/generic.aspx?genericContentID=49216 (accessed January 4, 2015).

16. "Housing Starts," *Investopedia,* accessed December 7, 2014, http://www.investopedia.com/terms/h/housingstarts.asp (accessed January 4, 2015).

17. *A Day Without a Mexican.* Directed by Sergio Arau. Mexico, D.F.: Altavista Films, 2004.

18. Tracie Cooper, "A Day Without a Mexican (2004)," *New York Times,* http://www.nytimes.com/movies/movie/306597/A-Day-Without-a-Mexican/overview (accessed May 20, 2015).

19. Cheryl Conner, "Business Lessons from Immigrant Entrepreneurs," *Forbes,* May 20, 2014, http://www.forbes.com/sites/cherylsnappconner/2014/05/20/business-lessons-from-immigrant-entrepreneurs/ (accessed January 4, 2015).

20. Ibid.

21. Ibid.

22. Thomas J. Donohue, "The State of American Business 2012," U.S. Chamber of Commerce, January 12, 2012, https://www.uschamber.com/speech/state-american-business-2012-address-thomas-j-donohue-president-ceo-us-chamber-commerce (accessed January 4, 2015).

23. Cheryl Conner, "Business Lessons from Immigrant Entrepreneurs," *Forbes,* May 20, 2014, http://www.forbes.com/sites/cherylsnappconner/2014/05/20/business-lessons-from-immigrant-entrepreneurs/ (accessed January 4, 2015).

24. Barry Chiswick, "Are Immigrants Favorably Self-Selected," *Migration Theory: Talking across Disciplines* (New York: Routledge, 2000), 61–76.

25. Interview with Andrés Panasiuk through electronic mail, February 16, 2015.

26. Ibid.

27. Jose Pagliery, "On the rise: Immigrant entrepreneurs (New Face of Entrepreneurship)," CNNMoney, May 8, 2012, http://money.cnn.com/2012/05/07/smallbusiness/immigration-entrepreneurs/index.htm?iid=HP_River (accessed January 4, 2015).

28. Ibid.

29. Ibid.

30. "Bringing Vitality to Main Street:: How Immigrant Small Businesses Help Local Economies Grow," Fiscal Policy Institute, January 2015, http://fiscalpolicy.org/wp-content/uploads/2015/01/Bringing-Vitality-to-Main-Street.pdf (accessed January 4, 2015).

31. Ibid.

32. R. Borges-Mendez, M. Liu, and P. Watanabe, *Immigrant Entrepreneurs and Neighborhood Revitalization* (Malden, MA: The Immigrant Learning Center, Inc., 2005), 4, 8, 20, 32.

33. Robert W. Fairlie, "Immigrant Entrepreneurs and Small Business Owners, and their Access to Financial Capital," SBA Office of Advocacy, May 2012, https://www.sba.gov/sites/default/files/rs396tot.pdf (accessed January 4, 2015).

34. Mike Handelsman, "4 Alternative Funding Sources," *Entrepreneur*, December 6, 2009, http://www.entrepreneur.com/article/204238 (accessed January 4, 2015).

35. Interview with Andrés Panasiuk through electronic mail, February 16, 2015.

36. Michelle Evans, "Arrival of Financial Cards to Latin America Led to Credit Binge," *Euromonitor International*, August 2, 2014, http://blog.euromonitor.com/2014/08/arrival-of-financial-cards-to-latin-america-led-to-credit-binge.html (accessed June 15, 2015).

37. "Remittances to Latin America Grow, but Mexico Bucks the Trend Faced with the US Slowdown," *The World Bank News*, October 8, 2013, http://www.worldbank.org/en/news/feature/2013/10/04/remesas-latinoamerica-crecimiento-mexico-caida (accessed January 4, 2015).

38. Michael Matza, "Many ways to help immigrant businesses, report says," *Philadelphia Inquirer,* January 15, 2015.

Chapter 11

1. Interview with Jesse Miranda, Springfield, Missouri, August 4, 2014.

2. John U. Ogbu and Herber D. Simons, "Voluntary Immigrants and Involuntary Minorities: A Cultural-Ecological Theory of School Performance with Some Implications for Education," *Anthropology & Education Quarterly*,1998,155–188, http://faculty.washington.edu/rsoder/EDUC310/OgbuSimonsvoluntaryinvoluntary.pdf (accessed August 6, 2014).

3. Interview with Jesse Miranda, Springfield, Missouri, August 4, 2014.

4. Ibid.

5. Ibid.

6. Malcolm Knowles, E. F. Holton III, and R. A. Swanson, *The Adult Learner: The Definitive Classic in Adult Education and Human Resource Development,* 6th ed. (Burlington, MA: Elsevier, 2005).

7. Interview with Jesse Miranda, Springfield, Missouri, August 4, 2014.

8. Ibid.

9. Ibid.

10. Telephone interview with Jessica Domínguez, January 8, 2015.

11. Ibid.

12. Ibid.

13. Ibid.

14. Ibid.

15. Paloma Esquivel, "Immigration lawyer known as 'the angel of justice' among Latinos," *Los Angeles Times,* August 20, 2012, http://articles.latimes.com/2012/aug/20/local/la-me -angel-of-justice-20120820 (accessed August 6, 2014).

16. Steve Lopez, "When Freedom Rings Hollow," *Los Angeles Times*, January 28, 2004, http:// articles.latimes.com/2004/jan/28/local/me-lopez28.

17. Paloma Esquivel, "Immigration lawyer known as 'the angel of justice' among Latinos," *Los Angeles Times,* August 20, 2012, http://articles.latimes.com/2012/aug/20/local/la-me -angel-of-justice-20120820 (accessed August 6, 2014).

18. Ibid.

19. Ibid.

20. Doug Lederman, "Higher Ed's Other Immigrants," *Inside Higher Education*, July 18, 2012, http://www.insidehighered.com/news/2012/07/18/us-study-examines-college -experiences-1st-and-2nd-generation-immigrants (accessed August 6, 2014).

21. Ibid.

22. Richard Fry and Paul Taylor, "Hispanic High School Graduates Pass Whites in Rate of College Enrollment, High School Drop-Out Rate at Record Low,*"* Pew Research, Hispanic Trends Project, May 9, 2013, http://www.pewhispanic.org/2013/05/09/ hispanic-high-school-graduates-pass-whites-in-rate-of-college-enrollment/ (accessed August 6, 2014).

23. Ibid.

24. John U. Ogbu and Herber D. Simons, "Voluntary Immigrants and Involuntary Minorities: A Cultural-Ecological Theory of School Performance with Some Implications for Education," *Anthropology & Education Quarterly*, no.173, (1998), http://faculty .washington.edu/rsoder/EDUC310/OgbuSimonsvoluntaryinvoluntary.pdf (accessed August 6, 2014).

25. Ibid.

26. Ibid.

27. Andrew Mytelka, "College-Going Rates for All Racial Groups Have Jumped Since 1980," *The Chronicle of Higher Education*, July 14, 2010, http://chronicle.com/blogs/ticker/ college-going-rates-for-all-racial-groups-have-jumped-since-1980/25533 (accessed August 6, 2014).

28. Molly Redden, "Hispanic Enrollment Jumps 24%, Making Those Students the Largest Campus Minority," *The Chronicle of Higher Education*, August 25, 2011, http://chronicle .com/article/Hispanic-Enrollment-Jumps-24-/128797/.

29. Alan Fram and Christine Armario, "Hispanics Place Higher Emphasis on Education, Poll

Reports," *Huffington Post*, July 20, 2010, http://www.huffingtonpost.com/2010/07/20/hispanics-place-higher-em_n_652605.html (accessed August 6, 2014).

30. Interview with Jesse Miranda, Springfield, Missouri, August 4, 2014.

31. Kimberly Hefling and Jesse J. Holland, "White Students to No Longer Be Majority at School," Associated Press, August 9, 2014, accessed August 9, 2014, http://hosted.ap.org/dynamic/stories/U/US_BACK_TO_SCHOOL_MAJORITY_MINORITY_AB RIDGED?SITE=AP&SECTION=HOME&TEMPLATE=DEFAULT&CTI ME=2014-08-09-13-51-17 (accessed August 6, 2014).

32. Interview with Jesse Miranda, Springfield, Missouri, August 4, 2014.

33. Ibid.

34. Ibid.

35. Ibid.

36. Pew Research, "Between Two Worlds: How Young Latinos Come of Age in America," Hispanic Trends Project, December 11, 2009, http://www.pewhispanic.org/2009/12/11/between-two-worlds-how-young-latinos-come-of-age-in-america/ (accessed August 14, 2014).

37. "Nepantla Art," Chicanoart.org, http://www.chicanoart.org/nepantla.html (accessed August 14, 2014).

38. Interview with Jesse Miranda, Springfield, Missouri, August 4, 2014.

39. Pew Research, "Between Two Worlds: How Young Latinos Come of Age in America."

40. Alexander W. Astin, *What Matters in College. Four Critical Years Revisited* (San Francisco: Jossey-Bass Publishers, 1993), 194.

41. Interview with Jesse Miranda, Springfield, Missouri, August 4, 2014.

42. Assemblies of God, "AG U.S. Adherents by Race 2001–2012." Obtained from Sherri Doty, Statistician, Assemblies of God National Resource Office, Springfield, Missouri, on June 25, 2014.

Chapter 12

1. Interview with Varun Laohaprasit, Bellevue, Washington, July 24, 2014.

2. Ibid.

3. *Casablanca.* Directed by Michael Curtiz. Los Angeles: Warner Brothers, 1942.

4. Rubén G. Rumbaut and Walter A. Ewing, *The Myth of Immigrant Criminality and the Paradox of Assimilation: Incarceration Rates among Native and Foreign-Born Men* (Washington, D.C.: Immigration Policy Center, American Immigration Law Foundation, Spring 2007), 6–10.

5. Alberto Mottesi, *América 500 Años Después: Hacia un Nuevo Liderazgo para el Año 2000* (Fountain Valley, CA: Asociación Alberto Mottesi, 1992).

6. Aarón Sánchez,"Ingobernabilidad," El Debate, 17 de Agosto de 2014, http://www.debate.com.mx/eldebate/noticias/columnas.asp?IdArt=13509158&IdCat=17502 (accessed August 18, 2014).

7. Ricardo Palma, *Tradiciones Peruanas, Tomo III* (Lima, Perú: Ediciones Culturales, 1973), my translation.

8. Carlos Torres y Torres-Lara, "Retos De La Consolidación Democrática Del Peru, La

'Institucionalizacion,'" my translation, http://www.asesor.com.pe/teleley/contenlegal .php?idm=2453 (accessed July 30, 2014).

9. Ronald Reagan, "A Time for Choosing," speech, 1964 National Convention of the Republican Party, San Francisco, California, October 27, 1964, http://www.reagan.utexas .edu/archives/reference/timechoosing.html (accessed August 1, 2014).

10. Barack Obama, "Remarks by the President at Univision Town Hall," Bell High School, Washington, D.C., March 28, 2011, http://www.whitehouse.gov/the-press-office/2011/ 03/28/remarks-president-univision-town-hall (accessed August 1, 2014).

11. Telephone interview with Jessica Domínguez, January 8, 2015.

12. Ibid.

13. U.S. Department of Homeland Security, "Deferred Action for Childhood Arrivals," http://www.dhs.gov/deferred-action-childhood-arrivals (accessed October 7, 2014).

14. Jeremy R. Corsi, "Children Crossing Border: 'Obama Will Take Care of Us.'" *WND Weekly*, July 25, 2014, http://www.wnd.com/2014/07/children-crossing-border-obama -will-take-care-of-us/ (accessed October 7, 2014).

15. Alan Greenblatt, "What's Causing the Latest Immigration Crisis? A Brief Explainer," NPR, July 9, 2014, http://www.npr.org/2014/07/09/329848538/whats-causing-the-latest -immigration-crisis-a-brief-explainer (accessed October 7, 2014).

16. Electronic mail correspondence from Jessica Domínguez, January 19, 2015.

17. Jim Treacher, "Obama: 'I Just Took an Action to Change the Law,'" *The Daily Caller*, November 26, 2015, http://dailycaller.com/2014/11/26/obama-i-just-took-an-action-to -change-the-law/ (accessed August 1, 2014), emphasis mine.

18. John Winthrop, "A Model of Christian Charity (1630)," The Gilder Lehrman Institute of American History, http://www.gilderlehrman.org/sites/default/files/inline-pdfs/A%20 Model%20of%20Christian%20Charity.pdf (accessed August 1, 2014).

19. Woodrow Wilson, 8th Annual Message, Washington D.C., December 7, 1920, http:// www.presidency.ucsb.edu/ws/?pid=29561 (accessed August 1, 2014).

20. John Winthrop, "A Model of Christian Charity (1630)," The Gilder Lehrman Institute of American History, accessed August 1, 2014, http://www.gilderlehrman.org/sites/default/ files/inline-pdfs/A%20Model%20of%20Christian%20Charity.pdf, emphasis mine.

21. Interview with Saturnino González, Tampa, Florida, November 2, 2014.

22. "2008 Republican Convention, Day 3," *C-SPAN*, September 3, 2008, http://www .c-span.org/video/?280790-1/2008-republican-convention-day-3; "Republican National Convention Day 2—Benediction: Rev Sammy Rodriguez," YouTube, Aug 29, 2012, https://www.youtube.com/watch?v=RDOxAnPwY4g (accessed December 28, 2014).

23. Esperanza, "Rev. Luis Cortés Story," *Esperanza:* Strengthening our Hispanic Community, http://www.esperanza.us/mission-impact/about-the-agency/luis-cortes-story/ (accessed May 4, 2015).

24. Samuel Rodríguez, *The Lamb's Agenda: Why Jesus Is Calling You to a Life of Righteousness and Justice* (Nashville: Thomas Nelson, 2013), 33.

25. Ibid., 42.

26. Ibid.

27. Ibid., 46.

28. Gabriel Salguero, "God's Politics: My Living Paradox,"*Beliefnet*, April, 2007, http://www.beliefnet.com/columnists/godspolitics/2007/04/rev-gabriel-salguero-my-living-paradox.html (accessed May 4, 2015).

29. "Catholic Church's Position on Immigration Reform," United States Conference of Catholic Bishops, August, 2013, http://www.usccb.org/issues-and-action/human-life-and-dignity/immigration/churchteachingonimmigrationreform.cfm (accessed December 28, 2014).

30. Donald W. Dayton, *Discovering an Evangelical Heritage* (New York: Harper & Row, 1976).

31. "Immigration 2009," National Association of Evangelicals, http://www.nae.net/government-relations/policy-resolutions/354-immigration-2009 (accessed December 28, 2014).

32. "On Immigration and the Gospel," Southern Baptist Convention, http://www.sbc.net/resolutions/1213 (accessed August 1, 2014).

33. Ibid.

34. "Statement on 'Immigration,'" General Council of the Assemblies of God, September 20, 2006, http://ag.org/top/about/immigration.cfm (accessed December 28, 2014).

35. "John Ashcroft on Immigration," *On the Issues: Every Political Leader on Every Issue*, March 29, 2014, http://www.ontheissues.org/Cabinet/John_Ashcroft_Immigration.htm (accessed August 1, 2013).

36. "Who We Are," Evangelical Immigration Table, http://evangelicalimmigrationtable.com/#about (accessed August 1, 2013).

37. *Evangelical Statement of Principles for Immigration Reform*, Evangelical Immigration Table, http://evangelicalimmigrationtable.com (accessed April 19, 2015).

38. Pew Research Center, "The Religious Affiliation of U.S. Immigrants: Majority Christian, Rising Share of Other Faiths," The Pew Forum on Religion and Public Life, May 17, 2013, http://www.pewforum.org/2013/05/17/the-religious-affiliation-of-us-immigrants/ (accessed August 1, 2013).

Chapter 13

1. Capitol Ministries, "What the Bible Says About Our Illegal Immigration Problem," *Members Bible Study: U.S. Capitol*, June 16, 2014, http://capmin.org/site/resources/bible-studies/6-16-14.html (accessed June 15, 2015).

2. John Herbers, "Religious Leaders Tell of Worry on Armageddon View Ascribed to Reagan," *New York Times*, October 21, 1984.

3. Paul Houston, "Reagan Denies Astrology Influenced His Decisions," *Los Angeles Times*, May 4, 1988, http://articles.latimes.com/1988-05-04/news/mn-2147_1_astrological-advice (accessed June 15, 2015).

4. Capitol Ministries, "What the Bible Says About Our Illegal Immigration Problem."

5. Ibid.

6. 2 Kings 22:1–20.

7. James K. Hoffmeier, *The Immigration Crisis: Immigrants, Aliens, and the Bible* (Wheaton, IL: Crossway Books, 2009), 105. Here Hoffmeier uses the feminine form of the word

nekhar, which I have generally not done in order to facilitate understanding for the casual reader.

8. Thomas Allen, "Stranger in the Old Testament," *TC Allen*, June 12, 2009, http://tcallenco .blogspot.com/2009/06/stranger-in-old-testament.html?m=1 (accessed June 15, 2015).

9. James K. Hoffmeier, *The Immigration Crisis: Immigrants, Aliens, and the Bible* (Wheaton, IL: Crossway Books, 2009), 51, emphasis mine. *Nokharim* is the plural form of *nekhar*.

10. Ibid., 52.

11. Ibid., 81, emphasis mine.

12. Matthew Soerens and Jenny Hwang Yang, *Welcoming the Stranger: Justice, Compassion, and Truth in the Immigration Debate* (Downers Grove, IL: InterVarsity Press, 2009), 82.

13. 1 Corinthians 10:11.

14. Matthew 1:1–16.

15. Matthew 2:14–15.

16. Luke 10:27.

17. Luke 10:29.

18. Luke 10:36.

19. Matthew 25:35–36.

20. James 1:27: "Religion that God our Father accepts as pure and faultless is this: to look after orphans and widows in their distress . . ."

Chapter 14

1. Ronald Reagan, "Farewell Address to the Nation," Washington, DC, January 11, 1989, http://www.reagan.utexas.edu/archives/speeches/1989/011189i.htm (accessed June 15, 2015), emphasis mine.

2. Steve Bostrom, "Escape to Freedom," *Northwest Passages*, Spring 2013, 23.

3. Interview with Ben Sterciuc, Kirkland, Washington, July 22, 2014.

4. Steve Bostrom, "Escape to Freedom," *Northwest Passages*, Spring 2013, 23.

5. Ibid.

6. Ibid., 24.

7. Interview with Ben Sterciuc, Kirkland, Washington, July 22, 2014.

8. Steve Bostrom, "Escape to Freedom," *Northwest Passages*, Spring 2013, 24.

9. "Elevation Church," www.elevationc.com (accessed August 18, 2014).

10. Steve Bostrom, "Escape to Freedom," *Northwest Passages*, Spring 2013, 24.

11. Ronald Reagan, "Farewell Address to the Nation."

ABOUT THE AUTHOR

Joseph Castleberry is president of Northwest University in Kirkland, Washington. He travels frequently as a conference speaker in churches around the world. As an Evangelical missionary, he served as a pastor, educator, and community development leader in Latin America for twenty years. His insight into intercultural relations, honed by doctoral studies in international educational development at Columbia University's Teachers College and practiced in close relationship with immigrants around the world, gives him a valuable vantage point for understanding immigration in today's America.

Dr. Castleberry has written two other popular books: *Your Deepest Dream: Discovering God's True Vision for Your Life* (NavPress/Tyndale, 2012) and *The Kingdom Net: Learning to Network Like Jesus* (My Healthy Church, 2013). He writes blogs in English (www.josephcastleberry.com) and Spanish (www.inmigrantesdedios.org) and contributes a regular column relating the Bible to immigration in the bilingual newspaper *TúDecides/YouDecide*.

Dr. Castleberry's immediate family includes his wife, Kathleen; Nathan, Jessica, and Emerson Austin; Roberto and Jodie Valdez; and Sophie Castleberry.

Follow Dr. Castleberry on Facebook at
www.facebook.com/joseph.castleberry
and on Twitter @DrCastleberry.
Send email to josephlcastleberry@icloud.com.

WORTHY®
PUBLISHING

If you enjoyed this book, will you consider sharing the message with others?

- Mention the book in a Facebook post, Twitter update, Pinterest pin, blog post, or upload a picture through Instagram.

- Recommend this book to those in your small group, book club, workplace, and classes.

- Head over to facebook.com/worthypublishing, "LIKE" the page, and post a comment as to what you enjoyed the most.

- Tweet "I recommend reading #TheNewPilgrims by @DrCastleberry // @worthypub"

- Pick up a copy for someone you know who would be challenged and encouraged by this message.

- Write a book review online.

You can subscribe to Worthy Publishing's newsletter at worthypublishing.com.

WORTHY PUBLISHING
FACEBOOK PAGE

WORTHY PUBLISHING
WEBSITE